SUPER NES® GAMES SECRETS

Volume 2

Super NES Games Secrets, Volume 2 is published by Prima Publishing, an independent publishing company. This book is not published by, authorized by, or associated in any way with Nintendo of America, Inc. This book is not related and should not be confused with any publication that is printed or distributed by Nintendo of America Inc. NINTENDO® is a registered trademark of Nintendo of America Inc.

The following are trademarks owned by Nintendo of America Inc.: Super Mario Bros.®, The Legend of Zelda: A Link to the Past®, Super Nintendo Entertainment System®, Super NES®, Super Mario World™, and Super Scope™.

Secrets of the Games Series Editor: Rusel DeMaria
Layout: Just Your Type, Matt Kim, Zach Meston, Rusel DeMaria
Editing and Proofreading: Kathy Mejia, Zach Meston
Cover Illustration: Matthew Holmes
Cover Design: Dunlavey Studio
Special processing, maps, and original drawings: Ocean Quigley and Zach Meston

Library of Congress Cataloging-in-Publication Data

DeMaria, Rusel, 1948-
Super NES games secrets Volume 2/ by Rusel DeMaria and Zach Meston
p. cm.
ISBN 1-55958-193-X : $9.99
1. Nintendo video games. I. Meston, Zach. II. Title.

GV1469.3.D458 1992 91-38523
794.8'15365--dc20 CIP

92 93 94 95 — 10 9 8 7 6 5 4 3 2

SUPER NES® GAMES SECRETS

Volume 2

Rusel DeMaria
and
Zach Meston

Prima Publishing
P.O. Box 1260 SNESB
Rocklin, CA 95677
(916) 786-0426

NOW AVAILABLE

Nintendo® *Games Secrets, Volumes 1, 2, and 3*
Super NES® Games Secrets, Volumes 1 and 2
Nintendo® Game Boy™ Secrets, Volumes 1 and 2
Sega Genesis® Secrets, Volumes 1, 2, and 3
TurboGrafx–16® and TurboExpress® Games Secrets, Volumes 1 and 2
GamePro Presents: Nintendo® Games Secrets Greatest Tips
The Legend of Zelda: A Link to the Past® Game Secrets (August)

COMPUTER GAME BOOKS

SimEarth: The Official Strategy Guide
Harpoon Battlebook
The Official Lucasfilm Games® Air Combat Strategies Book
Sid Meier's Civilization, or Rome on 640K a Day
Wing Commander I and II: The Ultimate Strategy Guide
Chuck Yeager's Air Combat Handbook
Ultima: The Avatar Adventures

...and more to come!

HOW TO ORDER:

Quantity discounts are available from the publisher, Prima Publishing, P.O. Box 1260SNESB, Rocklin, CA 95677; telephone (916) 786-0449. On your letterhead include information concerning the intended use of the books and the number of books you wish to purchase.

CONTENTS

The Complete Story on...

ACKNOWLEDGMENTS

Thanks to Adobe Systems for Photoshop, Microsoft for MS Word, Quark for Quark XPress, Byte by Byte for Sculpt 3D, and CE Software for their indispensable utilities like Quickeys and Disktop.

On a personal note, thanks go, as usual, to an incredible (and growing) team at Prima whose efforts complement ours; to Waterside; and to my family—Don and Elaine, Leslie and her newest future gamer, and all the rest in California; Marsha, Shan and Max.

—R.D.M.

Greetings to Mom, Henry, John and Kelly; Kristin Tesman and Randi Tesman, my ultra-nice cousins; Andy Eddy and Chris Bieniek, my buds at *VideoGames & Computer Entertainment;* Chuck Miller, Millie Miller, and Marci Rogers, my friends in the Enchanted Realms; Danny Han, a reviewer on the rise; Peggy Herrington, a fellow Amigan and genuinely nice person; Joel Pambid, who provided valuable help with Street Fighter II; and Julie Carlson, whose ROM board expertise saved me a lot of headaches. Thanks, Julie!

—Z.M.

We both thank our hard-working game player, Rio Roth-Barreiro, for his efforts.

INTRODUCTION

Super NES Games Secrets 2 is meant to get you farther than you've ever gotten in the games you love to play. By combining detailed descriptions with lots of graphics, this book not only tells you what to do, but often shows you, too. Like all books in the Secrets of the Games series, *Super NES Games Secrets 2* goes an extra step for you. In fact, you can read this book in three different ways:

1. As a guide to the games you don't yet own. What kind of game is it? Does it sound like fun? Learn about the games before you buy them.

2. As a strategy guide. How can you play this game successfully? Check the **General Strategies** section of each chapter for the most successful techniques and ideas. Then check the level-by-level, step-by-step **Strategy Session** and learn exactly how to go from the start to the finish of each game.

3. To learn the ultimate secrets. Even in the step-by-step descriptions, we hold back a little. We want you to try and figure it out on your own. But if you're still stuck, try our section called **The Secrets**. Often you'll find special strategies, passwords, or even powerful secret techniques in The Secrets.

Our section on **Superstar Sports Games** gives you winning tips on the latest Super NES sports titles.

We've provided a chapter of **Short Tips** to add to your fun. That's where you find some of the secrets, passwords, and nifty tricks hidden in your games.

Finally, we've written about the hottest **Peripherals** to hit the Super NES scene. Check them out!

I'd like to end with a personal statement. It's the same statement I've put in all my books. Video games are often violent in content. That's okay. They're games. Enjoy the games, but please remember what's important:

Respect the Earth.
Respect all Life.

—RDM

CHAPTER 1

The Addams Family

by Ocean

WHAT'S GOING ON?

The Addams Family mansion has been invaded by Abigail Craven and her two cohorts, Tully and The Evil Judge. They've kidnapped five family members and are looking for the Addams' hidden fortune. Gomez Addams has to find his family members, find the family fortune, and defeat The Evil Judge to make every "Thing" all right!

PLAYERS

The Addams Family is for one player only.

SCORING

You score points by jumping onto monsters and grabbing items. You receive 100 points for each monster, and 10 points for each item. If you bounce off more than one monster during a single jump, without touching the ground, the points will double (100 points for the first, 200 for the second, and so forth).

LIVES AND CONTINUES

You start the game with five lives. Each life has a number of Heart Units displayed on the left side of the screen. Each time you're hit by an enemy, you lose a Heart Unit. Lose all the Units and you lose a life. You earn extra lives by collecting 1-Ups. You also earn an extra life for every 50,000 points.

You start the game with two Heart Units (which means you can only survive two hits). You can earn another three Units during the game to give yourself a total of five Heart Units.

You have unlimited continues, but there's a catch. When you continue, you start back in the Hall of Stairs, not from where you lost your last life.

Whenever you defeat a Big Bad Guy (boss creature), you'll get a password. This password keeps track of all the family members you've saved, the number of Heart Units you have, and most importantly, the number of lives you had at the time you received the password. For example, if you defeat a Big Bad Guy with 20 lives in reserve, the password will start you with 20 lives. This excellent feature is the key to beating the game (as you'll see in the Strategy Session).

CONTROLS

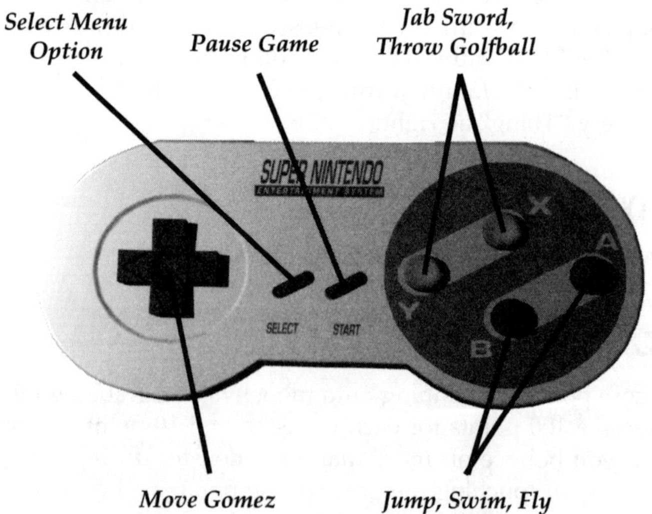

WEAPONS

You defeat creatures by jumping onto them from above. You can also pick up two different weapons during the game: the Sword and the Golfball. The Sword is a short-range weapon, while the Golfball is a long-range weapon. If you're hit by an enemy while holding a weapon, you won't lose a Heart Unit, but you will lose the weapon.

SPECIAL ITEMS

The **Dollar Sign** adds $1 to your Money total (read on for more Money info).

The **Fez** gives you the power of flight. Press A or B rapidly to soar into the air. The Fez lasts until you leave the current area, at which point the Fez blinks for a few seconds, and then disappears.

Invisible Points are worth 1,000 points each. Keep jumping into the air and you may find some!

The **1-Up** adds one life to your total.

Running Shoes make you run faster and jump farther. The Shoes last until you're hit by an enemy.

The **Shield** makes you invulnerable for a short time. You're surrounded by a "star trail" while the Shield is in effect.

The **Small Heart** replenishes one empty Heart Unit.

The number of **Dollars** you have is indicated in the lower-left corner of the screen. For each $25 you collect, you replenish one Heart Unit. For every $100 you gather, you get an extra life.

FRIENDS

Thing is your most helpful friend. He appears in several places around the mansion, inside Thing Boxes. Hit a Box from below and Thing will pop out to give you a helpful clue about the dangers ahead.

Lurch sits in the Music Room. Once you've rescued Granny, Uncle Fester, Pugsley, and Wednesday, come to this room and Lurch plays a tune to give you access to the final area of the mansion.

Granny, **Uncle Fester**, **Morticia**, **Pugsley**, and **Wednesday** are being held captive in the mansion. Rescue them all to win the game!

ENEMIES

The smaller enemies in the game don't have any names, but the Big Bad Guys do!

The **Big Bird** guards a Heart Unit. He flies around the screen.

The **Centipedes** guard a Heart Unit. There are three of these nasty buggers to deal with.

The **Fire Dragon** has captured Granny. He slithers around the screen and shoots hot fireballs.

The **Ghastly Goblin** has captured Wednesday. He flies around the screen and throws skulls at you.

The **Nasty Judge** is the final Bad Guy of the game. Defeat him to free Morticia!

The **Snowman** guards a Heart Unit. He throws snowballs and rolls around the screen in his un-natural form.

The **Witch** has captured Uncle Fester and hypnotized him. She flies around the screen on her broom and shoots fireballs at you.

STRATEGY SESSION

General Strategies

The most important maneuver to master is the Springboard Jump. Bounce off a creature while holding down the Jump button and you'll soar higher into the air than you would with a regular jump. You have to use the Springboard Jump at many points in the game to reach platforms and highly placed items.

Every area in the game has a name, displayed in the box at the top of the screen. We've labeled our Strategy Session by name to make it easy for you to follow along.

The Addams Walkthrough

The walkthrough is structured to take you on the easiest path through the game. Because the game is so huge (we literally could have written an entire book about it), there's no way we can provide a detailed walkthrough. You'll have to figure out some of the puzzles on your own. We will tell you how to solve some of the trickier puzzles, we'll take you to the secret rooms, and we'll provide maps for several areas. (Please note that the maps aren't proportionally correct. They merely show how the rooms are connected to each other.)

The Walkthrough is divided into four parts: Collecting 1-Ups, Collecting Heart Units, Saving Family Members, and Saving Morticia. Read on!

Part One: Collecting 1-Ups

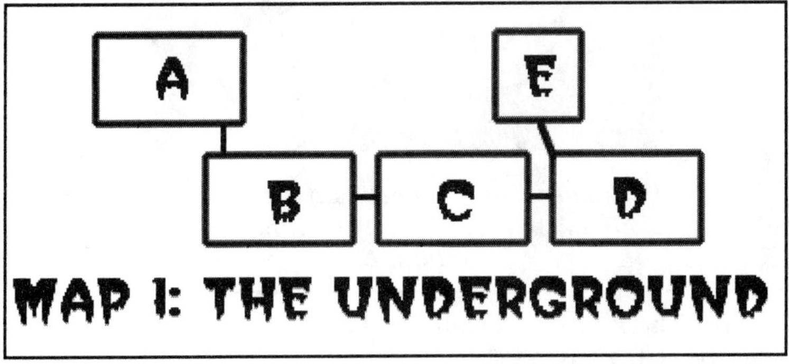

1A. The Addams Residence. You start the game at the front door of the mansion. Walk to the left until you find a gallows. Climb up the noose to spot a Fez floating in the air. Jump up and grab the Fez.

Soar up and right, collecting the Dollars scattered around the mansion. When you've collected all of the Dollars, land atop the chimney on the right side of the mansion and press Down. You'll enter . . .

The East Chimney. Drop down and walk to the left to find 12 Dollars. Use a Springboard Jump off a monster to grab the four highest Dollars.

1A. The Addams Residence. Push Down as soon as you appear back here. You won't go back into the East Chimney. Instead, you'll enter . . .

The West Chimney. This chimney is stocked with four 1-Ups. Nab 'em all and walk to the far right. Jump up and out to return to . . .

1A. The Addams Residence. Walk right and drop down to the ground. Walk to the right until you spot a hole in the ground. Drop into the hole to enter . . .

1B. The Underground. Drop to the bottom of the cave and hit the Thing Box for a clue. Press X or Y to return to the action. Walk to the left and you'll pass through the wall into a hidden room, with four Dollars and a 1-Up. Thanks, Thing!

Move out of the hidden room and walk to the right. Keep going until you find a tunnel leading upward. Instead of jumping into the tunnel, continue walking to the right. You'll

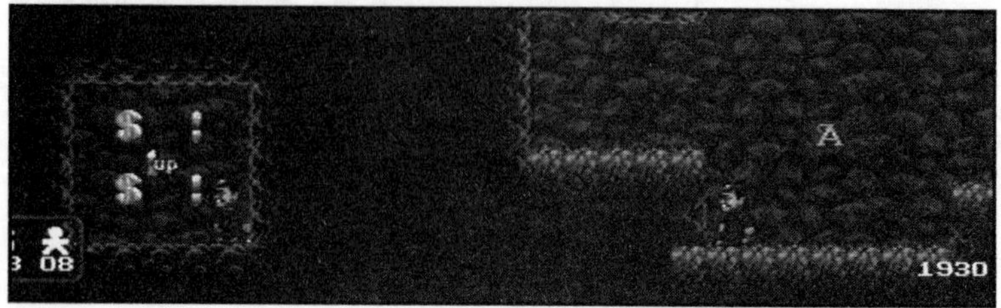

pass through the wall into an area with nine Dollars. From here, you simply walk right to enter Area 1C.

1C. Going Down Under. There's a 1-Up about halfway through the area that's tricky to reach. Use a Springboard Jump off the spitting plant on the right side of the 1-Up and you'll make it to the ledge.

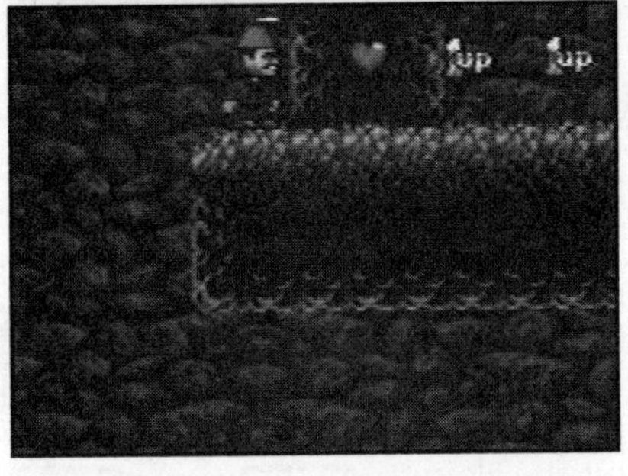

1D. Under the Tree. There are three well-placed 1-Ups in the upper-right corner of this area. To get to them, go to the lower-left corner of the area, where you'll find a grassy platform floating up and down. Drop onto the platform and ride it down, then leap to the right and into the hidden tunnel. Gather all the Dollars and the Fez. Use the Fez to fly back up into the upper-right corner and grab the 1-Ups.

Once you've gotten your 1-Ups, go into the upper-left corner of the area. You'll find a Thing Box next to the path to Area 5. Hit the Box, then walk to the left.

1E. The Old Tree. You'll appear in the "mouth" of The Old Tree. Don't jump up the branches just yet. Walk to the right and go through the door to enter the . . .

Hall of Stairs. Walk down the stairs into the lower-left corner of the area. Stand underneath the door to The Old Tree. Press

Up and you'll go through an invisible door into . . .

Pugsley's Den. In this secret room, you'll find three 1-Ups, Running Shoes, and a Heart. It gets better! Walk into the upper-left corner of the room and press Up to

enter a second invisible door! This one takes you . . .

Behind Stairs. There are six doors in this area (indicated on Map 2: Behind Stairs).

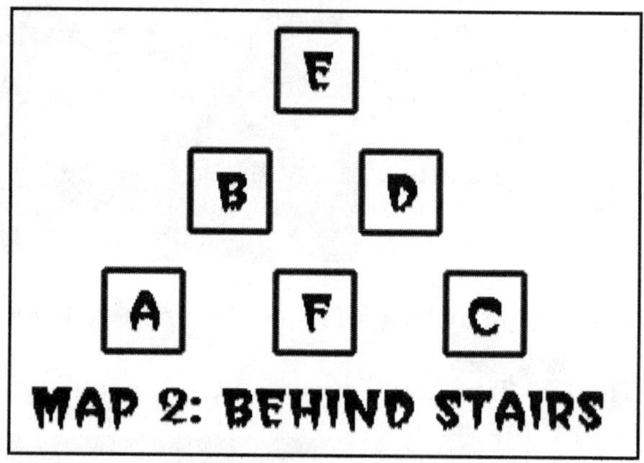

2A. Take Heart. This place is filled with Hearts (not to be confused with Heart Units). Grab them all for some points.

2B. Sports Room. This room's filled with Dollars and a few weapons. Take the 1-Up on the left side of the room, and take the Sword, but don't take the Golfball.

2C. Training Shoes. You normally can't reach the Shoes, but you can with the Sword from the Sports Room. Jump into the air and thrust the Sword upward to get the Shoes.

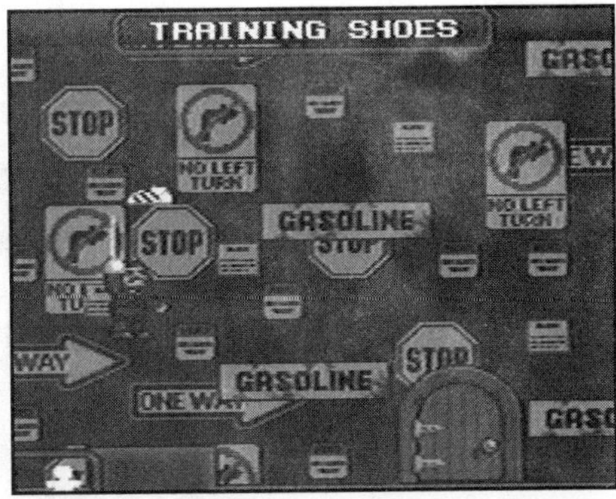

2D. The Hat Room. Jump across to the right. (If you miss the jump and fall to the door below, go through the door and go back into this room to try again.) You'll find a Fez on the other side. Take the Fez and fly back to the left. Exit the door and go to The Cloak Room as quickly as you can.

2E. The Cloak Room. Press the Jump button rapidly to fly upward with the Fez. You have to reach the upper ledge before the Fez disappears. If you don't make it, go back to The Hat Room and try again. If you do make it, grab the Dollars and go through the door to . . .

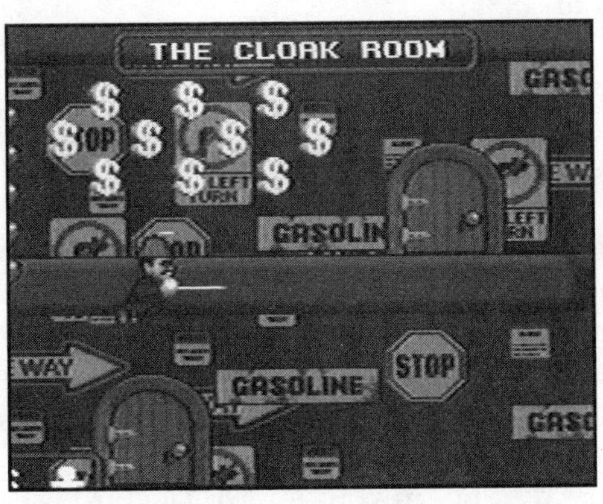

The 1-Up Room. It's obvious what to do in this area: run to the right and grab all the 1-Ups! There's a Running Shoe above the door on the right side, which takes you back to . . .

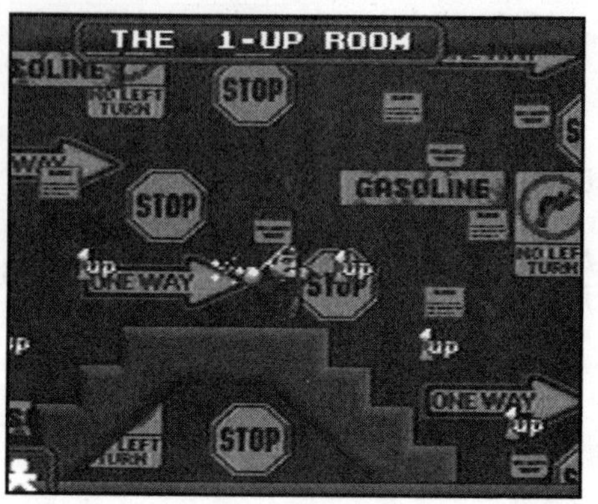

Behind Stairs. You've cleared out all of the rooms, and you should have a bunch of lives by now (at least 30). Leave through door 2F at the bottom of the area to go back to . . .

Pugsley's Den. Drop down to the door and go through to re-enter the . . .

Hall of Stairs. Jump up to the first door on the left side and open it. You'll appear at . . .

The Old Tree. Run to the left and jump up the branches of the tree until you see the Big Bird. Get ready to fight!

The Big Bird flies back and forth, soaring into the air, and then swooping downward. Hit the Bird on the head when it swoops downward, then bounce away from it (use a Springboard Jump off the Bird's head to get more distance in your jump). The Bird is easy to beat (as are most of the Bad Guys). When you defeat the Bird, you'll get a password. Write it down, because you'll be using it immediately.

After you get your password, reset the Super NES. When

the title screen appears, select the Password option and input your password. You'll reappear in the Hall of Stairs, with three Heart Units and as many lives as you had when you beat the Big Bird.

Now here's the cool part. Since you reset the Super NES, all of the 1-Ups you collected in Pugsley's Den (and The Underground) will have returned! It's not worth your time to go back to The Underground, but it is worth going back into Pugsley's Den and collecting more 1-Ups. By the time you come back out of the Den, you should have 50 lives or more.

Part Two: Collecting Heart Units

Hall of Stairs. Once you've raided the Den for lives, go to the door in the upper-right corner. Enter the door to walk into...

The Kitchen. It's possible to go left or right from here, but you want to go to the left. You'll go to the right later in the game, to rescue Granny. The left passage leads to . . .

The Pantry. Move to far left side of the area. Hit the Thing Box, then go through the door and into . . .

***3A. Penguin Problems.** The name of this area is an understatement! The penguins are nasty because they move fast and because they're small (which makes them hard to hit with a jump). What's worse, the ledges in this area are iced over, which makes you slip and slide. There's a Shield shortly into the area, high in the air. Stand on a high ledge and Springboard off a penguin to get the Shield.*

***3B. Slippery Slopes.** This area is filled with bouncing bulls (at least, they kinda look like bulls) and steep slopes. Jump onto the bulls and bounce over them to collect Invisible Points. (You'll usually need to use a Springboard Jump to collect the Points, but don't jump too high, or you'll hit the roof and take damage from the sharp icicles.)*

3C. The Icy Steps. This is a basic area, except for one tough jump about halfway through. It may seem like you need to Springboard off the bull to make the jump, but you don't. It's just a really tough jump to make.

3D. Rolling Snowball. This area has a group of rolling snowballs that can't be destroyed by hopping onto them. Your best bet is to leap the snowballs as they roll toward you.

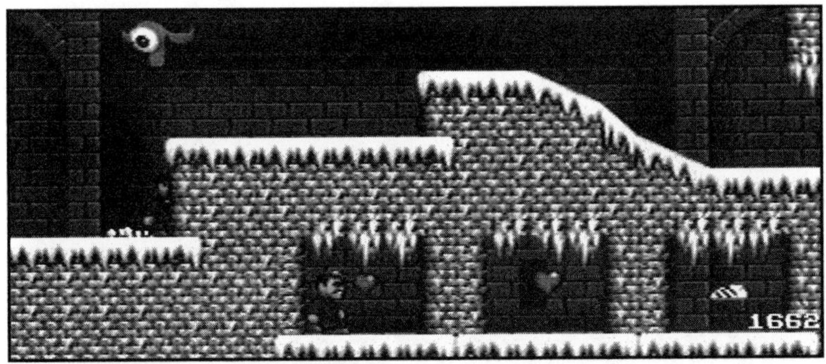

Near the end of this area is a secret tunnel. Inside the tunnel, you'll find two Hearts and a Running Shoe. The Hearts and Shoe are visible, even if you're not in the tunnel.

3E. The Ski Slopes. This is the final area before The Snowman, but it's not too tough. There are more snowballs to leap, and more bulls to bash. Keep going until you find the door to the Snowman (with a Thing Box above it).

3F. The Snowman. This guy actually starts out as a snowball, then transforms into a snowman. Hit the Snowman on the head, then leap to the left and jump over the snowball that the Snowman throws at you.

The Snowman turns back into a snowball and rolls to the left; jump over him to the right. When he hits the left side of the screen, four icicles fall from the top of the screen, Dodge the icicles and leap over the snowball when it rolls back to the right.

Repeat the attack pattern until the Snowman is iced! Write down your password, reset the Super NES and enter the password. You'll appear in the . . .

Hall of Stairs. Raid Pugsley's Den for 1-Ups, then go through the door in the lower-right corner to enter . . .

4A. The Conservatory. There are two secret rooms in this area. To enter the first area, walk right until you find a group of seven pots. Jump on top of the rightmost pot in the bottom row, and push Down to enter The Plant Pot.

The second secret room is farther along in the area, on the left side of a Running Show floating in the air. Walk to the left, against the wall, to enter The Privet. There are twelve Dollars to be had in this room.

Continue walking to the right until you see an On/Off Switch at

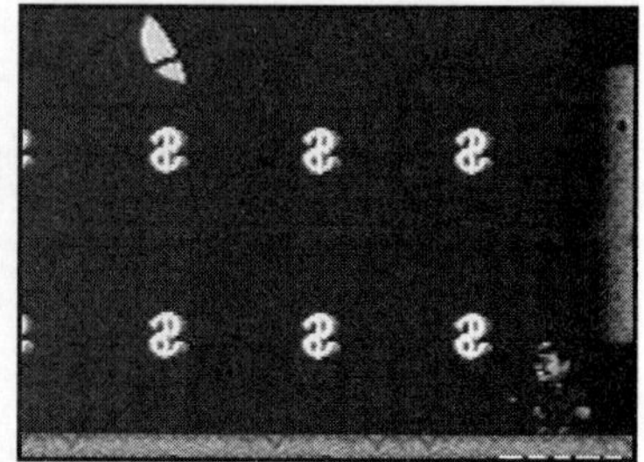

the top of the screen. Jump off a passing bird to leap up to the Switch. Hit the Switch, then drop back to the ground and walk to the right until you find a door. (If you didn't hit the Switch properly, it will be blocked by walls.) Go through the door.

4B. Thorn Pass. Walk to the right until you see a door at the top of the screen. Bounce off a bird to get up to the door.

4C. Wormy Way. This area has several walls that are toggled on and off by the Switches. If you find your progress blocked by a wall, walk back to the left and hit a Switch, then return to the right and the wall should be gone.

Near the end of the area, you have to climb some ropes that get smaller as you move to the right. Climb to the top of each rope and fall to the right. If you jump at the top of a rope, you'll hit the spikes on the roof and suffer damage.

4D. The Centipedes. This area is populated by three nasty centipedes. Stand on the far left or far right side of the screen and the creepy-crawlies can't touch you. Jump onto the body of any of the Centipedes to cause damage. Don't jump onto a head, or you'll take damage yourself.

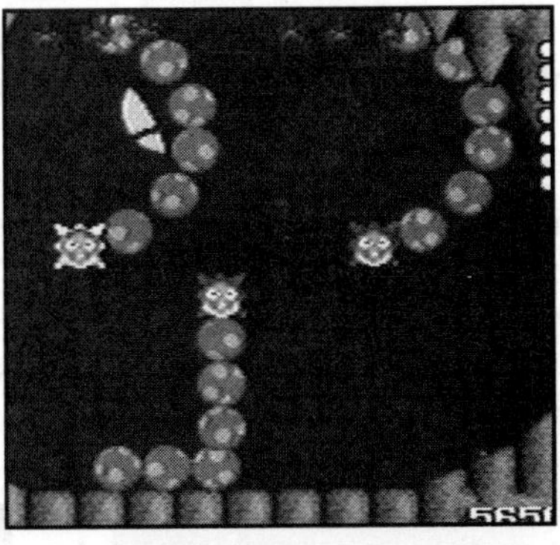

When you defeat the Centipedes, you'll earn the fifth and final Heart.

Write down your password, reset the Super NES, and enter the password to go back to the . . .

Hall of Stairs. Go into Pugsley's Den and the 1-Up Room to collect 1-Ups, then come back here and enter the door in the lower-right corner. It's time to start the Addams Family reunion!

6B. The Upper Tomb. Collect the Dollars, leap over the shaft on the right, and grab a second Dollar group. Return to the shaft on the left and drop down. Walk to the right and drop into the next Dollar area. Walk to the right and into the wall to collect a hidden Shield, then walk to the left.

6C. The Spooky Drop. Walk to the left and hit the Eyeball Switch to open the wall, then drop down the shaft. Aim to the left so you can collect the Heart before you fall to the bottom of the shaft and walk to the right.

6D. The Arch Vault. Walk to the right until you find an area with two giant stars moving up and down. Drop into the lower tunnel and hit the Eyeball Switch, then walk to the right. You'll find another Eyeball Switch at the far right side of the area, but don't hit it.

6E. Jester's Jump. Drop into the lower-left corner of the room and hit the Eyeball Switch closed. Jump back up the blocks and move over to the right side of the area. Drop into the lower-right corner and hit the Eyeball Switch open, then jump back up and into the tunnel on the right side of the wall.

6F. The Stone Steps. Collect the Fez about halfway through the area and fly to the right. If you lose the Fez, go back and get it again (you'll need it for the next area of the game). Grab the Running Shoe before you walk to the right.

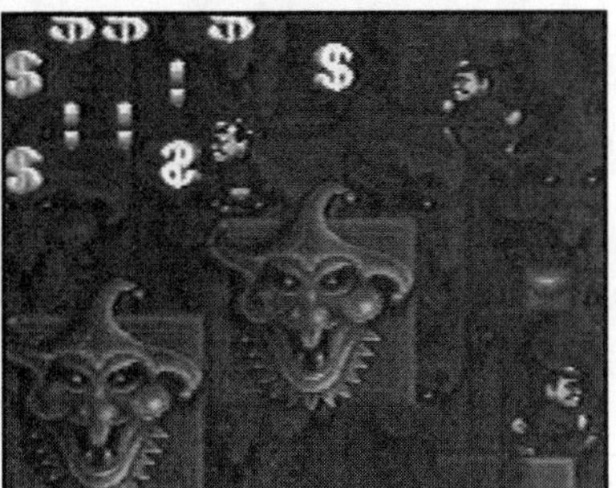

6G. The Crazy Crypt. On the right side of this area, you'll find a single Eyeball Switch. Hit the Eyeball Switch to cause a group of blocks to appear above it. Jump up the blocks to find a cache of Dollars at the top of the area. Grab the money and drop back to the ground.

6H. The Firing Fish. The trickiest puzzle in this area is the gap that's too small to walk through. Wait until the ledge floats to the left, then walk next to the gap and crouch down. The ledge will push you through the gap as it floats to the right.

6I. Chamber of Walls. This area's a breeze. Hit each Eyeball Switch in turn to open the walls blocking your way. Work your way into the lower-right corner of the room and walk through the tunnel to the next area.

6J. The Ante-Room. This is the final room before the Big Bad Guy, but it's surprisingly uninteresting. Just make your way to the right until you find a door with a Thing Box above it. This is the door to Area 6K.

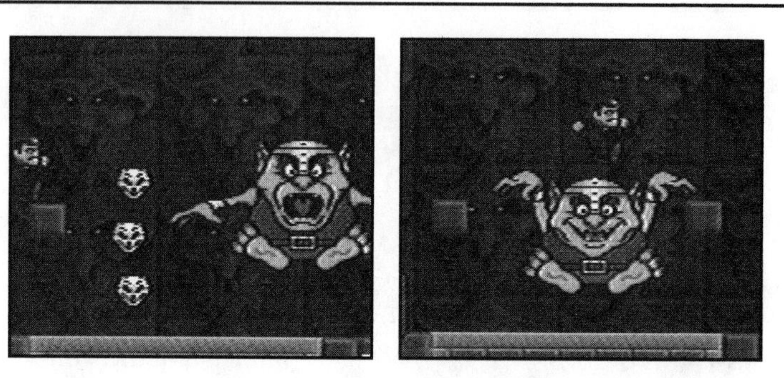

***6K. A Ghastly Goblin.** The Goblin moves in a clockwise pattern around the screen, stopping at eight different locations. When the Goblin is at the top of the screen, stay below him. When he floats to the bottom of the screen, use the blocks to jump onto the Goblin's Head. You can strike the Goblin three times while he's on the bottom of the screen. Repeat the attack pattern until you defeat him. Copy down the password, reset the Super NES, and enter the password to start at the . . .*

Hall of Stairs. Collect extra lives from Pugsley's Den and the 1-Up Room, then come back to the Hall and go into . . .

The Kitchen. Walk to the right to enter . . .

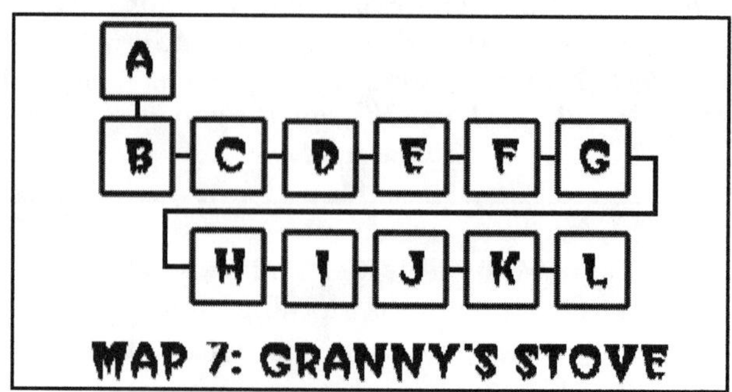

7A. Granny's Stove. There are two secret rooms here. To reach the first one, jump into the upper-right corner of the area. Walk through the tunnel to enter Now That's Tasty. Drop to the bottom of the room and walk to the left to re-enter Granny's Stove and collect the 1-Up.

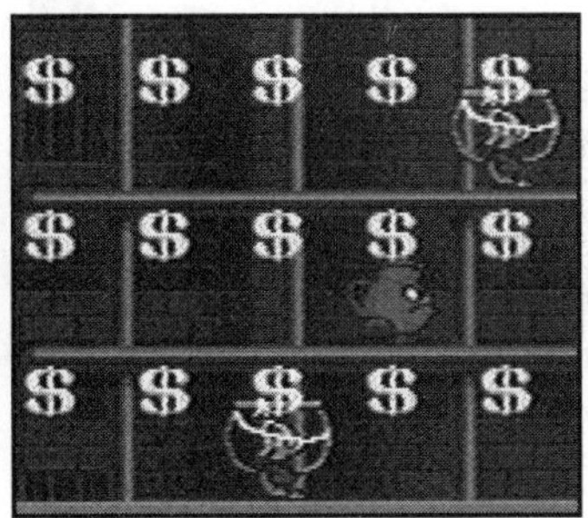

The second secret room is in the upper-left corner of the area, to the left of the On/Off Switch. Jump through the tunnel and you'll appear in The Cookie Jar. Grab the Dollars and exit the room.

Once you've explored both rooms, hit the On/Off Switch and drop back down to the stove. Stand on the stove and push Down to enter Area 7B.

7B. The Furnace. The Thing Box warns you that you can't jump onto the enemies in the oven areas (they're simply too hot). Heed Thing's advice!

At the bottom of the area, you'll find four Switches. Hit any of the Switches and you'll drop down to the bottom of the area. Walk right into the next area.

7C. The Grill. This is a simple area, with only a few distracting Switches. If you come to a wall, walk back to the left, hit a Switch, and return to the right. The Wall should be gone.

7D. The Hob. Drop to the bottom of the area and hit the Switch to make two blocks appear on the far left and far right sides of the screen. Jump onto the block on the right and wait for the ledge to slide your way. Jump onto the platform and leap up into the hole so you can continue upward.

Jump all the way to the top of the area to find a single Switch. Hit the Switch to the Off position, then jump to the right. Drop to the right and into the shaft leading to the next area. If you miss the drop, you'll have to fall all the way back to the bottom of the area and start over.

7E. The Oven. Don't hit any of the Switches in this area. Just keep moving to the right. When you reach the Heart, hit the Switch on the right to Off, then walk to the left. You'll go through the barrier and pick up the Heart. Hit the Switch back to On so that you can continue to the right.

Near the end of the area, you'll find a second Switch. Hit the Switch to Off, then walk to the right and through the wall to pick up Invisible Points. When you come out on the other side, jump up the hill and grab the Heart and four Dollars.

7F. Just Toast. This is a simple area, but there's a hidden room with a Fez. You can fly with the Fez into a hidden tunnel with a Heart inside. However, it's not really worth the trouble, and you should just press on to the next area.

7G. Oven Baked. There's nothing much to talk about in this area. There's a Heart and a few Dollars to the right.

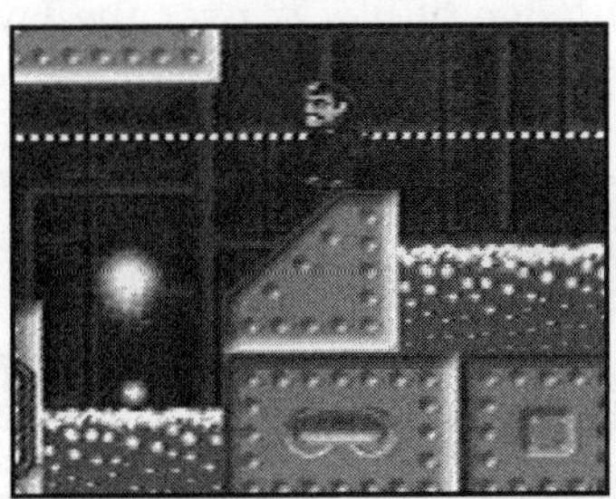

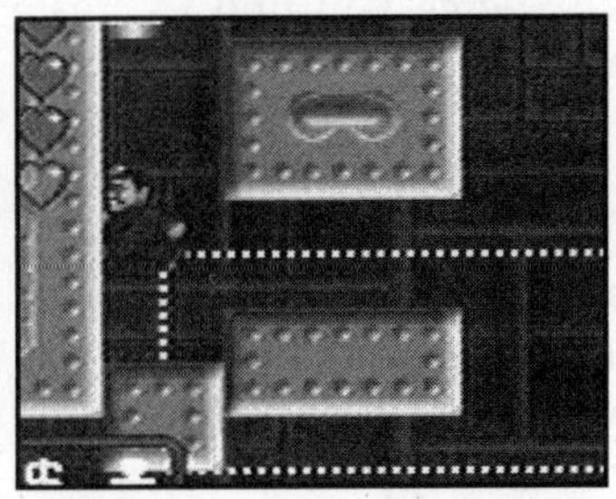

7H. Stir Fried. *The beginning of this area is tough. Here's what to do. Jump to the right and stand at the top of the slope (to the left of the second lava pit). Wait for the moving ledge to slide into the tunnel. Jump into the tunnel and follow the block to the left. When the block starts moving down, walk onto the block and jump straight up to hit the On/Off Switch. Timing is crucial!*

Once you've hit the switch, move back to the right. Ride the ledge up and right, then leap up and into the next section. There's a second Switch to hit in the upper-left corner before you can enter the tunnel to the next area.

7I. River of Lava. Jump to catch the Fez, then fly to the right. The Fez won't run out, so take your time and watch out for the fireballs erupting from the lava below. Grab the Running Shoe and you can fly to the right even faster.

When you reach the room of Hearts, fly into the blocks to break them. Collect the Hearts, then resume flying to the right. You'll find a second room with a single Heart farther to the right.

7J. Barbecued. You'll have to hit several Switches in this area, but it's not hard to figure out which ones. If you think you're stuck, walk around and look for ledges that may have appeared.

7K. The Last Oven. You're almost to the Fire Dragon, so things get really hot in this area. Near the end of the area, hit each Switch you find to create a ledge of blocks over the lava pits.

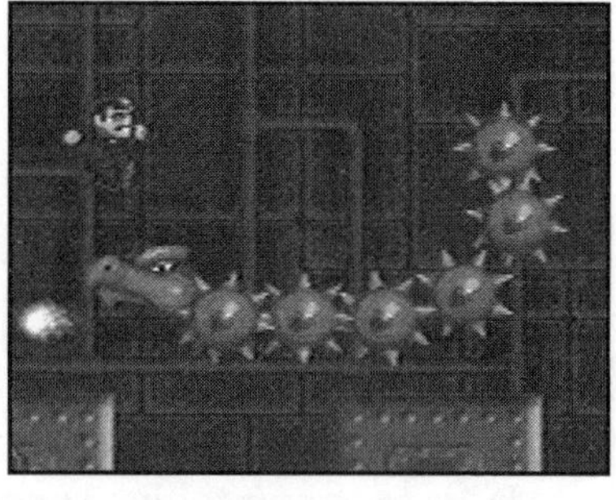

7L. The Fire Dragon. Stay on the left side of the screen. Duck and jump the fireballs that the Dragon exhales in your direction. When the Dragon comes out of the lava on the left side of the screen, jump up and hit him on the head. Don't touch his body or you'll take damage. You may not need to steer at the Dragon's head; instead, try letting him "curve" underneath you when you leap into the air.

When you defeat the Dragon, you'll free Granny. You know the routine by now: write down your password, reset the Super NES, and enter the password to go back to the . . .

Hall of Stairs. Go into Pugsley's Den and the 1-Up Room for your extra lives, then leap up to the door in the upper-left corner. Go inside and you'll find yourself in . . .

8A. Portrait Gallery. Start moving to the right. Halfway through the area, you'll come to a door. Go through the door to enter The Dark Room, a duplicate of the Portrait Gallery, only with no enemies! Gather all the Dollars, then return to the door and come back to the Gallery.

8B. The Armoury. There's a funky secret room in this area. Walk to the right until you find the single Switch with a unicycling enemy below it. Hit the enemy, then hit the Switch to create a mound of blocks to your left. Instead of jumping to the right (and entering the next area), jump

to the left. It'll seem as if you're jumping into thin air, but you'll end up in The Trophy Room, filled with Dollars and two 1-Ups. Grab the goodies and drop out of the bottom of the room to return to The Armoury.

8C. Hall of Clocks. The clocks in this area have huge pendulums. Jump over the pendulums when they swing to the left, or duck underneath them when they swing at you.

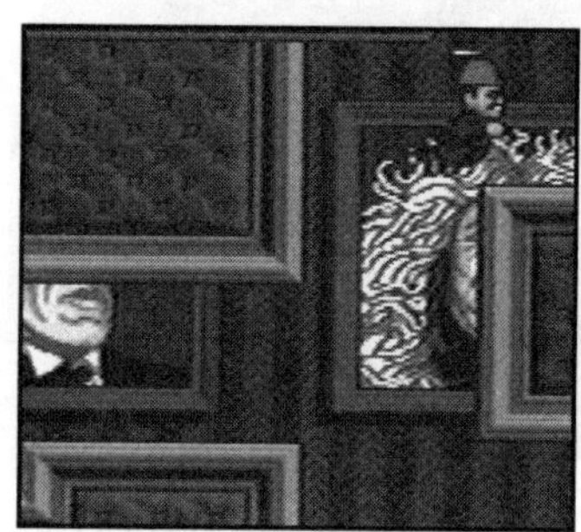

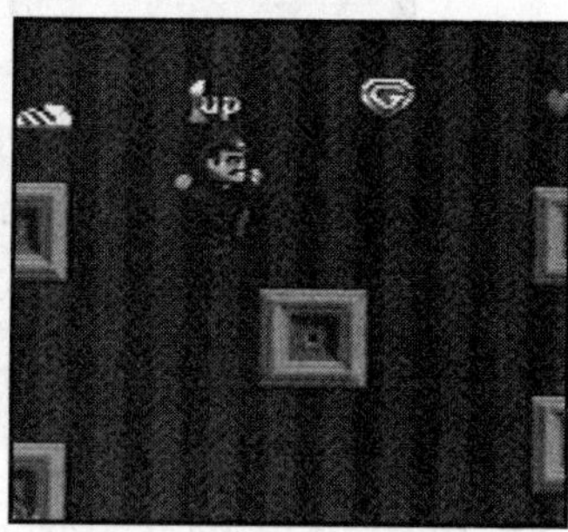

8D. The Weaponry. When you reach the group of red Springs near the end of the area, run straight across without stopping. If you stop, you'll bounce up into the spikes and take damage.

8E. Fly, Fly, Fly. Move to the right and collect the Fez, then return to the left and go back to . . .

8D. The Weaponry. Press the Jump button rapidly to fly straight up and into the high tunnel. If you make it, walk to the right and you'll go into The Closet, a secret room. Jump to the top of the room to find Running Shoe, a 1-Up, a Shield, and a Heart. Take all the items, then return to . . .

8E. Fly, Fly, Fly. Collect the Fez again and fly to the right. Watch out for the spikes on the ceiling and the floor. There are a few bombs near the end of the area, but they shouldn't cause you any problems.

8F. Lower Gallery. There's a wall in this area that you can scale easily if you hit a Switch to toggle on some blocks. Don't hit the Switch, though. Instead, use a Springboard Jump, off one of the teddy bears being spit at you by the bear rug, to get over the wall. Move to the right and you'll find a 1-Up. This 1-Up can't be collected if you hit the Switch!

8G. The Library. Jump into the upper-left corner of the area and go through the tunnel to find The Top Shelf (you get a clue about this room from the Thing Box). Grab the Dollars and go back into The Library, then make your way to the right and into the next area.

8H. The Reading Room. Walk in front of the book "Door O" and press Up on the controller to enter the secret room A Very Good Read. Bounce off the bookworm on the right to get to the door in the upper-left corner. Walk through the door and you'll reappear in The Reading Room. Walk to the right and go through the next door, into A

Secret Panel. This secret area is filled with Dollars, 1-Ups, and a few enemies. Grab all the items and leave through the door at the far right.

After you return to The Reading Room, move to the right and find the Fez. With the Fez, you can soar along the top of the screen until you reach the next area.

***8I. The Big Books.** Jump to the top of the screen and walk to the right, along the top of the books. When you reach the book entitled "Drop In," push Down on the controller to go into a secret room called A Better Read. You'll need the Sword to collect the 1-Up (jump and stab upward to collect it).*

8J. The Train Room. This area is filled with tricky jumps, but they become a lot less tricky if you stand on the engine of the train. This will give you some extra height to jump over the spike wheels in the air. Remember that you don't have to jump over everything; try ducking some of the wheels instead of

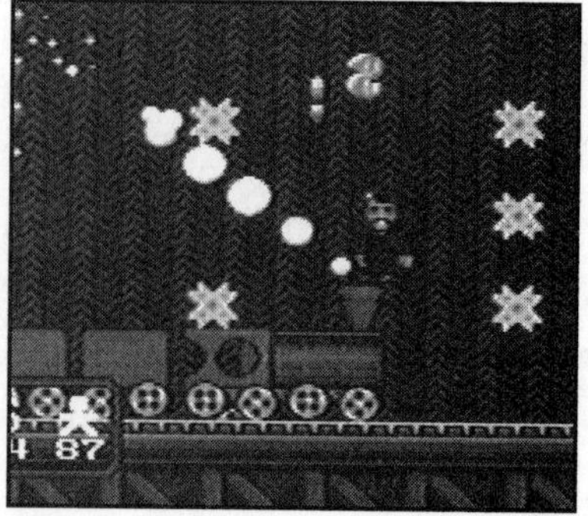

jumping them. At the end of the track, you'll find a few Hearts next to the door to The Witch.

8K. The Witch. Jump off Fester's head to hit the Witch as she swoops down to the ground, then stand underneath her when she's at the top of the screen. You'll be well positioned to dodge her fireballs. You can even stand on Fester as he walks back and forth on the screen, but this is dangerous. Keep bapping the Witch until she gives up the ghost and Fester is freed from her spell.

Write down your password, reset the Super NES, and enter the password again to return to the . . .

Hall of Stairs. Jump all the way to the top of the Hall and go through the door. You'll find yourself in . . .

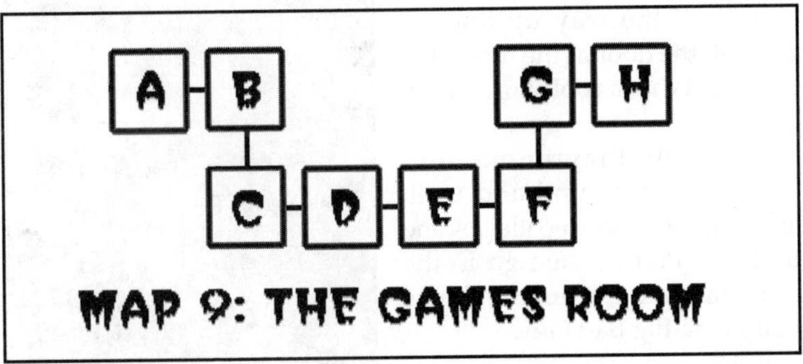

9A. The Games Room. If you'd come to this part of the mansion earlier, it would have been tough, but with five Heart Units and a lot of experience under your belt, you should breeze through here.

9B. The Toy Tower. Drop down to the next door and go through. Simple.

9C. Boom Boom Boom. As you may have guessed from the title, this area is filled with cannons. It's easy enough to jump off the cannonballs as you walk to the right. Don't go into the first door you find; continue to the right until you find a second door. Go into the door to find The Bonus Room. Gather the ten Dollars, then go outside and return to the first door. This door takes you to the next area.

9D. The Toy Tower. Wait for the bomb to explode, then walk to the right and go through the door. Very simple.

9E. Conker Cage. This area is filled with the devilish Conkers, but it's easy to make it through here. Keep going to the next area.

9F. Use the Spring blocks to jump over to the right side of the area. Bounce off the green monster and press Up as you bounce into the roof. You'll climb into a secret passage. Climb all the way up and go through the door at the top of the passage. What a cool shortcut!

9G. The Playroom. Drop down to the ground and walk left into the wall to collect some Invisible Points, then go to the right and find the door. It'll take you to the Big Bad Guy.

9H. Wacky Scientist. Stand on the far left or far right side of the room and jump onto the Scientist's head when the spinning blades are underneath him. When the blades stop rotating, get ready to dodge them. This Bad Guy is a real wimp, so you should thrash him easily.

Copy down the password given to you by Pugsley, then reset the Super NES and enter the password. You'll be back in the . . .

Hall of Stairs. Get the 1-Ups from Pugsley's Den, then jump to the door in the center of the room and go into . . .

The Music Room. Fester, Granny, Pugsley, and Wednesday will all be here. Lurch will play the tune to open the wall on the right side. Walk to the right and go through the door.

Part 4: Rescue Morticia

The Chain Room. Jump onto one of the chains above the door and climb to the right. Climb all the way to the top of the fourth chain, then jump to the right and go through the door.

When you emerge from the next door, climb up until you find the Heart. Take the Heart, then walk to the right until you find the Thing Box. Jump across the shaft to the stone Switch on the right. Hit the Switch and climb down the chain. Drop to the left, then walk to the right. Don't go through the first door you find. Instead, continue to the right and climb into the upper-right corner. Go through the door into . . .

Amazing Chains. Climb down the two chains, then walk to the left. One of the bricks will collapse. Leap to the right so you don't fall down the shaft. (If you do fall down the shaft, you'll end up in the Piranha Tank. Swim to the top of the Tank and go through a door, then make your way back to this point.)

Make your way across to the middle of the room, then climb up the chain. Look for the stone Switch below and to the right of the door through which you entered this area. Hit the Switch and jump back onto the chain.

Climb down, then to the right. Don't go through the door in the lower-right corner. Instead, climb to the top of the area, then go to the left. You'll see a second door. Watch out for the hidden shaft on the right side of the door. If you fall into the shaft, you'll drop back down to the bottom of the area! Go through the door and into the . . .

Hall of Chains. Climb the chains to the right. You'll come to a large gap. Jump across the gap and go through the door on the right side of the gap. (If you miss the jump and fall down the gap, you'll end up in the Piranha Tank.) The door takes you to . . .

The Steps Down. Walk to the right and climb down the steps.

Chain of Coins. Zigzag left and right to collect the Dollars as you fall. When you land at the bottom of the area, you'll find two doors. Go into the left door to find the . . .

Last Refill. Gather all the goodies by using the invisible blocks, then go back outside to the Chain of Coins and go into the right door. You'll appear in . . .

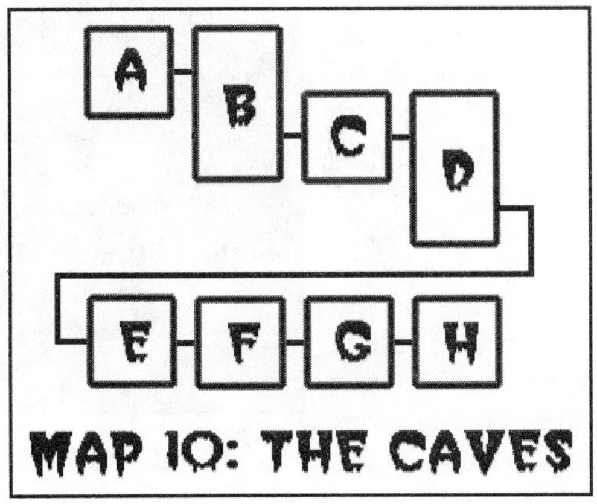

10A. The Caves. You have to take your time going through this area (as with all of the areas on Map 10). If you lose a life, you'll begin your next life at the start of the current area, no matter how close you were to the door into the next area.

There are a few tricky jumps in this area, but nothing too tough. Make your way to the right and go through the door.

10B. Down Deeper. Grab the Heart near the top of the area, then make your way down. Swim into the water to collect the Dollars, then swim up to the door and go through.

10C. The Catacombs. There are two doors in this area. The first door takes you to Rolling Stones, a bonus room with a group of Dollars. The second door takes you to Area 10D. Watch out for the cannons near the end of this area.

10D. The Mine Shaft. Halfway down the shaft, you'll see a strange Switch underneath a swinging mace. Hit the Switch to change the number from "0" to "1" and open the shaft leading farther down into the area.

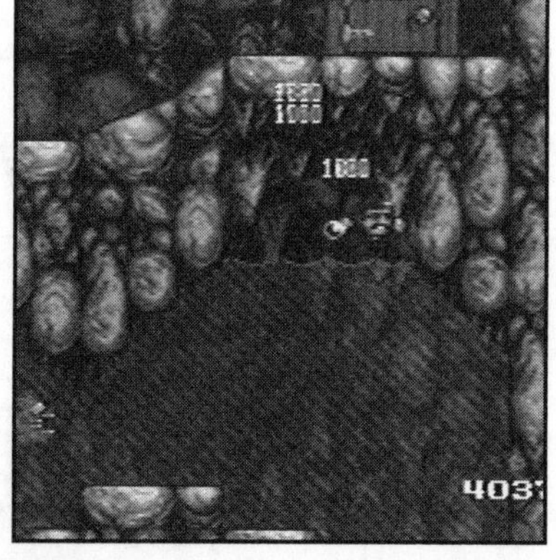

There's a large pocket of water at the bottom of the Shaft. Swim around to collect the Dollars, then jump into the air pocket below the door to grab some Invisible Points! Once you've picked up all the items in the water, go back up to the door and walk through.

10E. The Big Cavern. At the end of this area, there are Invisible Points hidden in the air around the two falling platforms. Jump high into the air to collect what you can before you go to the right and open the door.

10F. The Volcanoes. The namesake of this area doesn't appear until you're about halfway through. The volcanoes spew out four rocks during each "eruption." You can jump on top of the rocks to destroy them. In fact, if you're standing on a volcano when it goes off, the rocks will hit your feet and be destroyed instantly!

10G. To The River. There are four craftily placed Hearts near the end of the area. Springboard off the cannonballs fired by the cannon on the right to soar up and snag the Hearts. If you've still got several full Heart Units, you can ignore the Hearts and continue to the right.

10H. The Gondola. Jump onto the Gondola and it starts moving to the right. Jump over (or onto) the attacking creatures and enjoy the ride. (Don't bother jumping into the water. There's nothing to find.) When the Gondola reaches the right side of the area, jump to the right and go through the door. You'll pop into the . . .

Addams' Vault. There's nothing here except a nice graphic. Go into the Vault and you'll emerge in . . .

The Treasury. Run to the left and grab the Dollars until you hit the wall, then return to the right and keep going until you find the door. Go through and get ready for the final battle!

The Nasty Judge. This big nasty is the final boss, but he's easy to defeat. First, the Judge jumps on his bench a few times, causing gavels to fall from the top of the screen. Then he jumps to the left or the right side of the bench and waits a few moments before leaping back onto the bench and repeating his attack pattern.

Stand on one side of the bench and dodge the falling gavels. When the Judge leaps to one side of the screen, jump to the top of the bench, dodge the gavels, and jump onto the Judge's head. Pounce away from him, fall back to the ground, and wait for the Judge to resume his gavel attack.

Repeat this simple pattern until you defeat the Judge, rescue Morticia, and save the day! You'll be rewarded by a fireworks display above the mansion, followed by some neat pictures of the programmers and playtesters. A great ending to a great game!

SHH . . . THE SECRETS

Passwords

Use these passwords to start at various points in the quest. Remember to raid Pugsley's Den after using these passwords to collect extra lives.

&1YRT	Defeated the Big Bird (3 Hearts, 37 lives).
?1HZJ	Defeated the Snowman (4 Hearts, 49 lives).
L1KZR	Defeated the Centipedes (5 Hearts, 42 lives).

LZZ8V Defeated the Ghastly Goblin (58 lives, Wednesday saved).

LDRGR Defeated the Fire Dragon (66 lives, Granny and Wednesday saved).

LLY&W Defeated the Witch (87 lives, Fester, Granny, and Wednesday saved).

BLK6X Defeated the Wacky Scientist (92 lives, Fester, Granny, Wednesday, and Pugsley saved). Go to the Music Room and you'll enter the final stage of the game.

CHAPTER 2

Arcana

by HAL America

WHAT'S GOING ON?

Hundreds of years ago, the land of Elemen was ruled by the evil Empress Rimsala. Her Reign of Evil was brought to an end by a courageous group of magicians known as the Card Masters. For years afterward, Elemen lived in peace.

Now the land has been engulfed in civil war. Amidst the chaos, an evil magician is plotting to revive Rimsala and start the Reign of Evil again! There is only one Card Master left in the land, a young boy named Rooks. Help Rooks to learn the magical secrets of the Cards and stop Rimsala forever!

PLAYERS

Arcana is for one player only.

EXPERIENCE AND GOLD

You receive Experience Points (XP) and Gold Pieces (GP) every time you win a battle. The stronger the enemies you defeat, the more Experience and Gold you receive. Experience Points increase your personal statistics (Strength, Endurance, Intelligence, and Alertness). Gold allows you to buy weapons, armor and special items.

LIVES AND CONTINUES

There are no resurrection spells in Arcana. If a character dies, whether it's Rooks or someone else, the game is kaput and you have to resume play from a saved game (or start from the beginning).

There are three save slots in the Arcana cartridge. The game doesn't show the status of the saves, so take notes on each saved game. (You can also use just one save slot, but if you miss something during the game, you may not be able to go back for it later.)

CONTROLS

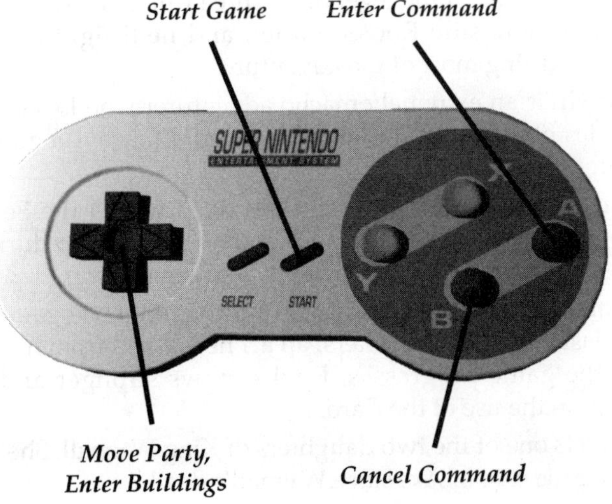

WEAPONS

There are five types of weapons: Axes, Hammers, Swords, Wands, and Whips. Look up the detailed list of weapons in the Arcana manual.

ARMOR

There are four types of Armor: Armor, Bracelets, Robes, and Shields. You'll find a detailed list of armor in the Arcana manual.

MAGIC

Everyone loves a good RPG spell, and Arcana's got a bunch of them. Read through the Arcana manual for a list of all the spells in the game.

SPECIAL ITEMS

Refer to the Arcana manual for a listing of special items.

FRIENDS

Axs is the last of the legendary Three Knights of Lexford. He fought alongside Rooks' father, and he'll fight alongside Rooks during most of the adventure.

Darwin is an extremely macho adventurer who loves to fight hordes of evil creatures single-handedly (always a good way to impress the babes).

Reinoll is an old man who lives deep within the Forest of Doubt. He's a master of magic, and he'll be of help during the quest (although he won't actually join your party).

Rooks is the character you play throughout the game. He's the last of the Card Masters, an art he learned from his father. As the game progresses, Rooks grows stronger and more adept in the use of the Cards.

Salah is one of the two daughters of King Wagnall. She's been under the care of Axs since Wagnall's death.

The **Sorcerer** guards the Crystal Sword with Axs. He makes a cameo appearance in the game: once you've finished the Balnia Temple, you'll never see him again.

Teefa is one of the two daughters of King Wagnall. After Wagnall was killed, she was protected by Darwin, but at the start of the game, she seems to be on Galneon's side. What's the deal?

ENEMIES

Galneon is the evil wizard who plans to return the Empress Rimsala to life. This pesky (and powerful) bad guy will show up at several points during the quest.

Rimsala is the queen of evil. Destroy her to save all of Elemen!

STRATEGY SESSION

General Strategies

• Arcana is an extremely combat-oriented game. There are no puzzles, no hidden doors, no secret rooms, just lots of areas to explore and wave after wave of enemies. If you're a hack-and-slash adventurer, this is the game for you. If you're a brainy adventurer, look at Arcana carefully before you buy.

• Keep track of your Gold and how much you need to upgrade your equipment. It's always worth going back to town and buying better armor and weapons to make your exploration easier.

• During combat, always attack the magic-using enemies first. Some of the magic-users near the end of the game can really wipe you out with Attribute and Sleep spells. The Sleep spells are particularly nasty, since sleeping characters just lie there and get hit. (Here's a strange quirk in the game; if an enemy swings at a sleeping character and misses, the sleeping character says "That's the best you can do?" and goes right back to sleep!)

• The Spirits are neat because they regenerate Hit Points and Magic Points as you walk around. Every time your party takes a step, the active Spirit regains one Hit Point and one Magic Point. Switch between the Spirits to keep them ready for battle.

• Make sure to explore each area on your own. If you use our maps to rush from item to item without exploring, you won't get into enough battles and your statistics won't improve enough for you to survive in the more difficult stages of the game.

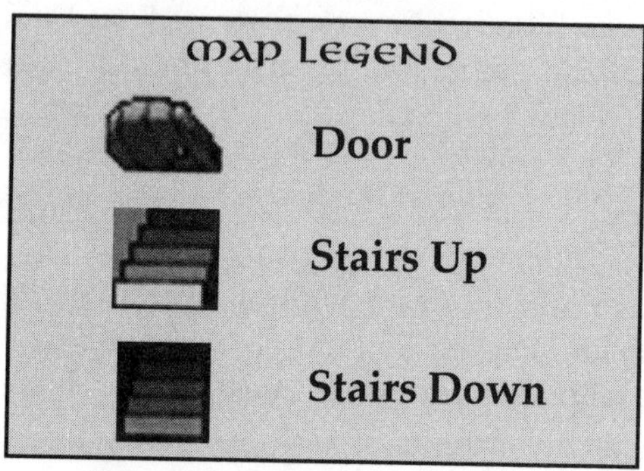

Chapter 1: The Journey Begins

Galia

You begin the adventure in the town of Galia, with the Wind Spirit, Sylph, in your party. Move her to the slot below Rooks by using the Formation option. This puts her into the back row of the party during battle, which keeps her out of close-range combat. She may be pretty, but she can't fight worth a lick.

Press forward on the Control Pad to try and leave Galia. You'll be stopped by Ariel. He'll explain that he's not working for the evil Galneon, unlike his traitorous father. (He sure doesn't seem that sincere, though.) He'll also introduce you to his apprentice, Princess Teefa, one of the daughters of King Wagnall. After some chitchat about the Balnia Temple, Teefa will join your group. Time to get some equipment!

Go into the Outfitter's shop and purchase two suits of Soft Leather, a Dagger, and a Staff. Equip Rooks with one Soft Leather and the Dagger, and equip Teefa with Soft Leather and the Staff. You'll have 50 Gold Pieces left. Exit the shop and leave Galia. Teefa will guide you to . . .

BALNIA TEMPLE

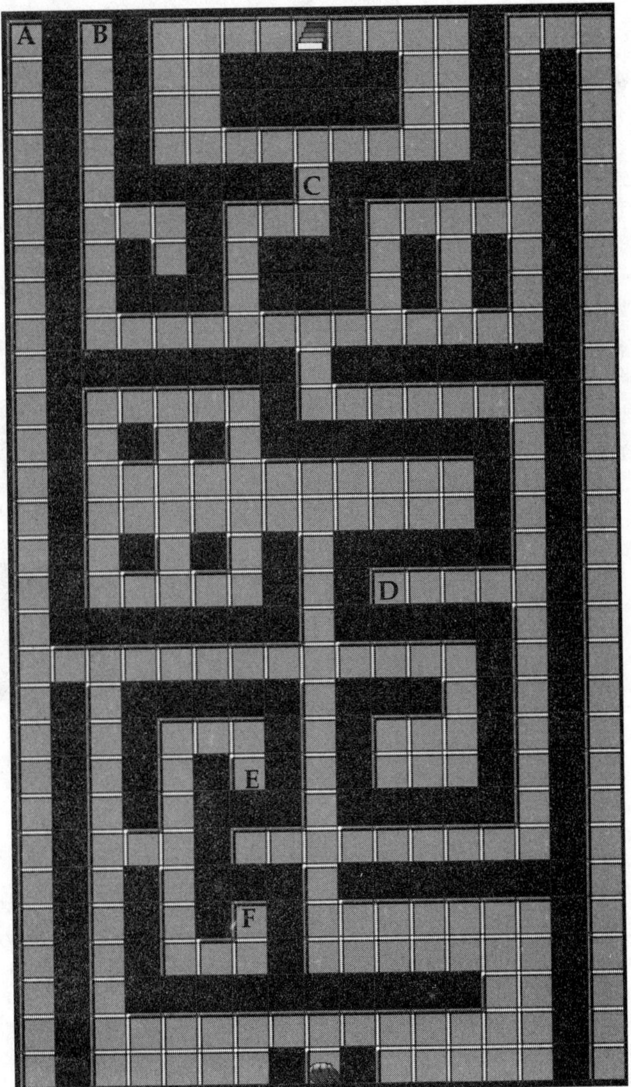

BALNIA TEMPLE LEVEL 1

A. 300 GOLD
B. 500 GOLD
C. STONE GUARDIAN
D. SLEEPING BAG
E. HERBS
F. SILVER FLASK

BALNIA TEMPLE LEVEL 2

A. AXS AND SORCERER
B. IRON GUARDIAN
C. RETURN RING
D. 500 GOLD
E. SLEEPING BAG
F. HERBS
G. SILVER FLASK

Fight a few battles near the Temple entrance to boost your Experience Points and Levels. This will familiarize you with the combat system while you "power up" Rooks and Teefa. Have Sylph cast attack spells during combat; there will be a lot of Earth creatures attacking, and Sylph's Wind spells work well against them. Rooks and Teefa should be able to reach Level 3 before you have to leave the Temple because of low Hit Points. Return to town, sleep at the Inn, and save the game.

When you've collected enough Gold Pieces, purchase a better weapon for Rooks. You need to be be well-armed before you go up against the Stone Guardian, who guards the stairway up to the second level of the Temple.

The Stone Guardian is an Earth enemy, so have Sylph zap him with attack spells during the battle. When the Guardian is beaten, you'll get some nice Experience Points and Gold, and you'll have cleared the way up to Level 2.

The enemies on Level 2 are tougher than the ones on Level 1 (of course), but they're not too bad. Explore, fight monsters, and build your Experience. Before you enter the room where Axs and the Sorcerer are, Rooks should be equipped with the Broad Sword, Ring Mail, and the Small Shield. Teefa should have a Whip, Hard Leather, and a Talisman. (Teefa will leave your party after you go through the door to meet Axs, but it doesn't matter if you un-equip her weapons or not. You might as well let her use them, so she'll do better in combat.)

As you enter the door, Rooks will feel a sting, but Teefa will say she feels nothing. Rooks will shrug it off and walk through the doors to find Axs, the last of the Knights of Lexford, along with the Sorcerer. These two are guarding the Crystal Sword, a magical weapon and one of the Three Treasures.

Ariel will arrive on the scene, and he and Teefa will show their true colors. They're on Galneon's side! Just say "No!" to Ariel's offer to join him. He and Teefa will attack you viciously, slaying poor Sylph and taking you down to just a few Hit Points, before the Sorcerer recovers and casts a nasty spell on the turncoats. They'll run away, but not before warning that your paths will cross again!

Chapter 2: Reinoll the Elder

Doraf

You'll regain consciousness in the sleepy town of Doraf. Axs will tell you the whole story, and the Princess Salah will join your party. Don't worry, she won't backstab you like the evil Teefa. Salah starts out at Level 7, with a good amount of Hit Points and Magic Points.

Leave Axs's house and visit the Spirit Healer to bring Sylph back to life. Then go to the Outfitter to equip yourself and Salah. Buy the Memory Wand for Salah to boost her Attack rating. Buy yourself Breast Mail (if you can afford it), a Large Shield, and the Broad Sword (if you don't already have it).

Once your party is equipped and ready, leave town and you'll walk to . . .

Draven Pass

A. Sleeping Bag
D. Herbs
B. MP Honey
E. Darwin
C. 400 Gold
F. Silver Flask

While walking through this small valley, you'll stumble upon Darwin (no evolution jokes, please) in the middle of a battle against two Gurgeons. Rooks will offer to help, but the studly Darwin will politely decline, and then wipe out his enemies. He'll leave, but not before warning you about the dangers in this area. Draven Pass leads into the next area . . .

FOREST OF DOUBT

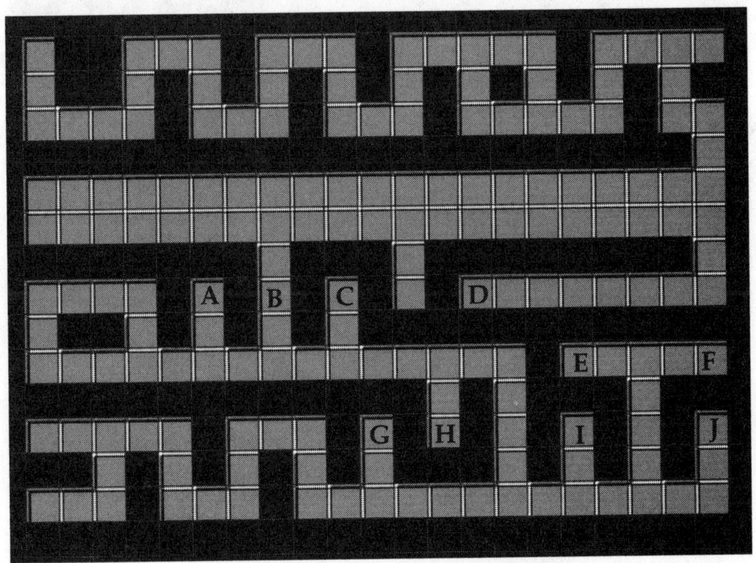

FOREST OF DOUBT AREA 1

A. WATER CARD
B. CYCLOPS
C. WATER CARD
D. RETURN RING
E. ENDURANCE HONEY
F. AGILITY HONEY
G. WATER CARD
H. NULL CARD
I. STRENGTH HONEY
J. INTELLIGENCE HONEY

There are several Cards and jars of Honey to be found in the chests scattered around the Forest. The Cyclops is a tough creature; after you defeat him, Darwin will reappear and ask if you want to join him on his quest. Say "Of Course!" and Darwin will join the party. Move him into the slot across from Rooks by using the Formation command. Darwin is a better close-range fighter than Salah, but he also has no weapons! You can return to town and buy him some equipment, although he won't be with your party long. It's up to you. (We decided not to buy any equipment for Darwin, saving the Gold for later.)

CRIMSON VALLEY

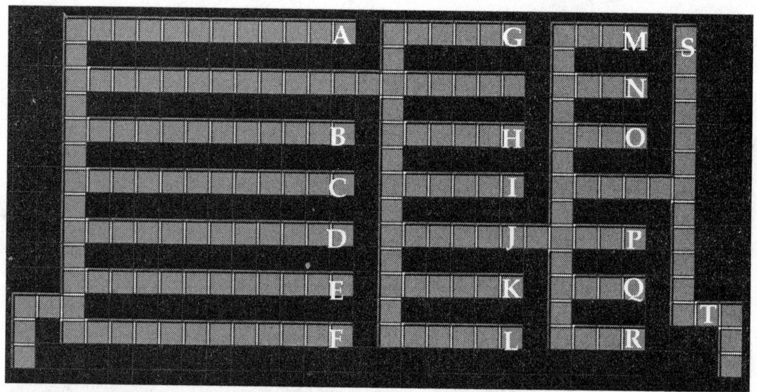

A. 100 GOLD
B. 150 GOLD
C. 200 GOLD
D. 250 GOLD
E. 300 GOLD
F. 350 GOLD
G. 400 GOLD
H. 450 GOLD
I. 500 GOLD
J. 500 GOLD
K. FIRE CARD
L. FOG CARD
M. STR. HONEY
N. INT. HONEY
O. END. HONEY
P. AGIL. HONEY
Q. RESTORE HONEY
R. MP HONEY
S. 300 GOLD
T. EFRITE

This Valley is loaded with treasure chests. Collect them all, then head toward the passage to Forest of Doubt 2. Before you can leave, you'll have to fight the evil Fire Spirit. When you win the battle, you'll add the Fire Spirit to your party. Darwin will leave after your victory, promising to join you again when the time is right.

As you'll notice, you can only have one Spirit in the party at a time. It doesn't make a big difference which one it is, since you can switch between them during combat.

FOREST OF DOUBT

This is a small area, and you shouldn't have any problems reaching Reinoll. Before you travel to his home, make sure you're stocked up on Herbs and Medicine. You'll be fighting a wicked opponent sooner than you think . . .

FOREST OF DOUBT AREA 2
A. TENT

REINOLL'S TREE

Wise (and rude) old Reinoll gives you some helpful info when you talk to him. He'll remind you that to defeat Rimsala, you need the four Spirits (Earth, Fire, Water, and Wind) and the three Treasures (Crystal Sword, Enchanted Jewel, and Spirit Sword).

Ariel and Teefa will bust down the door and crash the party, taking Salah captive and leaving behind Ariel's apprentice, Zerel. This guy knows how to fight, and he can take a ton of damage. Use Sylph to cast Dodge All spells, which improve your Avoidance, and use Efrite to cast Stomp All spells, which improve your Attack rating. If Zerel does a lot of damage, eat some Herbs to heal yourself. When Zerel goes down, you'll be ready for the next exciting chapter!

Chapter 3: Rescue

Doraf

When you return to Doraf, you'll see a note on the table from Axs. He's gone to the Ice Mine to find Salah. Now you've got two goals: find Salah and find the second Treasure.

Save the game at the Inn, then equip yourself at the Outfitter's Shop. You should have enough money to buy the Ice Blade and Seam Mail, which kick your Attack and Defense stats to new highs. While you're in a buying mood, purchase a Battle Axe to have in your inventory when you find Axs.

You can sell some of your older equipment, including anything you bought for Darwin while he was in your party, but don't sell anything of Salah's. She'll need it again once you find her.

The Ice Mine has three levels, each with a different name: Ice Mine (top level), Icicle Dungeon (middle level), and Polar Dungeon (bottom level). It's confusing at first, but the maps we've provided ought to keep you on the right path.

The Icicle Dungeon is tough, especially since you're fighting solo (the Spirits don't really count as members of your party). Keep switching back and forth between Sylph and Efrite to keep them fresh, and use your Heal spells. Bring Herbs, and a Return Ring, so you can get out of the Ice Mine quickly.

Your first task in the Mine is to find Axs. He's in a petrified state, but Rooks' magic is strong enough to return him to

ICE MINE

A. RETURN RING
B. MEDICINE
C. RETURN RING
D. RETURN RING
E. GOLD FLASK
F. 1,000 GOLD
G. FIRE CARD
H. EARTH CARD
I. AXS
J. INTELLIGENCE HONEY
K. FOG CARD
L. RESTORE HONEY
M. MP HONEY

normal. Once Axs is fighting at your side, the Mine becomes much easier to get through. Equip Axs with the Battle Axe you bought earlier, then return to Doraf to buy him some more stuff.

Hydra is a major enemy in the center of the Icicle Dungeon. Use Sylph to cast Dodge All spells, Efrite to cast Stomp All spells, and Axs to cast Offense Impair spells on Hydra. Have

A
B
C
D
E
F

Icicle Dungeon

A. Strength Honey
B. Endurance Honey
C. Hydra
D. Wind Card
E. Wind Card
F. Tent

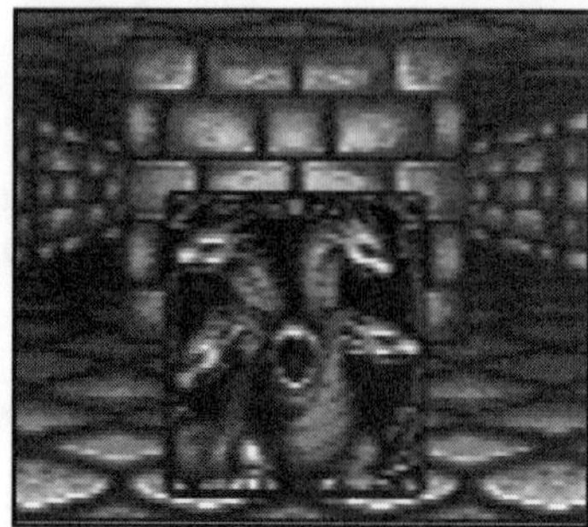

Rooks hack away with his weapon. When you defeat Hydra, Axs gives you the card of Marid, the Water Spirit. (It would've been great if Axs had given you the

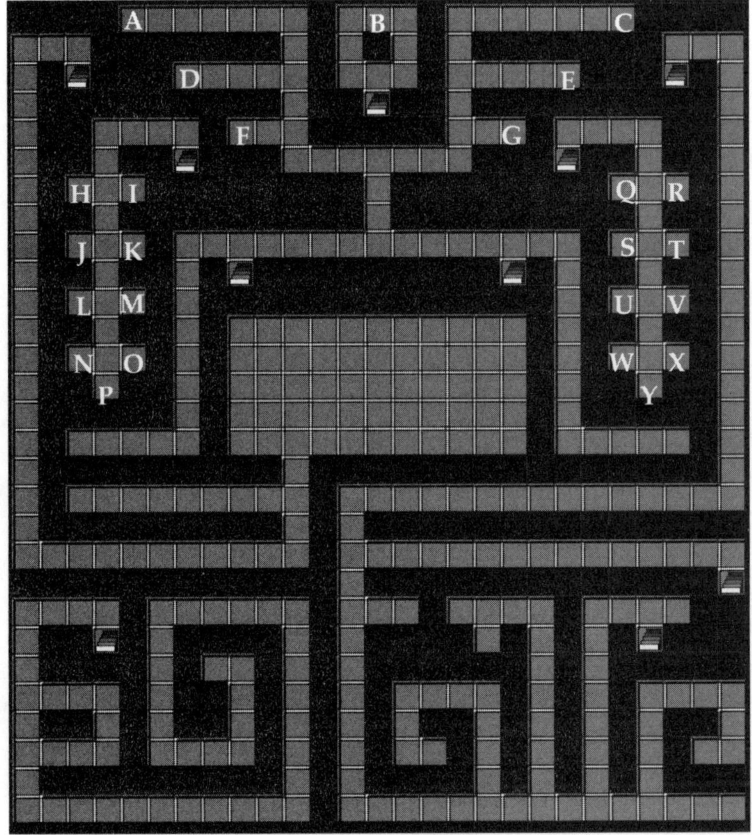

POLAR DUNGEON

A. RETURN RING
B. LAVA ROOM
C. RETURN RING
D. 100 GOLD
E. 200 GOLD
F. 300 GOLD
G. 400 GOLD
H. STRENGTH HONEY
I. ENDURANCE HONEY
J. INTELLIGENCE HONEY
K. AGILITY HONEY
L. STRENGTH HONEY
M. ENDURNACE HONEY
N. INTELLIGENCE HONEY
O. AGILITY HONEY
P. RETURN RING
Q. EARTH CARD
R. ENDURANCE HONEY
S. FIRE CARD
T. NULL CARD
U. WIND CARD
V. ENDURANCE HONEY
W. INTELLIGENCE HONEY
X. CALL AMULET
Y. RETURN RING

card earlier, but he's spacing out a bit in his old age.)

At the north end of the Polar Dungeon, you'll find the door to the Lava Room. The Arcana manual describes this area rather dramatically, but don't worry. You only have to fight one battle in here.

When you enter the Lava Room, you'll find Salah under an evil spell! Ariel has already taken the Enchanted Jewel, and you won't be able to take it back, because you'll have to fight another of Ariel's students, Sauza. Sylph should cast Dodge All, Efrite should cast Stomp All, and Marid should cast HP Restore All and Water 2. Axs won't help you in the fight (he's busy reviving Salah), so you've got to hack away at Sauza yourself. When Sauza bites the dust, you're ready to move on to . . .

Chapter 4: Confrontation

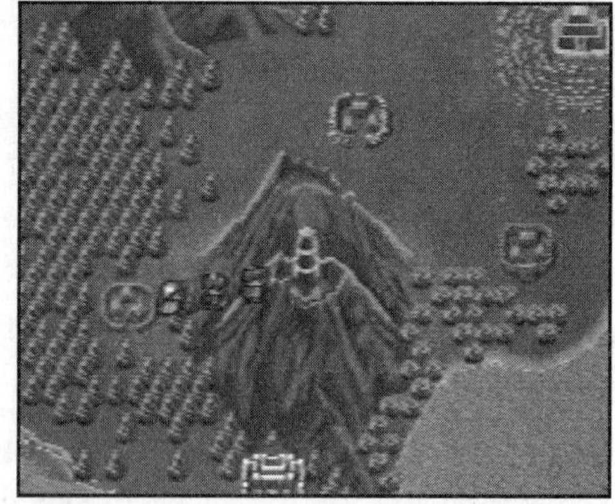

Elf Village

Visit the Outfitter's Shop and buy new weapons and armament. Remember to equip the new stuff! When you're ready, leave town and you'll walk to . . .

Stavery Tower

This massive structure is twelve floors high. The lower floors have lots of goodies to collect, but the higher floors are just tricky mazes without items to find. Here are the highlights of the Tower.

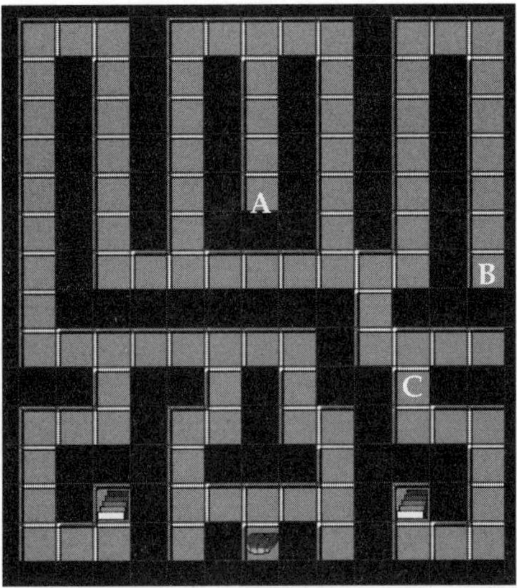

STAVERY TOWER LEVEL 1

A. TENT
B. TENT
C. DARAH

1st Floor: You'll encounter Darah. Defeat Darah and you'll earn the fourth and final Spirit Card: Dao, the Earth Spirit. Dao has lots of Hit Points, but his magical powers are somewhat wimpy.

2nd Floor: You'll find a door that seems impossible to open. Axs suggests you return to the Elf Village. Go back to Axs' house and you'll find Salah, recuperated and pre-

STAVERY TOWER LEVEL 2

A. SHAMAN ROBE
B. LOCKED DOOR
C. MEDICINE
D. GOLD FLASK

pared to join you on your quest. Go to the Outfitter's Shop and buy Salah some useful equipment, then return to the door in the Tower. Salah opens the door with her Royal Tears.

You'll also find the Shaman Robe. Equip Salah with this Robe, which is better than the Magic Robe for sale in the Elf Village.

3rd Floor: Find two powerful weapons: the Wish Wand (for Salah) and the Demon Axe (for Axs).

4th Floor: You'll discover that Dao is actually an impostor Spirit! You'll have to fight two Spirits, Darah (Water) and Barah (Fire), before you can have the real Dao in your party. Cast these spells during the battle: Dodge All (Sylph), Stomp All (Efrite), and HP Restore All (Marid).

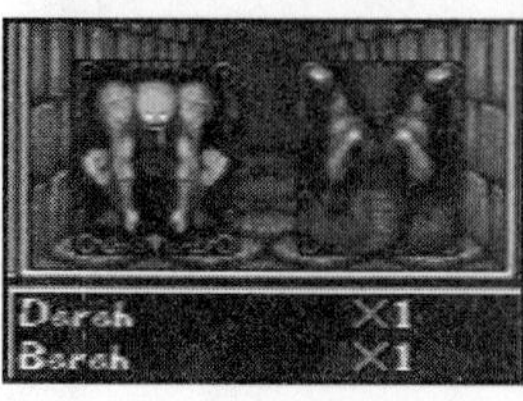

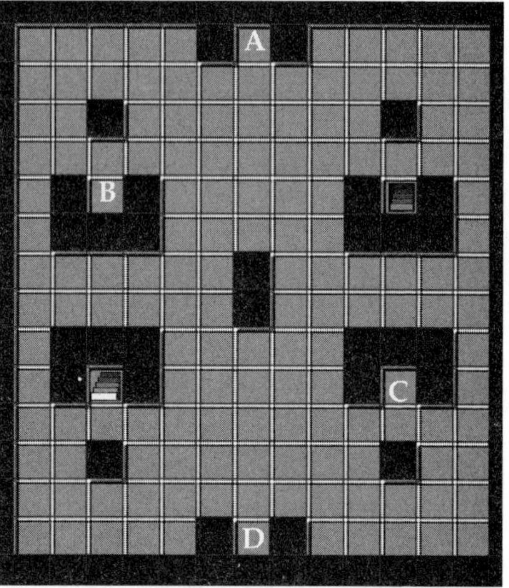

STAVERY TOWER LEVEL 3

A. DEMON AXE
B. 1,000 GOLD
C. 500 GOLD
D. WISH WAND

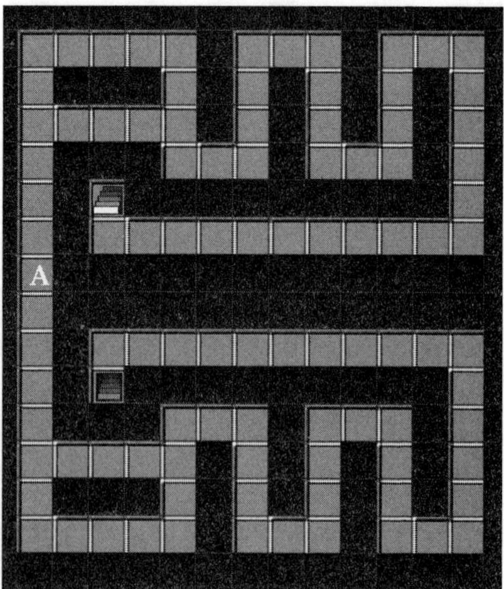

STAVERY TOWER LEVEL 4

A. DARAH AND BARAH

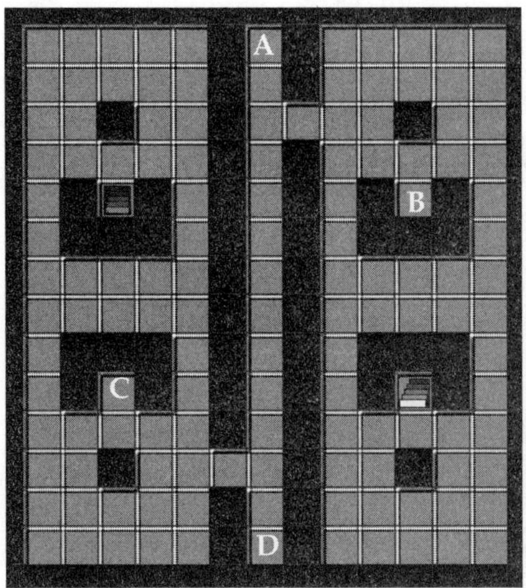

STAVERY TOWER LEVEL 5

A. 500 GOLD
B. DEMON SHIELD
C. DEMON MAIL

Ariel, moments before his gruesome death at the hands of Galneon.

Galneon!

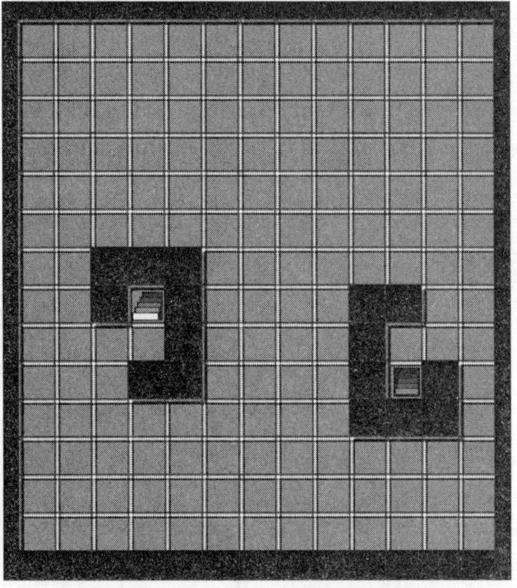

STAVERY TOWER LEVEL 6

STAVERY TOWER LEVEL 7

A. ARIEL

7th Floor: You'll pass by a door, but Salah will notice it, and you'll go through to encounter Ariel. Rooks has to fight Ariel alone (but with the help of the Spirit Cards). When you defeat Ariel, he collapses to the ground and tells you about Galneon's real plans. Before he finishes, Galneon shows up and wastes him! Galneon also tells Rooks about how he killed his father, getting Rooks so angry he runs from the room without Axs or Salah! You have to adventure onward by yourself.

8th Floor: You'll find Darwin. What the heck is he doing in the Tower?! Darwin joins your party, and you'll need his fighting skills. Unfortunately, you'll have to return to town for some equipment, since Darwin still doesn't have any armor or weapons.

STAVERY TOWER LEVEL 8

A. DARWIN

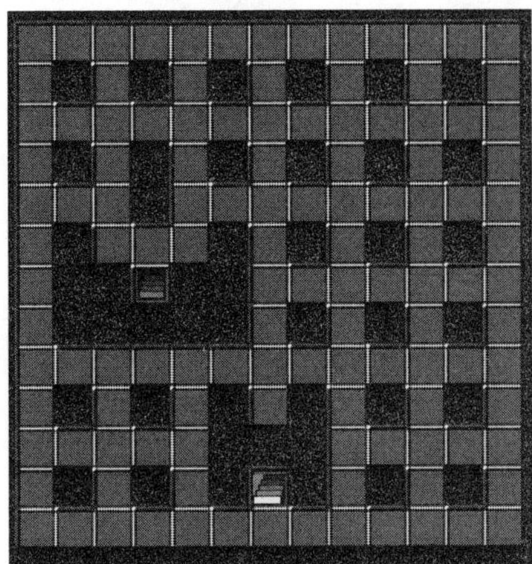

STAVERY TOWER LEVEL 9

She's back!

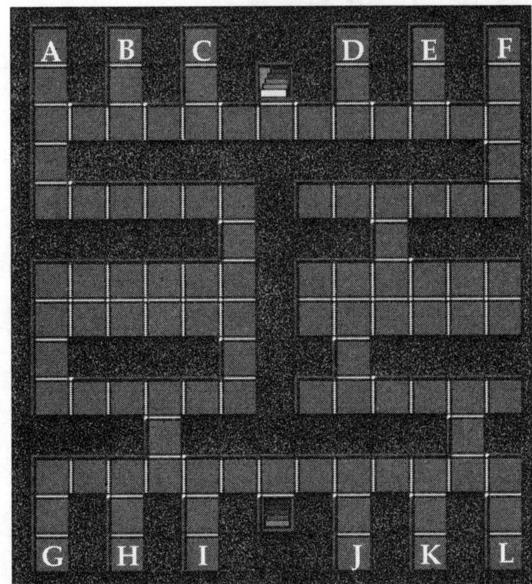

STAVERY TOWER LEVEL 10

A. STRENGTH HONEY
B. ROCOCO ARMOR
C. NULL CARD
D. CALL AMULET
E. RESTORE HONEY
F. MP HONEY
G. STR. HONEY
H. GOLDEN SWORD
I. END. HONEY
J. AGILITY HONEY
K. RETURN RING
L. MP HONEY

11th Floor: Galneon returns Teefa to you, but Teefa isn't exactly happy to see you; she'll attack the party. Defeat her and Darwin will leave the party to take care of her. You'll have to take care of yourself during the final journey to the 12th Floor.

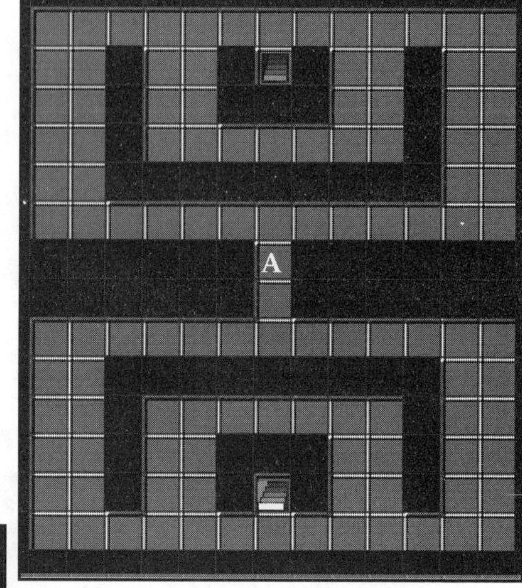

STAVERY TOWER LEVEL 11

A. TEEFA

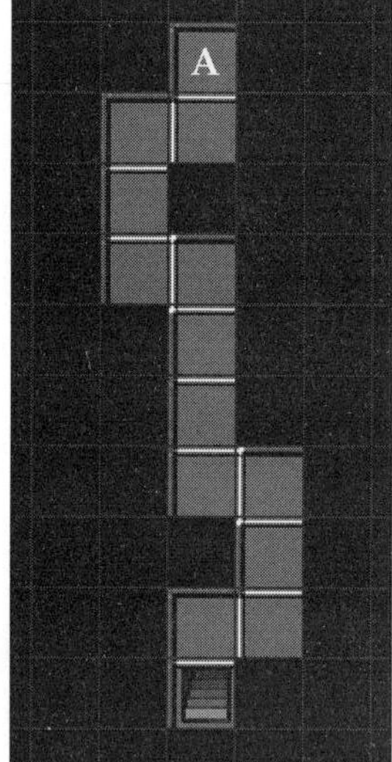

STAVERY TOWER LEVEL 12

A. GALNEON

12th Floor: You'll encounter Galneon. Axs and Salah will rejoin you, and Axs will take on Galneon by himself! After their incredible battle, you'll begin the final Chapter of the game.

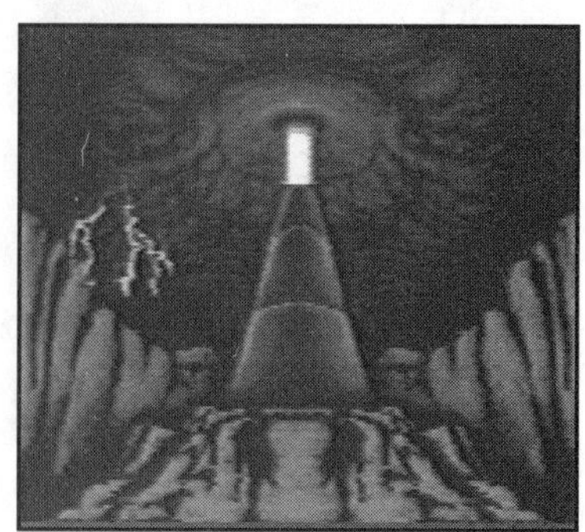

Chapter 5: Salvation

You'll regroup with Darwin and Teefa at the start of the Chapter. Go to the Outfitter's Shop and equip Teefa. Sell the Golden Sword and the Rococo Armor for a ton of Gold Pieces. Stock up on Fog Cards so you can avoid unwanted battles and press on toward Rimsala. And buy lots and lots of Herbs and Medicine. You'll need it all during the final battle with Rimsala. When you're ready, leave town and you'll enter . . .

BINTEL CASTLE

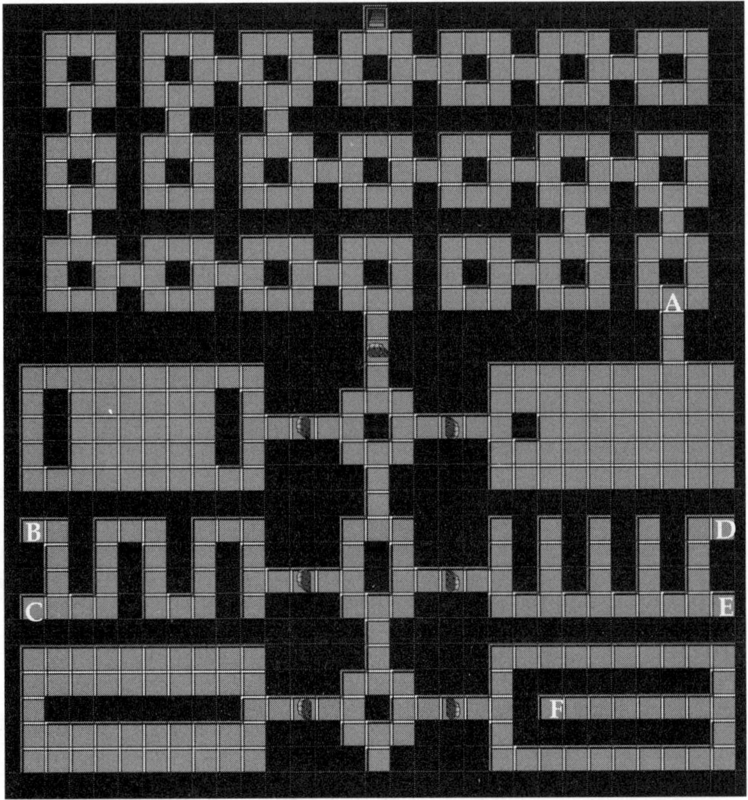

A. KARUL
B. SPIRIT STAFF
C. GOLD FLASK
D. ROBE OF VALOR
E. SILVER FLASK
F. DESIREE

There's some excellent equipment at various locations in the Castle. Make sure you retrieve it all before you encounter Karul, yet another of Ariel's apprentice fighters. Karul is a tough cookie, mainly because he's armed with the Crystal Sword. Defeat Karul and equip Rooks with the rock-hard Sword.

A Tunnel

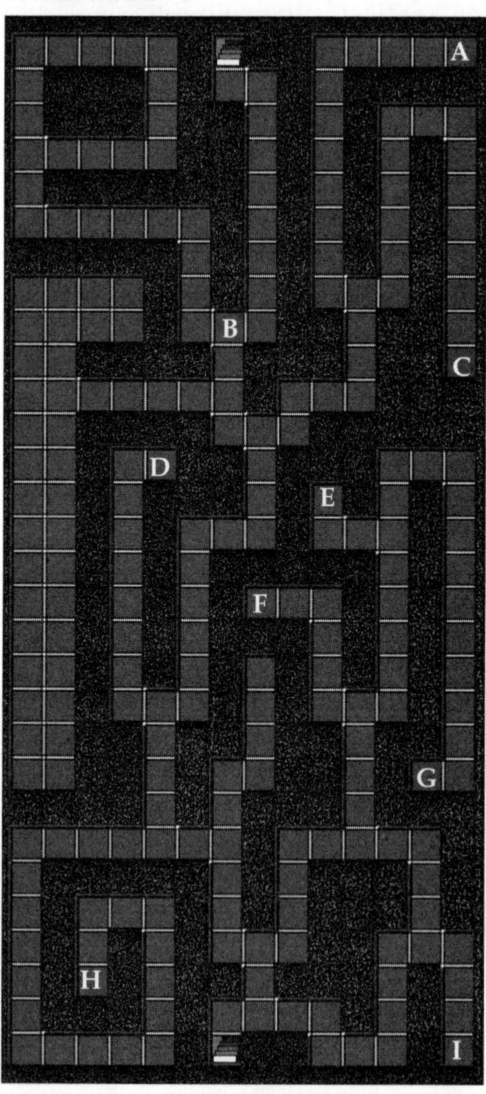

A. Moon Gauntlet
B. Galneon
C. Herbs
D. Return Ring
E. Gold Flask
F. Sleeping Bag
G. Medicine
H. Grand Shield
I. Earth Plate

In this dark and dingy underground locale, you'll encounter Galneon for the final time. After you defeat Galneon in his first form, he takes on a second form. After you defeat Galneon's second form, you get two additional Treasures: the Enchanted Jewel and the Spirit Sword. Equip Rooks with the Spirit Sword and forge ahead toward your final destination!

STAVERY TOWER

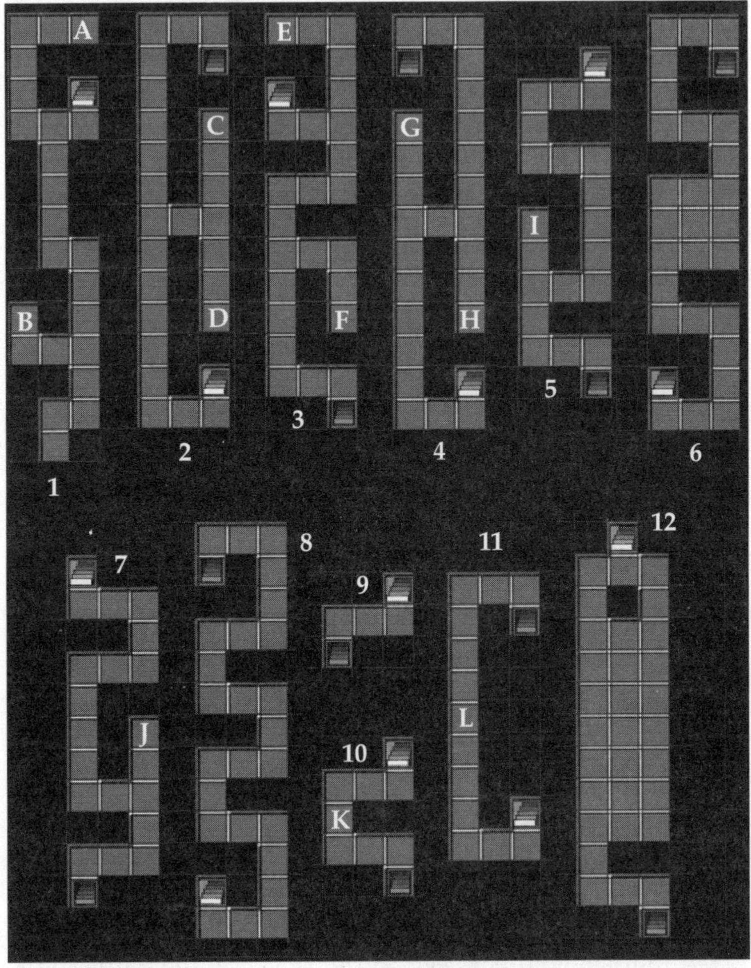

A. STRENGTH HONEY
B. RESTORE HONEY
C. RETURN RING
D. TENT
E. SPIRIT GAUNTLET
F. ENDURANCE HONEY
G. MP HONEY
H. GRAND ARMOR
I. GOLD FLASK
J. TENT
K. RED AND BLUE GUARDIAN
L. TIAMAT

There are a few items to find on the lower floors, but the higher floors are devoid of goodies, and they're also totally deadly!

10th Floor: You'll encounter two Guardians, Red and Blue, but you don't have to fight them, because Axs and Salah show up out of nowhere to keep them busy while you continue on. Thanks, guys!

11th Floor: A giant Tiamat dragon attacks you. Darwin and Teefa stay behind to fight the creature, allowing you to scramble ahead to the final encounter with Rimsala!

Rimsala

Before we go into the attack strategies, heed this advice: don't change your attribute! Remain as a "plain" Rooks, without any elemental attribute (Earth, Fire, etc.). If you take on an attribute, Rimsala casts Attribute spells that completely wipe you out.

Okay, now that you're warned, here's what to do. When Rimsala is in her "egg" form, switch to the Earth Spirit. Have him cast Smash 3 spells while you hack away with your weapon. Heal yourself when needed. When you do enough damage to Rimsala, Rooks cries out a magical chant, but Rimsala won't be harmed. Instead, she'll hatch and turn into her more powerful form! She'll attack and knock you down to a single Hit Point, and you'll pass out.

While you're unconscious, the three Treasures combine to form the Giant Sword! You'll regain consciousness and begin the final battle!

Use all of the Spirits in this battle, switching to another Spirit when the current Spirit is killed. Start out with Dao, casting Wall All spells. After he dies, switch to Marid and cast Accuracy Increase All. When Marid perishes, move on to Sylph, casting Dodge All spells. The final Spirit to use is Efrite, casting Stomp All. If Efrite dies, use the Restoration of Spirit spell to bring him back. You need to keep casting Stomp All spells, so that your attacks with the Giant Sword do lots of damage.

Keep using Herbs, Medicine, and Flasks as needed. Don't be afraid to cast the Heal 3 spell on yourself if you're running low on Hit Points, and keep hacking away at Rimsala. When Rooks repeats the chant, sit back and prepare for the ending sequence!

CHAPTER 3

Contra III: The Alien Wars

by Konami

WHAT'S GOING ON?

The date is February 14, 2636, Valentine's Day, but the alien Red Falcon doesn't have love on his mind. He's been thinking about revenge since his defeat at the hands of Earth's greatest warriors, Scorpion and Mad Dog. Red Falcon devastates the futuristic Neo City, turning it into his private war zone, and prepares to take over the Earth. Only two men can stop him: Jimbo and Sully, the great-great-great-grandsons of Scorpion and Mad Dog. Prepare for the most awesome battle in Super NES history!

PLAYERS

Contra III is for one or two players. The two-player mode is simultaneous.

SCORING

You rack up the points by blasting the enemy aliens. Of course, you're really just trying to play through the levels. Go for a high score to increase the number of lives you have (see Lives and Continues below).

LIVES AND CONTINUES

You start the game with three, five, or seven lives, depending on what you set at the Option Screen. If you're hit by a bullet or an enemy character, you lose a life. You earn an extra life when you score 20,000 points, and for every 60,000 points after that. You can have a maximum of 30 lives in reserve. In the two-player mode, if one player loses all his lives, he can steal one from the other player.

The number of continues you have depends on the difficulty level. In the Easy Mode, you only get three continues. In the Normal or Hard Mode, you get five. When you continue, you'll start from the beginning of the last Mission you reached.

CONTROLS

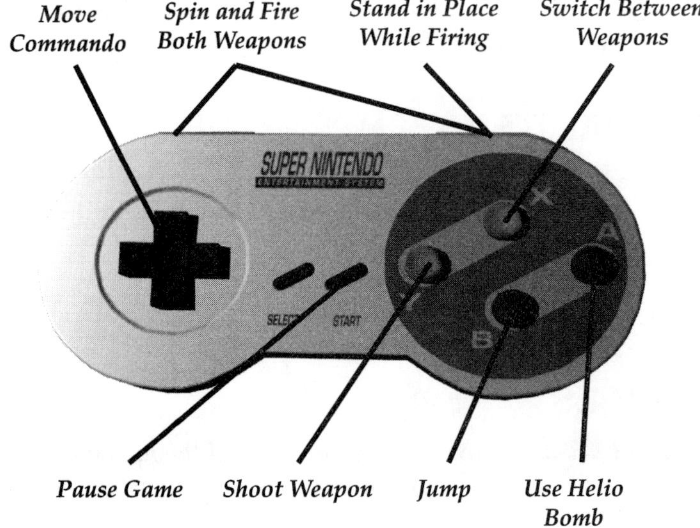

WEAPONS

You start the game with an ordinary assault rifle. It's a reliable weapon with an excellent rapid-fire rate, but you can do better. Shoot the Weapon Wings that float by to gain new weapons.

The **Barrier Shield** protects you from damage for several seconds. When the Shield goes from blue to red, it's about to disappear.

The **Crush Gun** fires a round of wicked explosive shells. The most powerful weapon in the game.

The **Fire Gun** provides a constant stream of flame to fry your enemies. A short-range weapon.

The **Helio Bomb** will destroy every enemy on the screen (along with providing an awesome graphic effect). You start each new life with one Helio Bomb. You'll lose all but one Bomb if you lose a life. These are great weapons to soften up the Bosses.

The **Homing Gun** fires a stream of homing missiles at every enemy on the screen. A great weapon for finding the weak spots on those tough-to-kill Bosses.

The **Laser Gun** fires a long, powerful laser beam. This isn't a rapid-fire weapon, so use with caution.

The **Spread Gun**, an old favorite from the previous Contra games, is back and better than ever. It fires a wide spray of bullets.

SPECIAL ITEMS

The Weapon Wings are the only special items in Contra III.

FRIENDS

None (unless you're playing a two-player game).

ENEMIES

You want enemies? You got enemies. Lots of them. You'll run up against a bountiful supply of mutants and monsters, looking grosser than ever thanks to 16-bit graphics. At the end of each Mission, you battle against a Boss alien. Defeat it to move on to the next Mission.

STRATEGY SESSION

General Strategies

• In Contra III, happiness is a warm gun. Keep firing! There's not a moment of dead space in the game, so keep your barrel hot.

• Here's an awesome tip for those of you with a rapid-fire controller. Set the X button to rapid-fire and you can shoot both weapons at once! Two awesome combos to try with this technique are Crush and Laser or Crush and Spread.

• Practice jumping while firing. You can use your jumping ability to avoid enemy bullets while sending out a spray of bullets that can pick off snipers stationed above you.

• Remember that when you hold the R button, you'll be rooted to wherever you're standing (or holding onto). This simple advice may prevent you from falling or walking to your death!

• If you're playing with a friend, fight cooperatively. One of you should cover the left side of the screen while the other covers the right side. Get to know where the Weapon Wings appear and plan who will get them. If you play your cards right, both of you can be armed with Crush Guns and Spread Guns, a wicked combination.

• The Mission walkthroughs are written for the Normal Mode of difficulty, but they work just as well for the Easy and Hard Modes. In the Hard Mode, there are more enemies, and both the enemies and their bullets move faster. We've included one Hard Mode-specific strategy in The Secrets. Remember that you have to beat Contra III in the Hard Mode to get the true ending.

Mission 1: The Streets of Neo City

Blast the first Weapon Wing that appears for a Barrier Shield. The Shield won't last long, but it'll keep you protected until you blast your way through the abandoned car.

Watch out for cannons popping out of the street. When one of these cannons appears, drop to the ground and its bullets will pass over you. Zap it into rubble!

The other tricky enemy at the start of this Mission is the Man-Faced Mutt. In the Easy Mode, the Mutts stay in the background, but in the Normal and Hard Modes, they attack you when you walk past them. Leap to the left and shoot them while you're in the air.

When you find the abandoned tank, jump into the driver's seat and roll to the right. Don't bother firing the cannon; the sheer weight of the tank will smash everything in your way until you reach the wall. Two shots from the tank destroys the wall.

Speaking of tanks, you'll encounter an enemy tank shortly after blasting down the wall. Stay close to the tank and its bullets will pass harmlessly overhead (these aliens haven't yet heard of adjusting their aim).

When the screen stops scrolling to the right, jump onto one of the cement ledges. A bomber plane will fly onto the screen and drop some wicked weaponry. Flame on!

Use the ledges above the flames to climb to the right. Watch out for the pillars of fire! The most dangerous area is the single stone pillar with a huge column of flame curving overhead. When the flame roars past, jump onto the top of the pillar. Wait for the flame to rush past again, then continue to the right.

Beast Kimkoh is the beastly Boss. Stand just to the left of Kimkoh's head and fire away at his heart. Use any Helio Bombs you've got to cause extra damage. Watch out for the occasional bullet. Keep shooting until Kimkoh explodes!

Mission 2: Maria Calderon Highway

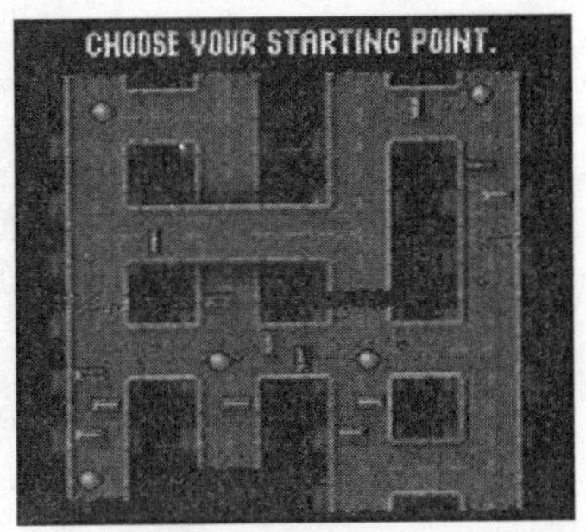

This is the first of the two top-down Missions in the game. (Check out the awesome Mode 7 effects!) The key to winning this Mission is to take your time. There's no time limit, so move slowly and cautiously from target to target. (Use the SELECT button constantly to see where you're located. The radar arrows aren't as useful as the full map.)

The Fire Gun is the best weapon to have in this Mission, because it can shoot through barriers. In other words, you can hit the aliens, but they can't hit you. Start in the lower-left corner of the Highway, since the target there leaves behind a Fire Gun when you destroy it.

There are land mines scattered all over the Highway. The mines don't explode immediately, so if you walk onto one, run away before it explodes.

Use the B button to hit the ground whenever a bullet is headed your way. This maneuver won't protect you from the enemies themselves, just their bullets. You can't move while you're in the prone position.

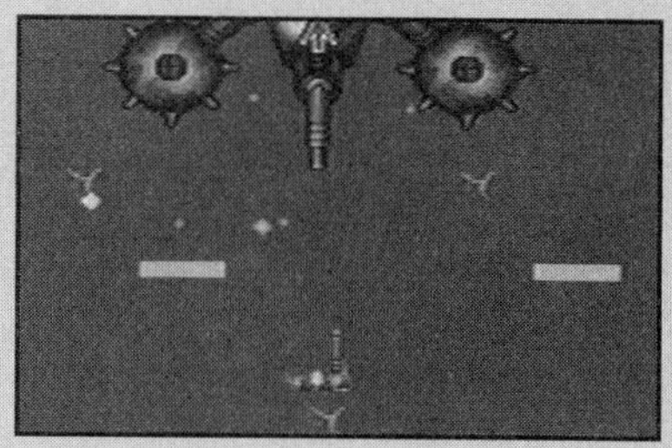

After you've destroyed all of the targets, get ready to fight the Boss, Metallican! When it first appears, aim for its rear-mounted cannon. (The Homing Gun or Laser Gun work best.) Once you've destroyed the cannon, go for the round pods around Metallican's body. Keep moving to the right to avoid Metallican's attacks.

Once the pods and cannon are destroyed, Metallican flies into the air and crashes down on your head! Start moving down the screen when Metallican goes up, and keep going downward until he lands. (In the Hard

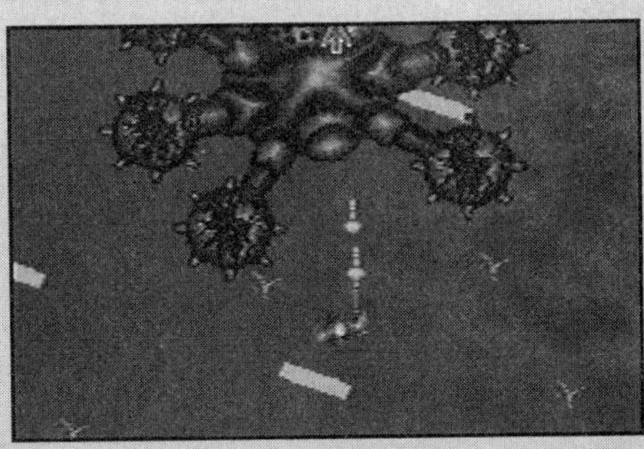

Mode, you have to walk in different directions, because Metallican can crush you even if you're walking downward.) Shoot his red "weak spot" until he flies into the air again. Repeat your attack pattern until the Metallican is crushed!

Mission 3: The Old Cyber Steel Mill

The Fire Gun is the best weapon to use during the first part of this Mission. Use it to toast the attacking aliens (particularly the flying aliens, who try to pick you up and drop you off the bottom of the screen). Keep moving to the right until the Chrome Dome appears!

Chrome Dome is a simple Boss to beat. Jump onto either end of the rotating rod and aim for the red plate at the base of the Dome. When the drill comes out of the top of the Dome, jump onto the girder at the top of the screen. Wait until the drill recedes back into the Dome, then grab the rod again. Keep blasting the Dome until it starts to blow up; leap onto the girder before the Dome plummets out of the sky. Move all the way to the right side of the screen, and you'll stay clear of the group of missiles launched onto the screen after you destroy the Dome.

After dodging the missiles and climbing up a screen or two, you'll be attacked by the Tri-Transforming Wall Walker. Keep

moving up the wall, and dodge (or shoot) the missiles that the Walker fires toward you.

After a long climb, the Wall Walker changes into a second form. The best strategy here is to climb to the top or bottom of the wall. Wait for the Walker to

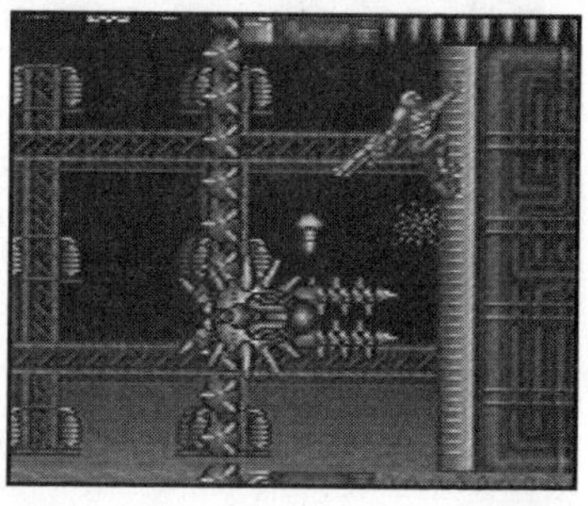

start closing in on you, then quickly climb to the opposite end of the wall and shoot the Walker while its red section is exposed. Keep doing this until the Walker has fallen and can't get up!

Climb to the top of the wall, shooting the Snipers on the left side of the screen along the way. When you reach the top, start shooting upward. You'll hit a Weapon Wing with a Laser Gun power-up inside. Snag it unless you've got better weapons already.

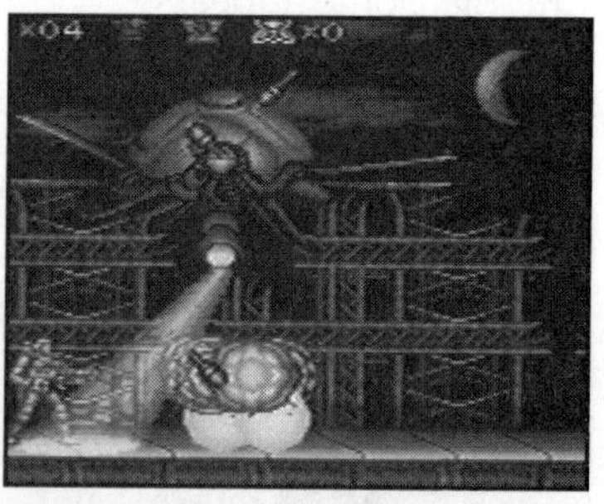

Run to the right until you see the moon in the background. The Megasquito will appear. Stand on the far left side of the screen and the Megasquito's bombs won't be able to hit you. Fire at the Megasquito when it opens its red eye, but watch out for the Mutants jumping down at you!

Once you've destroyed the Megasquito, keep going to the right. Blast your way through the door, then through the cannons and Mutants, until you reach the Robo-Corpse Twins. These guys are a tag-team of ugliness!

Climb up to the roof and shoot at the Twins from the sky. Aim for the red Twin, because he's got a dangerous roof attack. If the red Twin jumps onto the roof, get as far away from him as possible to dodge the bullets he fires at you.

Shoot the Red Twin first!

After you do enough damage, you'll blow up the legs of the Twins. Climb to the roof and they'll be unable to reach you. Destroy them both and prepare for the final Boss of the Mission, the Robo-Corpse himself!

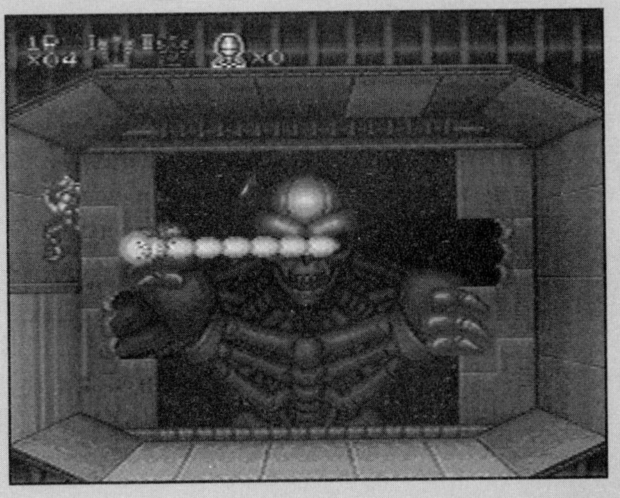

After the beams dissipate, the Corpse spouts a huge fire stream from his mouth. Follow behind the fire stream, continuing to shoot the Corpse. Climb in a clockwise direction to stay behind the fire stream.

When the fire stream has spun around the screen twice, the Corpse coughs up six time bombs and closes the doors to protect himself. You've got three seconds to get as far away from the bombs as possible. If you manage to get clear, the explosions won't harm you. If you're too close, you're toast.

When the Corpse opens the doors again, climb back to the left side of the screen and repeat your attack pattern. Keep blasting until the Corpse goes down for the count!

Mission 4: The Battle of the Blazing Sky

In the first part of this Mission, you'll be attacked by the Psycho Cyclers. Shoot 'em from below. If a Cycler lobs a bomb at you, jump off the cycle and you can avoid the explosion.

Once you blow up the Cyclers, you'll exit the tunnel and hit the mean streets. Your first major fight outside is against the battle tank. Keep shooting away at the tank to cause damage, and to destroy the tank shells it fires at you. Jump into the air every once in a while to shoot down the jetpackers.

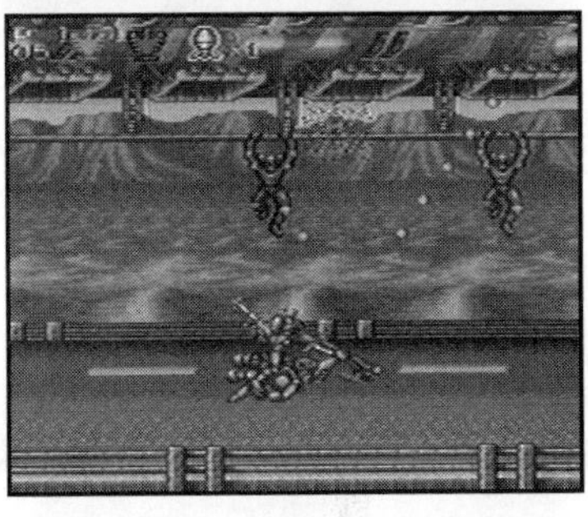

After you blow up the tank, a huge alien battleship will pass overhead! This battleship is armed with some nasty enemies, starting with the turrets. Use the Flame Gun to destroy them.

The monkey aliens are the next major enemies. Stay in the middle of the screen, hold the R button, and use the Flame Gun to toast the bad guys. Go for the gray monkey. Once you destroy him, the red aliens stop coming.

There's an alien Boss to fight as soon as the battleship flies off the right side of the screen. Keep shooting the Boss in its "head," and jump to avoid its lashing legs. After you blow the Boss up, a helicopter flies onto the screen. Jump off the cycle and grab onto the helicopter.

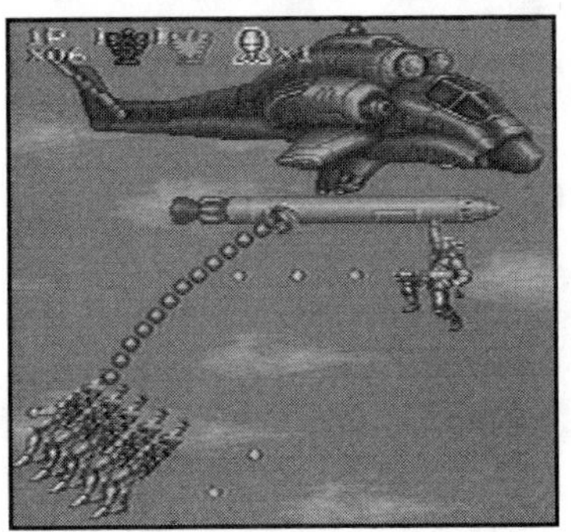

When the helicopter reaches its maximum altitude, an armored alien soars onto the screen. Move away from the alien as it latches onto the missile, then shoot it as it swings back and forth below the chopper. If the alien climbs up to the missile, leap over the spinning blade he lobs at you. Keep firing until this metallic mutha' explodes!

After you beat the armored alien, the helicopter launches the missile you're hanging onto. Jump from missile to missile until the battleship appears on the screen.

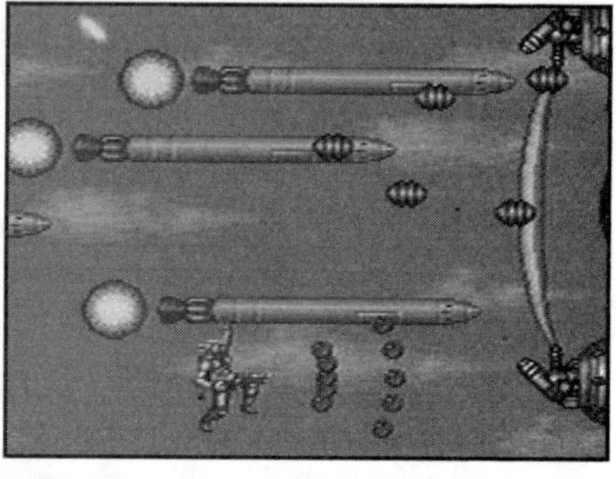

Your first task is to destroy the cannons at top and bottom of the battleship. To destroy the cannon at the bottom, hold onto the lowest-flying missiles and shoot to the right. To destroy the cannon at the top, hold onto the highest-flying missiles and jump into the air. The cannons defend each other, so when you're attacking one of them, you'll be shot at by the other. Stay as far to the left side of the screen as possible.

Once both cannons are destroyed, start shooting at the red engine of the battleship. The battleship shoots at the missiles to destroy them, so keep jumping from missile to missile. Stay at the top of the screen to avoid a nasty fall. When the battleship blows up, the entire screen goes white, but don't worry. After a few moments, you and the helicopter will reappear on the screen.

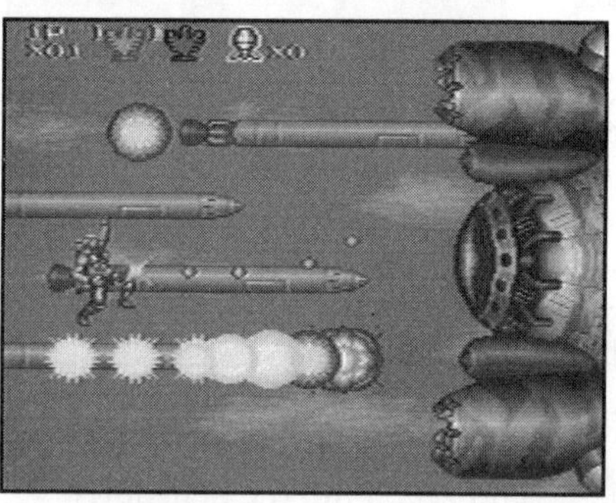

Mission 5: The Mucho Grande Badlands

This is the second of the top-down view Missions. It's way harder than the last one, thanks to some really narrow pathways to particular targets. The hardest target to reach is the one in the upper-left corner; for this reason, we suggest you start in that area, so you can destroy it first.

The target in the lower-right corner of the map is a tough kill. Move onto one of the swirling squares and hold down the B button. Keep firing your weapon and you'll hit the target every time you spin toward it.

Once all the targets are destroyed, you'll face off against a giant Boss in the middle of a sand pit. Shoot the Boss in the eye to cause damage. You can run away from the snakes that the Boss sends after you, or you can destroy them with a strong weapon (Crush Gun or Laser Gun).

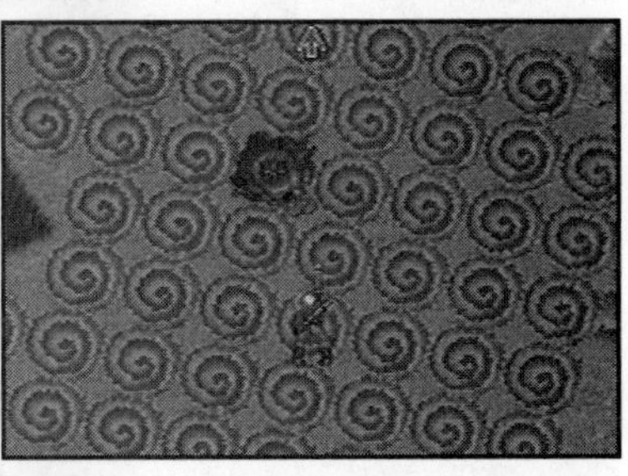

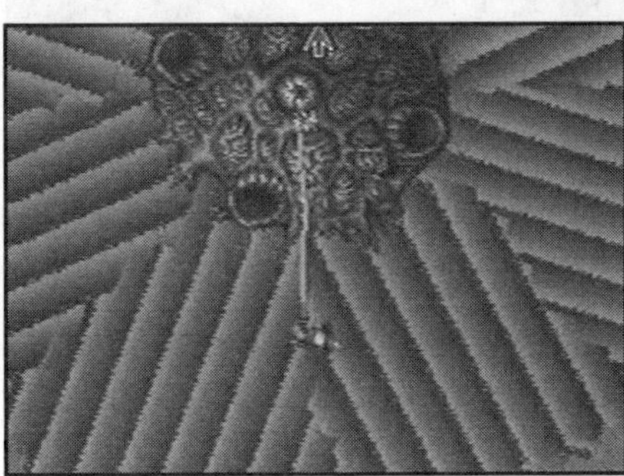

After you've caused enough damage, the sand pit starts to spin! When you stand on the sand, you'll slowly be sucked toward the Boss (and instant death). The trick is to hit the L button to counteract the spinning sands. If you do this correctly, you can continually shoot the eyeball of the Boss. Remember to back away from the Boss if you get too close. Use the strongest weapons you've got!

Mission 6: Red Falcon's Main Base

Since this Mission is a never-ending stream of Bosses, we'll skip the walkthrough format and go right to the strategies. Fight on!

Para-Slug

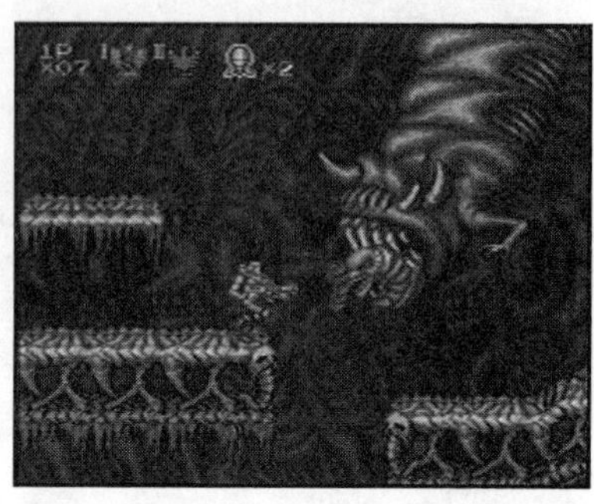

Use the Spread Gun (found inside the Weapon Wing that appears almost simultaneously with the Slug) and walk to the end of the ledge. Shoot the Slug rapidly in the jaw. Robo-Slug spits out alien embryos, but if you're positioned properly, the Spread Gun will destroy them as soon as they appear.

After the Slug, you'll see alien mouths at the top and bottom of the screen, spitting out spiky spores. The Crush Gun is the best weapon to use against the mouths, although the Homing Gun also works well.

Red Falcon's Heart

Get up close to the Heart, hold down the R button, and fire away with the Spread Gun. (The alien pods to the left of the heart will eventually blow up if you keep shooting.) Shoot until the heart goes boom!

"Mole" Boss

When the Boss slides to the left, jump straight up and you'll land safely on the Boss's legs. When the Boss slides back to the right, walk a few steps to the right and start firing your Laser. The Boss will open his armored stomach (allowing your Laser

to damage him) and shoot fireballs into the air. Dodge the fireballs and watch the Boss's eyelids. When they open, get ready to jump over a deadly laser beam.

The only other attack in this Boss's arsenal is when he burrows into the ground. If the Boss burrows, run to the far left side of the screen and wait for the Boss to come back onto the screen. (He'll always slide to the left after coming out of the ground.)

Vicious Slave Hawk

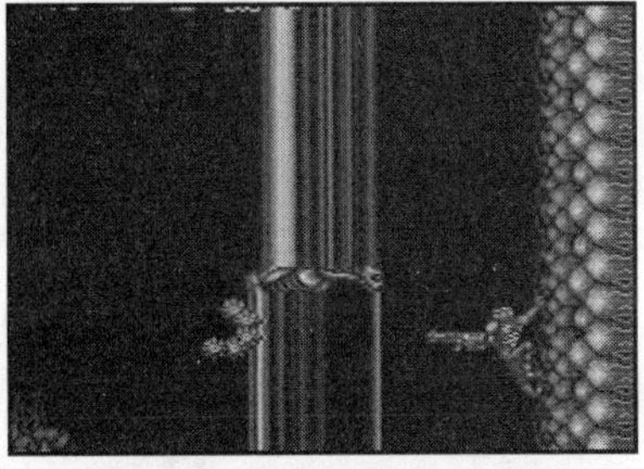

The Crush Gun or Laser Gun is best against the Hawk. Keep climbing up and down the wall to avoid the Hawk as he bounces left and right. Shoot him in the head to cause damage.

After taking enough hits, the Hawk switches into his second attack pattern, "beaming out" a la Star Trek, and then "beaming in" to attack. Climb to the middle of the screen when the Hawk beams out. Climb downward as soon as he starts to beam in, and fire at him before he beams out again. Keep repeating this pattern until the Hawk bites the dust. (You can also climb to the bottom of the screen, then climb upward and shoot when he beams in.)

Red Falcon's Head

Your first task is to destroy the alien snakes on either side of Red Falcon's head. The Crush Gun is best suited for the job, since it does the most damage, followed by the Laser. The snakes can

stretch all the way across the screen, so you've got to eliminate them as soon as possible.

Once you've toasted both snakes, move to the middle of the screen and start shooting Red Falcon's eyes. Turn left and right to shoot the attacking aliens as they drop to the ground. After both eyes have been blown to bits, go for Falcon's brain. Keep shooting until the head starts to blow up.

Red Falcon's Brain

The Brain is surrounded by eight rapidly rotating spheres. When you shoot a sphere, the Brain will attack using that sphere. The eight spheres are as follows.

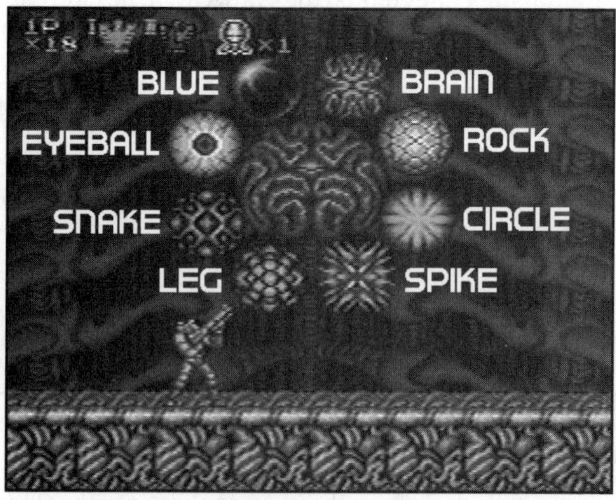

Blue Sphere: *Don't bother shooting the Brain, just dodge the bouncing blue spheres (seven of them in all). Use any Helio Bombs you've got before you die.*

Brain Sphere: *The big Brain floats back and forth on the screen, surrounded by a mass of smaller brains. Shoot through the smaller brains to uncover to uncover the big Brain. Use a Helio Bomb to destroy all of the smaller brains and leave the big Brain completely vulnerable to attack.*

Circle Sphere: *Eight spheres spin around you while the Brain floats overhead. The spheres will slowly close in on you. If you've got a Helio Bomb, use it to destroy the spheres around you. Otherwise, you're dead.*

Eyeball Sphere: *The Brain shoots out a steady stream of bouncing eyeballs. Stand on the far left side of the screen and blast the Brain.*

Leg Sphere: *The Brain sprouts legs and walks back and forth on the screen. Stand on the far left side of the screen, jump into the air, and shoot the Brain.*

Rock Sphere: *The Brain lands on the right side of the screen and sends groups of rocks flopping across the screen. Jump into the gaps between each group of rocks and shoot to the right.*

Snake Sphere: *A huge snake crawls along the bottom of the screen. Crawl along the ground and stay underneath the "arches" in the snake's back.*

Spike Sphere: *The Brain drops a downpour of Spike Spheres, power-ups, and Helio Bombs at you. It's possible to collect some great power-ups here, but you may need to sacrifice a life or two in the process.*

Stand below and to the left of the rotating spheres, hold down the R button, and aim diagonally up and right. Shoot your gun when the sphere you want is in front of your weapon.

You should aim for the Brain Sphere or the Leg Sphere, since the Brain is practically harmless with these spheres. (If you've got a controller with slow-motion, this is an excellent time to use it.) The Brain takes a ton of punishment, so keep up the attack!

SHH . . . THE SECRETS

The Final Battle (Hard Mode Only)

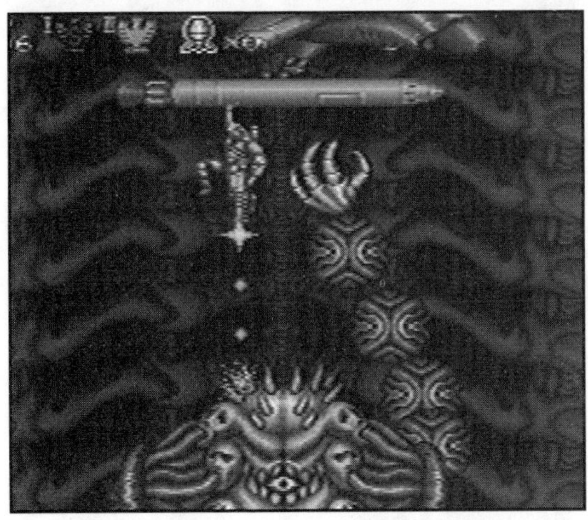

In the Hard Mode, after you're picked up by the helicopter, Red Falcon's Brain comes back to life! It encloses itself within a solid metal shell and pursues the helicopter.

Jump into the air to avoid the metal shell and the long arms it lashes out at you. If Red Falcon swings its left arm, jump to the right; if it swings its right arm, jump to the left. Keep firing downward, but don't make the mistake of holding the controller Down when you jump, or you'll fall to your doom. When you blow up Red Falcon, you'll get an excellent ending sequence! Good work!

Power-Up Trick

Find an area on a Stage where enemies constantly appear on one side of the screen (but not both, or this trick won't work). Aim toward that side of the screen and tape down the fire button (or activate your rapid-fire joystick if you have one). Now do something for a while (we usually go outside and shoot some hoops or read the latest issue of GamePro). Your points will slowly build up as the enemies run onto the screen and are shot by your rapidly firing weapon. As your points build up, your extra lives also build up. Eventually, you'll have 29 lives in reserve. Here are two power-up locations we've found. How many can youdiscover on your own?

Stage 1: When you reach the first wall, shoot the soldier and the two guns, but don't destroy the wall. Turn to the left and shoot the soldiers that run onto the screen.

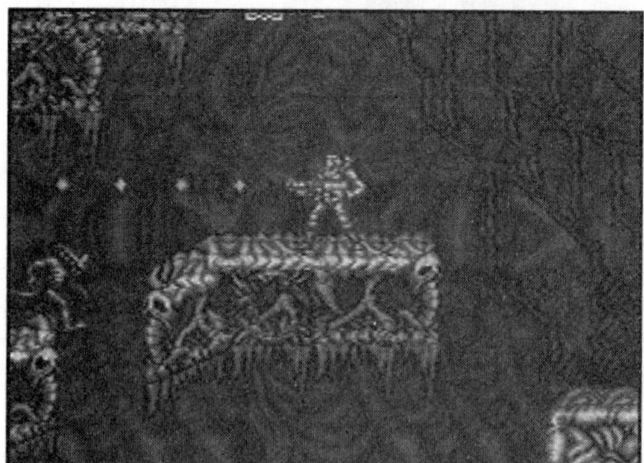

Stage 6: Stand on the ledge to the left of the tunnel that leads to the heart. Face left and fire rapidly. Aliens will leap at you from the right, but they won't reach you.

CHAPTER 4

Final Fight

by Capcom

WHAT'S GOING ON?

Metro City is overrun with crime, and ruled by the Mad Gear gang. Mike Haggar, former Street Fighter, has been elected Mayor and vows to clean up the streets. The Mad Gear gang kidnaps his daughter Jessica, threatening her life if Mike doesn't cooperate with them. Mike and Cody,

Jessica's boyfriend, must fight their way through Metro City to rescue Jessica from the Mad Gear's clutches!

PLAYERS

Final Fight is for one player only.

SCORING

It's easy to score points in Final Fight—just beat the stuffing out of anyone who gets in your way. The more points you score, the better your chances of earning extra lives (see below).

LIVES AND CONTINUES

You start the game with six lives. Each life has a Strength Meter. When you are hit by your enemies, or use your Super Move, the Meter decreases. When the Meter runs out, you lose a life. If you lose all your lives, the game is over!

You have three continues. When you continue the game, you'll resume play at the beginning of the last Stage you reached (there are five Stages in all).

WEAPONS

Some of your enemies carry weapons that you can use. Knock down the enemy and pick up the weapon. You can also find weapons inside crates and drums. If you are hit, you'll drop your weapon, and it may disappear!

CONTROLS

There are so many moves in Final Fight that we decided the best way to indicate the moves was simply to list the button presses needed to use them. Read on!

B and Left or Right then Y
Flying Kick (Cody)

B then Y
Jump Kick (Haggar)
Jump Kick (Cody)

Y then Left/Right
Shoulder Throw (Cody)

Y
Head Butt (Haggar)
Knee Bash (Cody)

B then Y and Down
Lunge (Haggar)
Knee Drop (Cody)

B then Y and Down
Pile Driver (Haggar)

Y and B
Super Spin (Haggar)
Super Kick (Cody)

Any Direction and Y
Back Drop (Haggar)

SPECIAL ITEMS

There are 19 Special Items in the game: 10 Food Items (these restore your Strength Meter) and 9 Bonus Point Items (these give you extra points).

Barbecue: Refills the entire Strength Meter.
Curry, Hamburger, Pizza: Refills 1/2 of the Strength Meter.
Apple, Banana, Grapes: Refills 1/4 of the Strength Meter.
Gum, Soda, Vitamins: Refills 1/9 of the Strength Meter.
Diamond, Gold Bar: 10,000 points.
Necklace, Ring: 5,000 points.
Dime, Money: 3,000 points.
Hammer, Hat, Radio: 1,000 points.

FRIENDS

You don't have any friends where you're going, which is deep into Mad Gear territory. Watch your back, dude!

ENEMIES

Some of your enemies are almost harmless thugs, while others are buffed individuals with powerful weapons. The most dangerous enemies are the Bosses!

Thrasher is the Boss of Stage 1 (The Slum). He'll attack with his own gang of thugs.

Katana is the Boss of Stage 2 (The Subway and Park). He uses two deadly swords to slash his opponents to bits.

Edi-E is the Boss of Stage 3 (The West Side). He's armed with a billy club and a rapid-fire gun.

Abigail is the Boss of Stage 4 (The Bay Area). He doesn't have a weapon, but he's so tough he doesn't need one.

Belger is the Boss of Stage 5 (Uptown). He's the leader of the Mad Gear gang. Defeat him and you'll save Jessica.

STRATEGY SESSION

General Strategies

• Choose Cody as your fighter if you want a speedy character. Choose Haggar if you want a powerful character. We normally use Cody because of his extra speed, which is more useful in the later Stages, when lots of thugs are attacking at once!

• Keep your enemies to one side of you. If you get surrounded, even the wimpiest thugs will strike you and do damage. This is something you definitely want to avoid on the higher Stages, where Food Items are few and far between. Try backing up into a wall and forcing your enemies to come to you.

• Don't use your Super Move too much. Save it for emergencies (when you're surrounded by thugs, for example) and the Bosses (especially Abigail, who can't be defeated without using the Super Move).

STAGE 1: THE SLUM

Stage 1-1

This Stage is just a warm-up. Your enemies are weak, and there aren't many of them to fight. Near the end of the Stage, back yourself up against the cement wall and your enemies will be forced to approach you from the left. This will allow you to pummel them with no trouble.

Stage 1-2

In this Stage, you'll encounter two tough enemies for the first time.

The Fat Guys (Bill Bull, G.Oriber, and Wong Who) bull-rush from the sides of the screen. They'll plow you down if you stand in one place for too long. You can use the Shoulder Throw and Flying Kick very effectively against them. Just don't let them get too far away from you, or they'll attack!

Holly Wood is armed with a knife and recovers very quickly after being knocked down. The best strategy against him is to keep on punching. When he tries to get up, he'll stand right into your barrage of fists and get knocked down again! You may also knock the knife away from Holly. If you do, pick it up and use it. If you press the B button when an enemy is at long range, you'll throw the knife at him; if the enemy is at close range, you'll stab him. Try to stay within stabbing range of your enemies.

Stage 1-3

On the way to the end Boss, you'll encounter Sid, who leaps high into the air and attacks with jump kicks. When Sid jumps over you, turn around and punch him out of the air!

The end Boss is Thrasher, a mighty large man! Pop him a few times with punches, then move away before he can retaliate. After he takes some damage, he'll leap over to the cement wall and whistle. Several

thugs will come onto the screen to answer his call. Watch Thrasher closely as you fight off the thugs. When Thrasher jumps, jump away from him, or he'll hit you with a powerful kick!

Thrasher will return to the wall several more times during the battle. As long as you avoid his kick attack, you'll wear him down quickly. Keep wailing away on Thrasher until he goes down for the count!

STAGE 2: SUBWAY AND PARK

Stage 2-1

You won't encounter anyone tough on the subway platform until you get near the end of the Stage. Andore Jr. uses a bull-rush attack similar to the Fat Guys. Use punches and Flying Kicks to take Andore down.

Stage 2-2

There are several groups of thugs riding in the subway train. You can walk up to the thugs and start punching before they even start to react. You can also play it cool and let the thugs come to you.

The end of the Stage is tough. You'll be attacked by Andore and El Gado. This Andore is tougher than the one in Stage 2-2, and El Gado has a wicked jump attack which he'll use if you get too far away from him.

If one of the barrels contains a Pipe or Sword, use it to swipe at Andore and Holly until they both run out of energy. If you don't get a weapon, stay on the right side of the screen and use Flying Kicks to knock Andore and Holly out. When all your foes are beaten, the train will screech to a halt!

Stage 2-3

This small Stage has a barrel right at the start, filled with Barbecue. Grab it, because you'll need the energy! When you reach on the right side of the substage, move up and right and let your enemies come to you. If you can get a knife from El Gado, this Stage will be a breeze.

Stage 2-4

The wrestling ring in this Stage is the lair of Katana, the Boss. Katana fights with a sword in each hand, and he'll cut you to ribbons if you try to attack him head-on.

Stay above or below

Katana and knock him down with punches. Don't pick up either of his Swords, or he'll attack you ferociously! Stay away from him and use a Flying Kick when he charges you.

Sometimes, Katana will pause for several seconds after getting up off the canvas. If you're quick enough, you can grab Katana and use a mighty Shoulder Throw to rack up extra damage.

Katana is a very tough Boss, so expect to lose lots of lives fighting him. When you finally beat him, you'll move on to the first Bonus Stage!

Bonus Stage 1

The goal of this Bonus Stage is simple: totally destroy the car! Pick up the Pipe and start swinging at the front of the car. You'll know you'll finished bashing the fender if it makes a metallic sound when you strike it, instead of a "bashing" sound.

When you're done with the front, move to the left side of the car and smash it to pieces. Finally, walk over to the right side of the car and start swinging. This part of the car takes longer to destroy than the others. When you've completely destroyed the car, you'll get lots of bonus points!

STAGE 3: WEST SIDE

Stage 3-1

Near the start of this substage, you'll be attacked by Andore and Andore Jr. Junior is tougher and will take longer to defeat. Use Flying Kicks to keep the Andores away, or get them both on one side of the screen and attack with punches. Watch out, because the Andores are faster and smarter in this Stage.

Once you defeat the Andores, move to the right and smash your way through the door of the club. Inside this sleazy establishment, you'll be attacked by El Gado, Holly Wood, and the Fat Guys. Because of the large number of enemies that attack, you should arm yourself with a Knife from one of the Holly Woods. If you don't, Flying Kicks will keep the Fat Guys and the knife thugs on the ground and out of your face.

Stage 3-2

This mini-stage is a cage match against two Andores! Grab the Sword or the Pipe and move into the upper-left or upper-right corner of the cage. Continuously swing your weapon and the Andores should keep walking into it! If you get punched (and disarmed), grab another weapon. If you use up all of the weapons without defeating the Andores, you're in trouble!

Stage 3-3

More malicious mayhem takes place in this Stage. The parking lot of the club is filled with thugs and other most dangerous enemies. You won't meet anyone here that you haven't defeated before, so getting through here should be easy.

The Boss is Edi.E, a corrupt cop with a strange name! Pick up the gum that Edi.E spits out (blech!) for some extra energy, then start attacking.

Use rapid punches on Edi.E to knock him down, then move above or below him and let Edi.E come to you again. Don't stand in front of him or he'll club you into submission!

After you've done some damage to Edi.E, he'll start running back and forth on the screen, trying to get away from you. If he manages to line up with you horizontally, he'll pull out a gun and start shooting! You can't punch these bullets away, and they will cause major damage. Slow Edi.E down by grabbing him as he's running, then using a Shoulder Throw. Repeat the Throw attack until Edi.E is beaten.

STAGE 4: BAY AREA

Stage 4-1

This Stage isn't broken up into substages. Instead, it's just one long Stage of attackers! At several points during the Stage, you'll encounter huge groups of enemies.

The first group is made up of Fat Guys. Use the Flying Kick (and a few Shoulder Throws) to thin out their ranks. After you defeat them all, move to the right and punch open the barrels for some goodies. Defeat the two Andores and move to the right again.

When the trees appear in the background, three barrels will roll at you from the right side of the screen. If you've got a weapon, smash the barrel rolling towards you (there's usually an item inside it). If you don't have a weapon, jump over the barrel.

Shortly after the first group of barrels, a second group will roll onto the screen, this time from the left. Be ready for them!

After the barrels, you'll be attacked by a group of leaping thugs (Sids and Billys). Punch them to the sides of the screen, then bash them into submission!

You'll enter a vandalized bathroom after beating the leapers. This bathroom is teeming with thugs and tough guys, but you've already beaten them before, and you should be able to defeat them again.

When you get through the bathroom, you'll have to fight more thugs, and a large group of knife-men (El Gado and Holly Wood). Keep fighting your way to the right. When you see the Statue of Liberty in the background, you've almost reached the Boss.

The most dangerous thugs in this section of the Stage are the red Holly Woods that throw explosive firebombs. To get past these thugs, move to the top of the screen and punch the thug that runs at you. Punch the firebomb out of the air before it hits the ground, then wait for the other firebombs to burn out before you start moving again.

When you see a sign that says "Way Out," you've reached Abilgail. This Boss is extremely tough, and he has a long reach that prevents you from using the Flying Kick.

Keep moving around the screen until you're surrounded by thugs (and Abigail), then use the Super Move. Continue dodging and using the Super Move until thugs stop coming onto the screen. Now it's just you and Abigail!

Move to the left side of the screen. If Abigail's at the bottom of the screen, move into the upper-left corner. If Abigail's at the top of the screen, move into the lower-left corner. You should always stay on the opposite side of the screen from Abigail.

When Abigail charges you, use the Super Move. You'll need good timing to hit Abigail. When Abigail is knocked down, move to the opposite side of the screen (up or down) and wait for Abigail to attack again.

Repeat this attack until Abigail runs out of energy. You're guaranteed to lose a life from using so many Super Moves, but it's the only way to defeat this rock-hard Boss and move to the final Stage!

Bonus Stage 2

This Bonus Stage is pretty simple. Run to the right and use Flying Kicks on the glass panes as they come onto the screen. You'll need to move up and down to line yourself up with each group of panes, but it's easy to do. Smash all the panes to earn more bonus points!

ROUND 5: UPTOWN

Stage 5-1

Two groups of barrels will roll at you at the beginning of this Stage. When you see a ONE WAY sign in the foreground, be ready for the barrels to appear!

Fight your way off the street and into the building. In here, you'll see the occasional chandelier on the ceiling. Move underneath the chandelier, then move to the bottom of the screen. The chandelier will drop to the ground and shatter, leaving behind a Barbecue,

which fully restores your Strength Meter!

When you see a black elevator door, you're almost at the end of the Stage. Fat Guys and Andores will attack. Force them off the screen with Flying Kicks, then punch them 'til they drop!

Stage 5-2

A boring, but challenging, Stage. You'll be attacked by Fat Guys, Andores, firebombers, and a brigade of common thugs. Keep punching, keep fighting, and keep winning!

Stage 5-3

There are a few more chandeliers in this Stage. When you reach the door at the far right side of the Stage, move into the lower-right corner and keep punching. Your enemies won't be able to attack you without walking right into your punches, and you'll knock them all out.

Stage 5-4

There are Food and Money Items hidden behind the pillars in the foreground. Move to the middle of the screen, then move behind the pillar and press the Y button to pick up the Item.

At the end of this Stage, you'll meet Belger, the final Boss. Don't try punching him on his chair. You'll just hit Jessica and lose Strength! Instead, move into the chair and you'll smash it. Now Belger will have to attack on his own two feet.

It really helps to be Cody at this point, because you'll be able to punch away the arrows that Belger fires at you. If you're Haggar, you'll need to jump and dodge the arrows to get within attacking range.

Belger's got a large group of thugs that will attack you during the battle. If you're Cody, move into the lower-right corner of the screen and stay there. Keep punching to knock away Belger's arrows and to knock out the attacking thugs. Once the thugs stop coming, you can concentrate on Belger.

Belger is extremely tough, but don't use your Super Move. Move above or below Belger and he'll jump to attack you. Punch him in the air and you'll knock him backwards. Don't get too close or Belger will skewer you with an arrow!

When you defeat Belger, he'll crash through the window and you'll see the ending sequence. Congratulations! This was your Final Fight . . . for now!

SHH . . . THE SECRETS

Configuration Screen

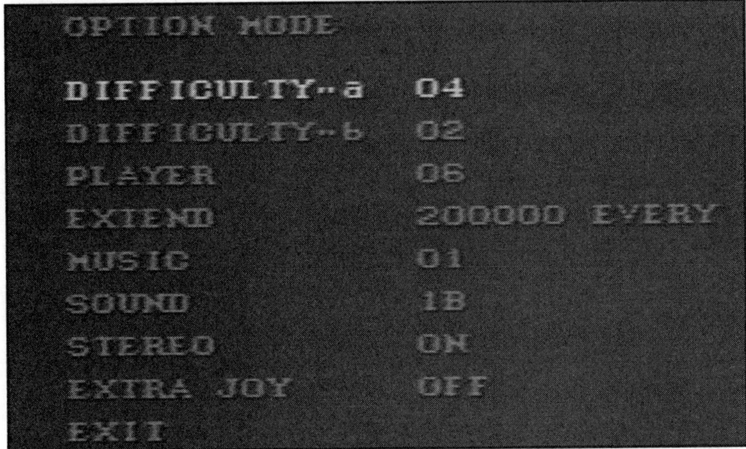

Hold down the L and R buttons and press Start. You'll enter a configuration screen that lets you change several game options. Here are the options, from top to bottom, and their effects.

DIFFICULTY A: Sets the overall difficulty of the game, with 1 being the lowest difficulty and 8 the highest.

DIFFICULTY B: Sets the timer speed, with 1 being the slowest speed and 4 the fastest.

PLAYER: Sets the number of lives you start the game with. 1 is the lowest number, 9 is the highest.

EXTEND: Sets the point level at which you receive an extra life. There are four settings: Nothing (hardest), 100000 Only, 200000 Only, and 200000 Every (easiest).

MUSIC: Selects a musical track to play. Use the R button to play the selected music track.

SOUND: Selects a sound to play. Use the R button to hear the sound.

STEREO: Changes the sound and music from Stereo to Mono.

EXTRA JOY: With this option ON, pressing the A button uses the Super Move. With this option OFF, you must push B and Y to use the Super Move as usual.

EXIT: Leave the configuration screen.

CHAPTER 5

Lagoon

by Kemco/Seika

WHAT'S GOING ON?

You're the good guy, Nasir, the Champion of Light. The bad guy is Zerah, an evil mage who hopes to cast the realm of Lakeland into eternal darkness. It's your job to stop Zerah and put an end to his evil schemes!

PLAYERS

Lagoon is for one player only.

EXPERIENCE AND GOLD

You receive Experience Points (XP) and Gold Pieces (GP) every time you win a battle. The stronger the enemy you defeat, the more Experience and Gold you receive. Experience Points increase your personal statistics (Hit Points [HP], Magic Points [MP], Strength, and Defense). Gold allows you to buy weapons, armor and special items.

LIVES AND CONTINUES

Some games have resurrection spells, but Lagoon isn't one of them. If you die, the adventure is over and you have to Continue or End the game. The Continue option starts you from your saved game.

Lagoon has a single save slot. The save slot is named after the area where you saved the game. It's a good idea to save the game constantly.

CONTROLS

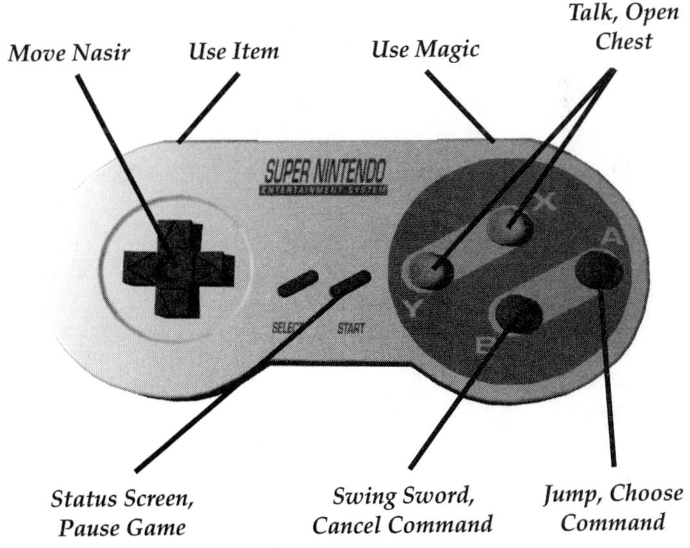

WEAPONS

There are five weapons in Lagoon, all of which are swords. From weakest to stronger, they are: Short Sword, Silver Sword, Magic Sword, Force Sword, and Moon Blade.

ARMOR

There are five suits of armor in Lagoon. From weakest to strongest, they are: Bandit Armor, Gold Armor, Sonic Armor, Thunder Armor, and Moon Armor.

MAGIC

There are sixteen magic spells in the game. You select spells by combining two types of magical items: Crystals and Staffs. There are four of each. The four Crystals are: Fire, Wind, Water, and Thunder. The four Staffs are: Earth, Sky, Star, and Moon. The following list shows the various combinations and the spells they become.

Crystal	Staff	Spell
Fire	Earth	Fireball
Fire	Sky	3-Way Fireball
Fire	Star	Fire Fall
Fire	Moon	Fireball Dragon
Wind	Earth	Wind Cutter
Wind	Sky	Wind Blaster
Wind	Star	Typhoon
Wind	Moon	Earthquake
Water	Earth	Water Hammer
Water	Sky	8-Way Water Hammer
Water	Star	Water Rush
Water	Moon	Water Dragon
Thunder	Earth	Thunder Ball
Thunder	Sky	Homing Thunder
Thunder	Star	Thunder Bolt
Thunder	Moon	Explosive Thunder

SPECIAL ITEMS

All of the special items are mentioned in the Walkthrough below.

FRIENDS

Your best friend is Mathias, the mage who raised you from a baby. Mathias won't join you on your adventures, but he'll show up several times to guide you along.

People in the villages and towns are always friendly. Talk to them for hints, tips, and special items.

ENEMIES

Thor seems like a friend through most of the game, but he turns out to be the Champion of Darkness. You'll have to help him during the game, even though you know of his evil ways. (He's not really evil, he's just being manipulated by Zerah.)

Zerah is the evil mage who stole Thor away from Mathias. He raised Thor to be stronger than Nasir, so that Darkness would rule Lakeland. Defeat Zerah to win the game!

STRATEGY SESSION

General Strategies

• Save constantly! There's no telling when a particularly nasty attack will knock your Hit Points down to zero. You've only got one saved game, but you can usually backtrack to get any items you've missed.

• If you take a lot of damage, stand still to let your Hit Points and Magic Points recharge. The Shiny Ball makes you recover HP and MP faster, but it also costs a whopping 10,000 Gold, and it's only available in Atland. We finished the game without it, and you can, too.

• If you're facing your enemies, and don't swing your weapon, they'll bounce off you without doing damage (in most cases). Use this to your advantage by pushing enemies out of your way. Enemy bullets can damage you whether you're swinging a weapon or not, so avoid them.

Hint Book Corrections

Kemco/Seika sells a hint book for Lagoon, but it's really a map book. This chapter has far more strategies than the hint book. If you already have the hint book, or are planning to buy it, be aware that there are several errors. We've listed the errors, and corrections, below.

Page 3: The chest labeled "Healing Pot" should be labeled "30 Gold."

Page 11: The chest labeled "Shiny Stone" should be labeled "70 Gold."

Page 17: The chest labeled "Sky Staff" should be labeled "120 Gold."

Page 27: The location labeled "Warp to Page 35" should be labeled "Warp to Page 30."

Page 33: The chest labeled "Elixir" should be labeled "200 Gold."

Page 42: The chest labeled "Bright Stone" should be labeled "250 Gold."

The Walkthrough

Atland

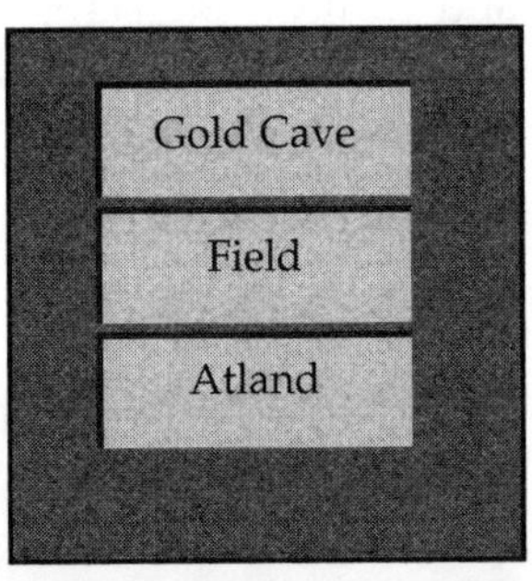

You start the game with 100 Gold, so walk to the Armor Shop in the Northwest corner of town and buy yourself some Bandit Armor. Equip the Armor, then walk to the Mayor's House in the Southwest corner of town and go inside. The Mayor's wife steers you to the Church in the center of Atland.

Walk into the Church and look for the Mayor. Walk up to him and start talking. After some interesting plot developments, you'll end up on the Field, near the entrance to the Gold Cave. Talk to the poor sap on the ground to find out what's going on.

After you've returned to Atland, walk to the Mayor's House and go inside. The Mayor gives you 300 Gold. Walk back to the Armor Shop and buy the Short Sword and Iron Shield. Equip them both and you're ready for battle. Save the game, leave town, and walk to the . . .

Gold Cave

Items to Collect: 20 Gold, Healing Pot (1st Floor); 10 Gold, 30 Gold (2nd Floor)

Goals: Rescue Giles, Defeat Samson

You're pathetically weak when you first enter the Cave, but so are the monsters. Walk around and beat up on monsters to increase levels. Look around for all the treasure chests; this is a sure way to build up your XP.

Once you've rounded up all the items, go to the 2nd Floor and walk to the stairs in the Northeast corner. Climb up the stairs and follow the path until you're outside. Climb upward to find Giles. He asks you for the Healing Pot; give it to him and he'll ask you to take him to Atland.

Giles is a real slowpoke, and it's possible for him to get stuck behind walls if you get too far ahead of him. Stop walking every so often to let Giles catch up with you. (Giles doesn't take damage from monsters, fortunately.)

When you get back to town, Giles mentions the Faith Healer. Walk into the Southeast corner of town and you'll see Giles standing in front of her house. Go into the house to get Samson's Key. You should have a good amount of GP by now, so walk to the Weapon shop (in the East part of town) to buy a Healing Pot and Shiny Stone. Once you've bought them, return to the Gold Cave.

Go to the locked door in the Northeast corner of the 1st Floor. Use the key to open the door. You're in Samson's room! If you're not at Level 5 or higher, this battle will be too hard, and you should come back when you're stronger. (The skeletons on the 2nd Floor are excellent for building XP.)

Samson moves fast, but all you have to do is move directly beneath him and hack away at his right leg. He gets in a few shots, but you should be able to defeat him before he defeats you. Use the Healing Pot if your Hit Points get too low.

When Samson croaks, you get the Fire Crystal. Walk North and go through the door to enter the . . .

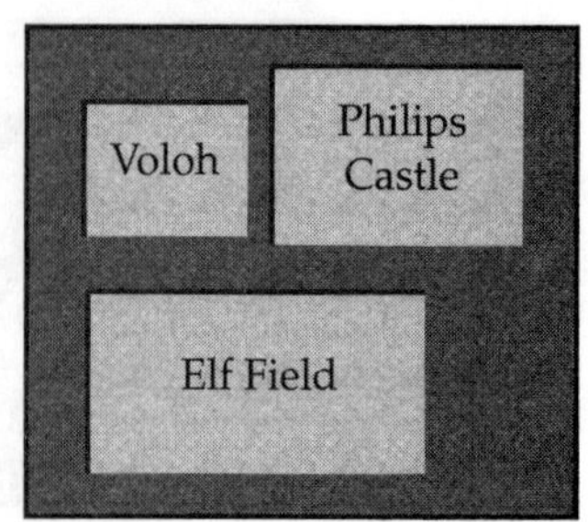

Elf Field

As soon as you leave Samson's room, the tunnel caves in. There's no turning back now! Walk to the Northwest corner of the Field and look for the entrance to . . .

Voloh

Talk to the old man next to the town entrance to learn about three Tablets. After that, go to the Mayor's House in the Northeast corner of town. Volunteer to rescue the elves trapped in the Philips Castle. The Mayor gives you the Movable Mantle and the Earth Staff. Go to the Magic screen and select the Fire Crystal and Earth Staff. Now you can cast Fire Balls with the R button. (Fire Balls are very effective against the monsters in the Elf Field.)

Look for the blue dude near the town entrance and talk to him. This is Thor. He'll give you the Tablet of Faith and start following you. Leave town and return to the Elf Field.

Follow Thor as he walks to the South. When he stops, talk to him and you'll get the Tablet of Wish. Now you have to find the third and final Tablet. Walk to . . .

Philips Castle

Follow the path as it winds toward the Castle. Watch out for the second vertical bridge; the middle of the bridge will collapse and fall as you walk over it. Save the game before crossing the bridge, then leap over the middle.

After you cross the collapsing bridge, walk West until you come to a small gap. Jump across the gap and open the chest for the third Tablet! Return to Voloh and the old man will tell you the spell needed to open the door of the Castle.

Go back to the Castle and follow the path all the way to the North. Walk up to the door and the spell will take effect.

Philips Castle

Items to Collect: 200 Gold, Gold Armor, Key of Prison (1st Floor); 100 Gold, Large Shield (2nd Floor); 100 Gold, 200 Gold, 70 Gold (Basement)

Goals: Rescue Elves, Defeat Natela

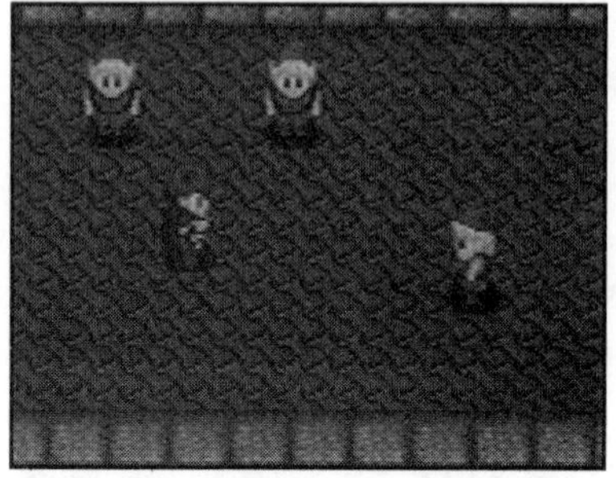

Once you've found the Prison Key, go to the Basement and find the prison in the Southwest corner. Open the prison and give the Mantle to the elf in the middle. He'll give you the Philips Key.

Go up to the 2nd Floor and use the Key to unlock the door in the middle of the area. You should be up to Level 11 before you enter the room and go into battle.

There are two ways to attack Natela: the brainy method or the brawny method. In the brainy method, you move close to Natela, dodge the fireballs, and strike him when he's not firing. The brawny (and more effective) approach is to wait at the bottom of the screen, and slash like mad when Natela attacks. Make sure your Elixir is equipped and ready to use. When Natela is defeated, you'll earn the Silver Sword.

Return to the front door of the Castle and go outside. Walk to the right and you'll find a second door. (The door was locked until you defeated Natela.) Go through the door and walk onto the crest. You'll teleport into a new room. Walk out the door and you'll be in the . . .

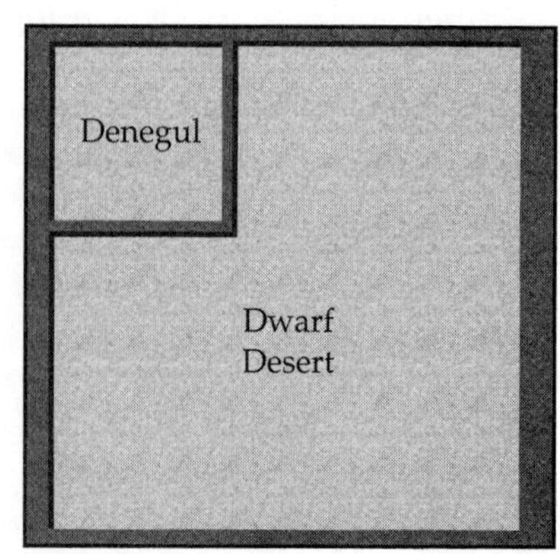

Dwarf Desert

The monsters out here are rough! Don't waste any time getting through the desert and making your way into...

Denegul

Go to the Armor Shop and buy Sonic Armor. If you don't have 1800 Gold, return to the Desert and beat up on the wandering monsters until you've got the Gold. Once you've bought your Armor, look for the elder on the West side of Denegul. He'll give you the Sky Staff and the Ancient Book. (You can read the Book by selecting it and pressing the L button.)

Search the Northwest part of town to find Thor. He'll ask you to look for his Pendant. No way?! (Way!) Leave town and go back into the Desert. Walk down to the teleport room in the Southeast corner and teleport back to Philips Castle.

Walk all the way to Voloh and talk to the elves. One of them will give you Thor's Pendant. Leave town and return to Denegul. Give Thor his Pendant and he'll give you the Powerful Mirror. Leave Denegul and return to the Dwarf Desert. Journey up to the Northeast corner and you'll see the entrance to the Dwarf Cave. Use the Mirror to destroy the rocks in front of the cave and go inside.

Dwarf Cave

Items to Collect: 120 Gold, Magic Sword, Protective Ring, Wind Crystal

Goal: Defeat Eardon

Your first task is to find the Silence Cave. Walk to the North end of the cave and pluck the Moon Stone out of the wall (press X or Y to take the Stone). Walk back out of the cave and

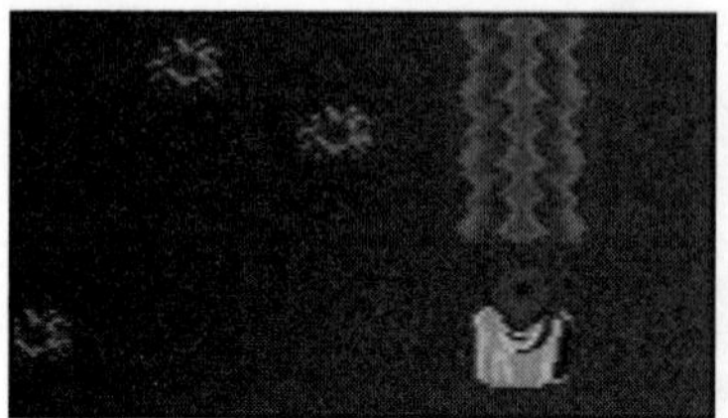

search for the teleport square that zaps you back to the entrance of the Cave. (Search along the East wall of the area where you found the Magic Sword.)

Walk back to Denegul and talk to everyone. You'll find a man who wants to see the Moon Stone. When he sees it, he gives you the Freezing Pot. Go back to the Dwarf Cave and keep going North until you find a lava bridge! Use the Freezing Pot to solidify the bridge. Walk across the bridge and go into the next area.

You'll find Princess Felicia, but she's taken away by an evil babe. Walk North and search around to find a door. If you aren't at Level 14 or higher, go back to the lava areas of the Cave and power up, then return here. Go through the door to fight Eardon!

Eardon's a tough boss, with an attack pattern that's difficult to explain. He'll follow you around the room, but he won't always go in the same direction. Your best bet is to lure Eardon into the Northwest corner of the room, then run below him. When his head comes out, leap over the fireballs he spews and slash him before his head retracts. Eardon takes a lot of punishment, so keep up the fight!

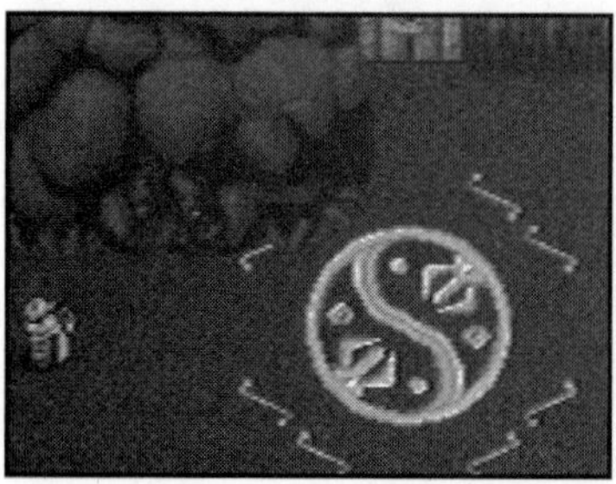

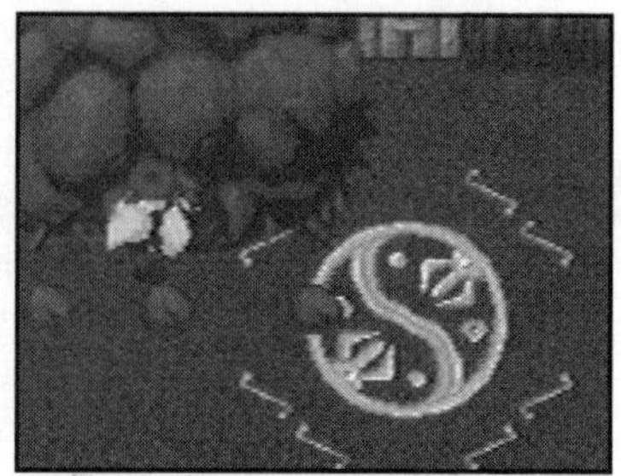

After you defeat Eardon, walk North to leave the room and go into . . .

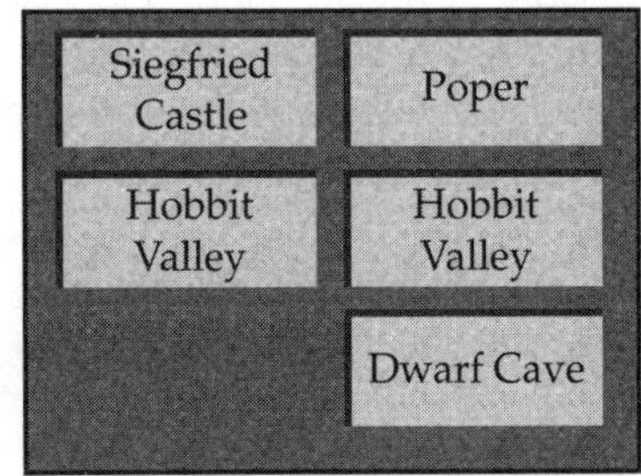

Hobbit Valley

Walk North and make your way to . . .

Poper

Go to the Church and talk to the priest. He'll mention the Mint in Siegfried Castle. Guess where you're headed next?

Siegfried Castle

Items to Collect: Defensive Ring, Force Sword (1st Floor); Maxim Shield, Mint, Power Ring, Thunder Armor (Basement).

Goals: Find the Mint, Defeat Duma

Take the time to collect all of the items listed above, even after you've found the Mint. You'll need all of the equipment in here before you take on Duma.

Once you've cleaned out the Castle, go back to Poper and give the Mint to the priest in the Church. He says that the spirits are pleased and want to talk with you. Walk through the glass above the priest to reveal a secret door.

Go through the door and walk down the tunnel, talking to each spirit in turn. The last two spirits give you the Star Staff and Duma's Key.

Return to the Castle and look for Duma's room in the middle of the 1st Floor. Go inside with your handy Key and get ready for a fairly easy battle. Avoid Duma's clapping hands, leap over his fireballs, and whack him in the head. You'll win two items when he's beaten: the Water Crystal and the Key of Siegfried.

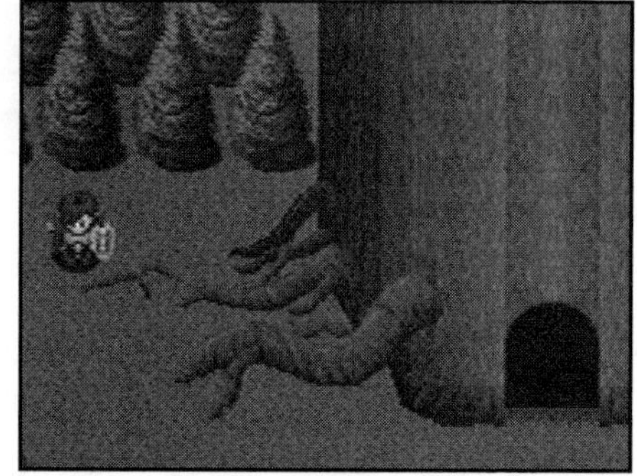

Use the Key to open the door in the Northwest corner of the 1st Floor. Make your way to the top floor and you'll meet up with Thor and Zerah. After you're done talking with them, walk onto the crest and you'll teleport to the Gnome Tree. Stand here to let your HP and MP recharge, then walk into the Tree.

Lilaty

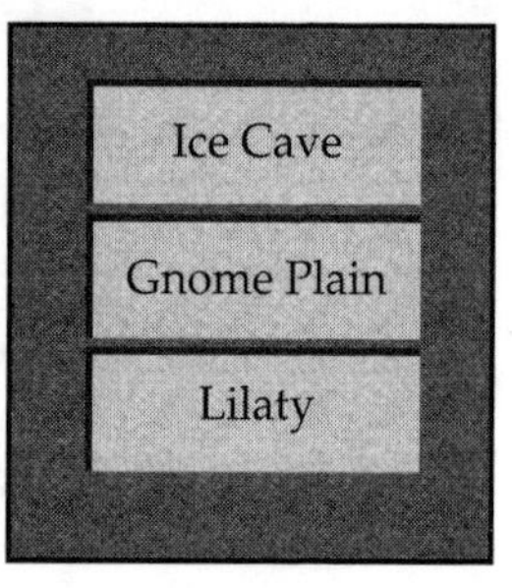

Talk to the elder on the West side of the village to learn about the Nymphs and receive the Angel's Bell. Walk up to the Northeast corner and talk to the female elf to receive the Truth Fire. Equip the Fire and find the lying elf. When he asks if you believe him, say No. He'll give you the Fur Mantle for finding him out. Equip the Mantle and make your way to the . . .

Ice Cave

Items to Collect: 200 Gold, Bright Stone

Goal: Defeat Thimale

Collect the items and power up to Level 22 or higher, then walk to the Northwest corner of the Cave and go through the door into Thimale's room. Avoid the large rolling ball and destroy the six smaller domes. (You can jump over the ice bullets the domes

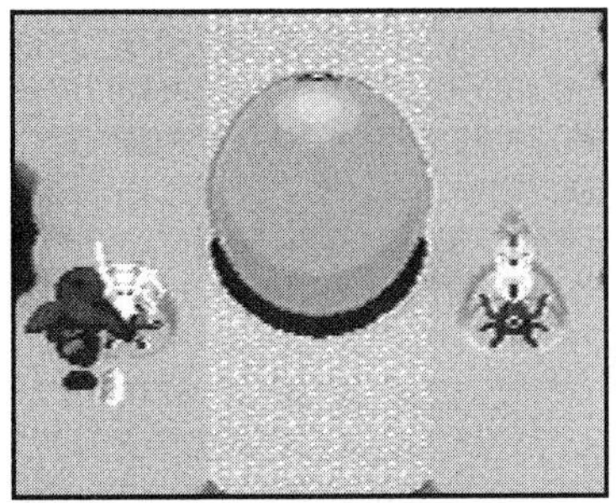

fire at you.) Once you've destroyed the domes, attack the rolling ball. Jump into the air to strike the monster in the middle of the ball. Use the Elixir and Healing Pot when needed.

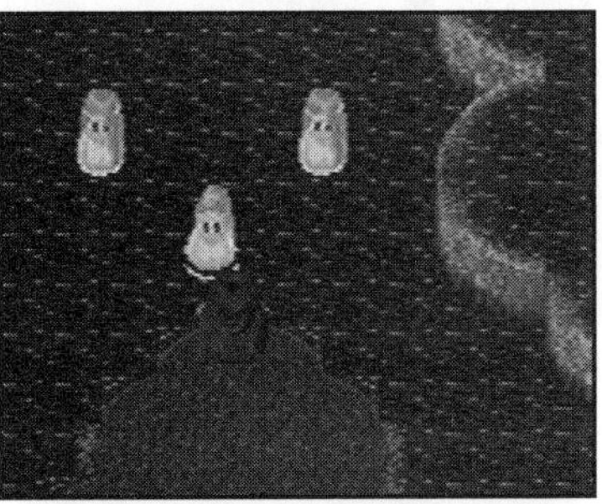

When you beat Thimale, you earn the Life Ball. Hang onto this item until the end of the game! Walk North and enter the Nymph Spring. Stand on the tip of the island and use the Angel's Bell to summon the Nymphs. They give you the Moon Staff and transport you to Phantom Hill.

If you're not up to Level 24 yet, power up by whacking the red hawks. You'll get 90 XP for every one you defeat. Once you're charged up, make your way to the top of the hill. Look for a small hole. Walk onto the hole and you'll fall into Ella's room.

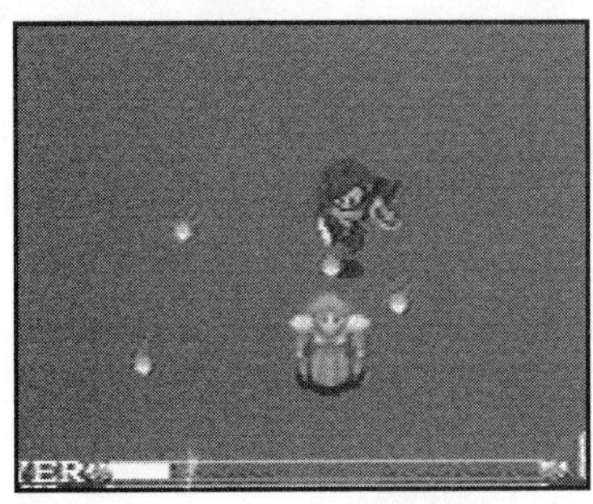

Put on the Power Ring and go straight for Ella. Leap over her fireballs and strike rapidly. The more damage she takes, the faster she teleports around the room, so defeat her quickly.

When she dies, you'll reveal some hidden stairs. Climb up the stairs to the top of the Hill, then walk to the right and leap over the gap.

Zerah appears and challenges you to a fight. Before you can do anything, Mathias shows up! Sit back and watch these two mages go head-to-head. After the battle, talk to Zerah. He'll fly off the screen. Talk to Mathias to learn the story of your life, and to receive the Thunder Crystal.

Mathias uses the last of his strength to blow you up to the clouds. Make your way to the northern-most cloud and jump off to arrive at your final destination . . .

Lagoon Castle

Items to Collect: 250 Gold, Curing Ring, Elixir, Moon Armor, Moon Shield, Statue

Goal: Defeat Thor and Save Lakeland

Your first goal in the multi-floored Castle is the Silence Terrace. Look for the window, and stand in the moonlight on the floor. Use the Moon Stone and it becomes the Moon Blade!

Next, explore the Castle and find the Statue, which you need to free the Princess from her prison. You'll probably stumble into two people (behind a force field) who tell you more about the Statue and the Princess.

With the Statue in hand, look for the Princess's room. Stand on the crest of the floor, facing Felicia, and use the Statue. You'll

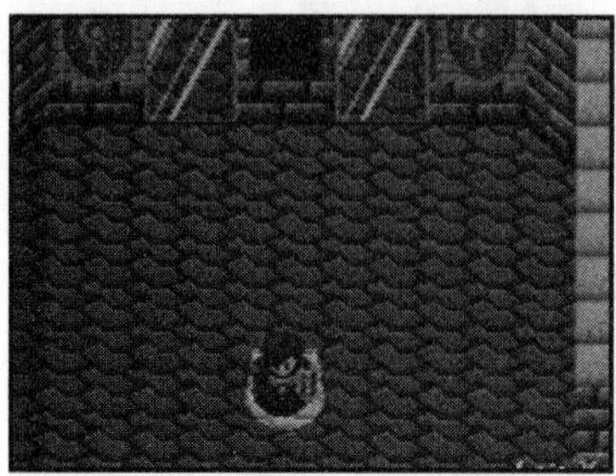

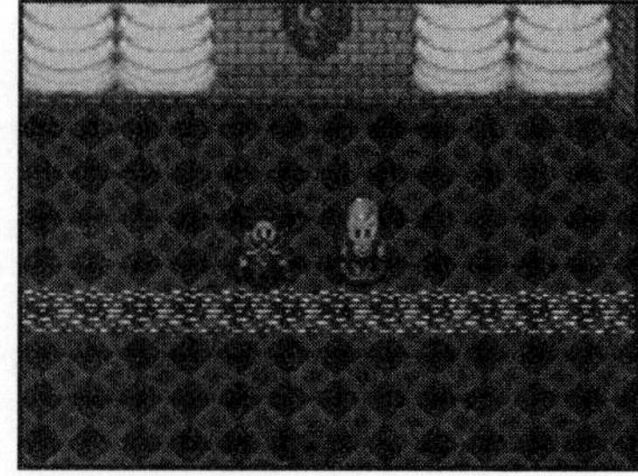

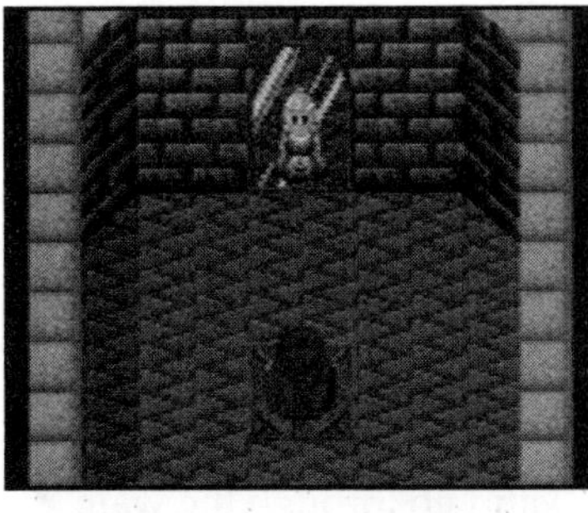

shatter the prison and set Felicia free. Walk North and through the door that Felicia was trapped inside.

Find the Moon Armor in this section of the Castle before you enter Battler's room. You should also power up to Level 29 or higher (the huge knights give some excellent XP).

In the fight against Battler, don't bother going after the egg-shaped guardians; go straight for Battler and slash him into oblivion. Once you beat him, walk North and through the door. When you appear outside, walk North and jump off the end of the pier.

When you land, walk Northwest and go down the stairs. You'll enter the final area in the game, a huge underground maze. We've provided a map of the maze so you can find your way to the door. Before you go enter the final battle, get yourself up to Level 32 or higher by slicing and dicing the creatures in the maze. You need the added strength!

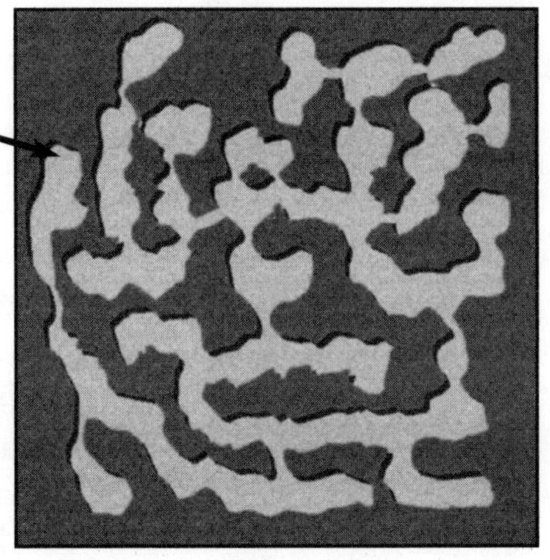

The Final Battle

When you enter the room, you'll see a bizarre glass sphere shooting fireballs. Jump over the fireballs and slash the sphere. After

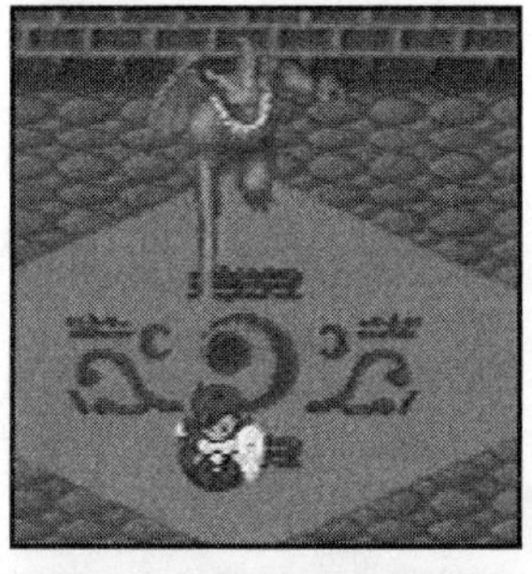

you do enough damage, the sphere shatters, and the creature inside attacks!

The creature looks tough, but he's a wimp. Slip on your Curing Ring and slash the creature. He'll hit you, but you can strike faster and do more damage. When you kill the creature, it falls to the ground, and the North wall collapses. Take off the Ring (to conserve MP) and go through the wall.

It's Thor and Zerah! You get to fight Zerah first. He's a real cream puff; just leap over his fireballs and smack him with the sword. When he's defeated, Thor appears in the middle of the room and starts attacking.

You have to walk through the spinning stars around Thor and strike him before the stars push you back to the edge of the room. The stars spin in a clockwise direction, so walk in that direction and wind your way to Thor.

When you've done enough damage, Thor transforms into a huge hawk! Move into the lower-left corner of the room and put on the Curing Ring. When Thor flies onto the left side of the screen, jump up and slash the glass sphere between his claws. You'll suffer damage, but the Curing Ring will heal you. If you run out of MP, use the Shiny Ball (if you have it).

After you defeat the hawk, Thor will collapse to the ground. Talk to him and receive Thor's Pendant, then walk South to fight the evil creature once again. The creature is a different color, but attacks as it did before. Put on the Curing Ring and equip the Life Ball to prevent yourself from dying if you run out of HP. Defeat the creature again and you've completed the game!

CHAPTER 6

Legend of the Mystical Ninja

by Konami

WHAT'S GOING ON?

Get ready to play the strangest game ever seen on the Super NES. You take on the role of Kid Ying (or his mentor, Dr. Yang), fighting through nine levels of wackiness in ancient Tokyo (known as Edo). Prepare for some truly bizarre action!

PLAYERS

The Legend of the Mystical Ninja is for one or two players. The two-player mode is simultaneous.

SCORING

You don't score points in this game; you're just trying to play through each of the levels (known as Warlock Zones).

LIVES AND CONTINUES

You start the game with three lives. Your strength is measured by the Life Line at the top of the screen. Every time you're hit by an enemy or a bullet, the Life Line decreases. If the Life Line goes empty, you lose a life.

There's a Timer at the top of the screen. The Timer starts counting down as soon as you appear in a Zone. You've got to finish the Zone before the Timer runs out or you'll lose a life for being so slow.

When you lose all of your lives, you can continue the game from the last Warlock Zone you reached. You've got an endless number of continues.

If you find a Travel Logbook Shop, get a password. Enter this password at the start of your next playing session to begin the game from the last Warlock Zone you reached.

You also get a password if you lose the game and choose to End instead of continuing. This password starts you from the beginning of the Warlock Zone, with no items, whereas the Logbook password starts you from inside the Travel Logbook Shop, with all the items you've collected to that point.

CONTROLS

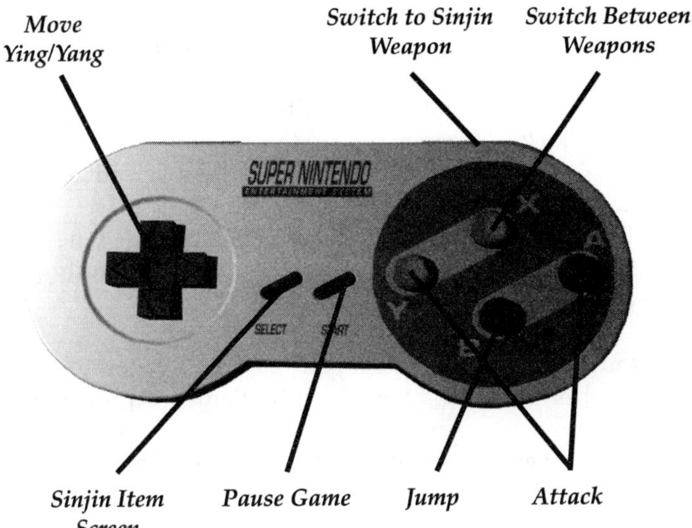

WEAPONS

Kid Ying starts the game with the Not So Peaceful Pipe. By collecting Lucky the Cat, Ying upgrades to the Extended Not So Peaceful Pipe and the Yokohama Yo Yo. Ying can even throw money at his enemies! The Lethal Coins are excellent missile weapons, and should be used liberally on the Boss of each Warlock Zone. Unfortunately, you lose a few bucks every time you throw one.

Dr. Yang starts the game with the Pan Flute. By collecting Lucky the Cat, Yang upgrades to the Mega Flute and the Party Whistle. Yang is armed with Shooting Stars, which are similar to Kid Ying's Lethal Coins in two ways: they're missile weapons, and they cost you money every time you throw one.

In addition to their standard weapons, Ying and Yang can buy Bombs from Stores. Bombs are helpful against some Bosses, but almost useless against others.

Finally, Ying and Yang have special Jutsu powers. These powers can only be used in the second (Side-View) half of a Zone. Ying and Yang have four Jutsus, varying in power from No. 1 (weakest) to No. 4 (strongest).

SPECIAL ITEMS

Most of these items are obtained by attacking the enemies wandering around each Zone. A few of them are bought in Stores. All of them are useful!

The **1-Up** gives you an extra life.

The **Clock** adds some time to the Timer.

Gold Coins build up your bucks. When you hit an enemy, he'll usually drop a Gold Coin.

The **Golden Cat** increases the size of your Life Line.

Hamburger, Pizza and **Pizza Slices** automatically restore your Life Line when it gets too low.

The **Heart** refills your Life Line completely.

Lucky the Cat upgrades your current weapon to the next level of strength. Every eighth enemy you hit will drop a Cat.

The **Power Pot** always has a special item inside. Break the Pot to collect the goodie.

The **Scroll** increases your Jutsu power. You have to collect ten scrolls for one use of Jutsu.

The **Straw Sandals** make you run faster and jump higher. You can wear up to three pairs of Sandals.

FRIENDS

Almost everyone in a Zone is dangerous, but there are three women who aren't. These women, called Bonus Babes, add to your money if you touch them. You'll lose a big chunk of dough if you hit them with a weapon.

ENEMIES

Most of the monsters in the game have names. Look through your Legend of the Mystical Ninja manual for a full rundown.

STRATEGY SESSION

General Strategies

You should always accomplish the five tasks listed below before you go to the Side-View section of a Zone. Any other tasks should be considered secondary (except in a few special cases, as you'll read about later).

1. ***Get a password at the Travel Logbook Shop.***
2. ***Power up your weapon to the highest level.***
3. ***Purchase three pairs of Straw Sandals.***
4. ***Purchase armor.***
5. ***Purchase Jutsu.***

To power up your weapon, simply wander around and bash everyone who appears on the screen, to collect Gold Coins, Lucky Cats, and Scrolls. The stronger your weapon becomes, the easier it becomes to power up.

Maps

For each Warlock Zone, we've provided a detailed Map of the Top-View section. The Map shows all of the locations you can visit. Here's what the symbols on the map indicate.

Arrows: Horizontal screens are always connected, but you must use particular paths to move between screens vertically. These paths are shown by the arrows.

Boxes: Each box on the map is approximately one screen in size.

Kid Ying: The little Kid Ying on each map shows the "starting position" where you first appear in each Zone.

Walls: A thick black line between two horizontal boxes indicates an impassable wall.

Locations

The following is a complete list of the different locations you'll find during the game. These locations are almost exactly the same from Zone to Zone; differences are mentioned in the Map Legend of each Zone. Read on!

Candy Shop

Buy some candy and recharge your Life Line. $40 buys the cheapest sweets, $80 the most expensive. The higher the price, the more your Life Line recharges.

Casino

In the Casino, you roll three dice and bet on whether the total of the dice will be low (10 or less) or high (11 and up). You can bet any amount of money, which means you can make, or lose, more money here than in any other location.

Concentration Game

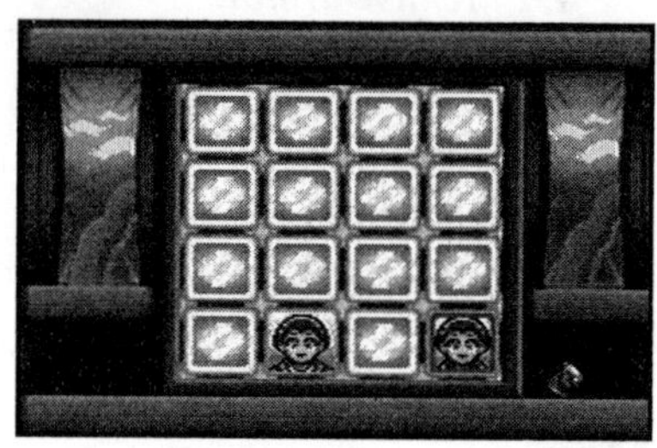

It's the old match-the-cards contest, but you only get to make two mistakes before the game is over. It's almost impossible to make money in this game, so skip it if you're trying to build your bucks.

Employment Office

There are three jobs available: Mole ($100), Paint ($80) and Goblin ($60). Goblin is the hardest of the jobs, and Paint the easiest (which means that you should choose Paint to make the most money). Mole is a cute game, but you can't make money at it unless you manage a perfect score (which is wickedly difficult).

Fortune Teller

This old man will tell your future for a mere $20. If the future is bad, you'll be attacked by a crowd of enemies when you walk outside. If the future is good, you'll find five Bonus Babes outside. If there's nothing of interest in your future, you won't find anything outside at all. Your fortune is different each time you visit.

Game Center

There are three different games in the various Game Centers. Each Center has two games available for play. Each game costs $100. The games are Break Down The Wall (a ball-and-paddle

game like Breakout or Alleyway), Hockey (a Pong-like game available only in the two-player mode), and Gradius (which is the entire first level of the classic NES game!).

There aren't any strategies for the first two games, but here's what to do in Gradius. Use the Speed-Up Option twice, then power up with Missiles. After that, save the Power Crystals to get Options. (The Options are pods that float around your ship and fire lasers.)

House

A House always has a citizen inside. Sometimes, these citizens give you clues about the Zone. Other times, they'll just say something weird or tell a bad joke ("What's better than jail? Bail!").

Jutsu School

The burly teacher in the Jutsu School can teach you one of two different types of Jutsu. There are four different Jutsus, numbered from No. 1 (the weakest) to No. 4 (the strongest). The stronger the Jutsu, the more it costs to learn. You've got to have a full Life Line, along with the necessary cash, to learn a Jutsu.

Lottery

A game of chance, the Lottery is generally a loser. If you're going to gamble, do it at the Casino, where the odds of making money are 50/50.

Motel

Stay here and refill your Life Line. The more expensive the room you stay in, the more your Life Line will recharge.

Question Palace

This location appears in Zone III only. You'll be asked some simple questions about the first two

Zones. The questions start repeating after a short time, so you'll memorize the answers in no time. You win $300 if you win the game.

Race Track

A gambling location. If you pick the top two horses in the correct order, your $20 bet (you can't bet more or less than $20) will be multiplied by the odds of the one-two finish that you chose. You can make over $300 on a single race if you're lucky.

Sauna

A Life Line recharge location. $100 buys you a refreshing soak in some hot wa-wa. It doesn't matter whether you choose the Men's or Women's sauna (although choosing the Women's sauna results in a cute graphic sequence).

Secret Maze

For $100, you can venture into the Secret Maze. The Maze is a real cinch. Once you've found the Map, pressing the B button shows all of the tunnels in the Maze, whether you've explored them or not.

Sideshow

This location costs $100, and it's kind of funny the first time you see it. After that, it's a bore (and a waste of money).

Store

A Store always has three items for sale. There's a Store in each Zone that sells Straw Sandals (the most important of the special items). You'll also find Pizza and Armor in Stores. Buy everything you can afford!

Sushi Joint

Similar to the Candy Shop, but with rice cakes and fish instead of sugary treats.

Travel Agency

The Agency appears in Zones I and II only. In Zone I, the Agency takes you to Zone II. There are three travel packages; the more expensive the package, the more your Life Line will recharge. In Zone II, the Agency gives you a little information about the Zone (and nothing else).

Warlock Zone I: Mystical Ghost

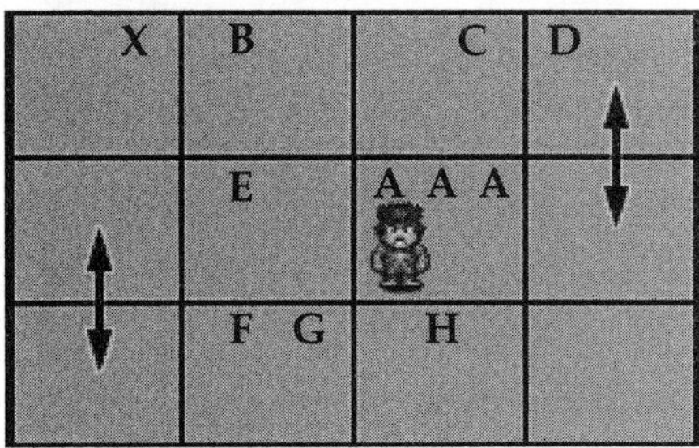

Map Legend

A. **House.**
B. **Secret Maze.**
C. **Candy Shop.**
D. **Employment Office.**
E. **Store.**
   Straw Sandals ($20), Pizza ($30), Bomb ($30).
F. **Fortune Teller.**
G. **Casino.**
H. **Travel Agency.**
X. **Door to Side-View.**

Top-View Tips

- Several locations are closed down until you defeat the Mystical Ghost. Come back to the locations after you've defeated the Ghost.

Side-View Tips

- Look for the Temple Bell about halfway through the level, at the top of the

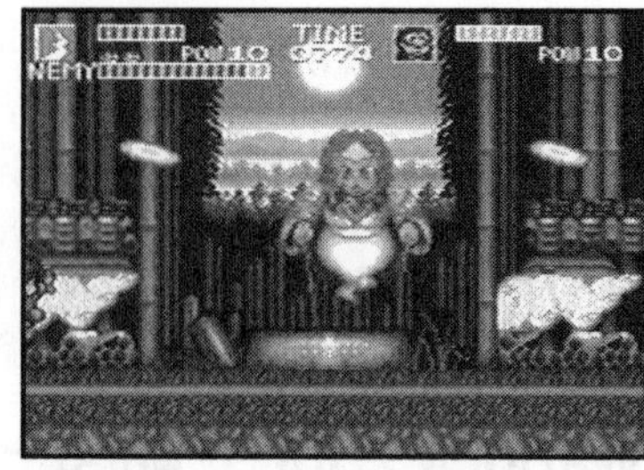

area. Whack the Bell with your weapon, and all of the Fire Ball Ghosts turn into special items.

- The Mystical Ghost attacks by throwing plates at you. Hit the plates with your weapon and they'll bounce back at the Ghost. You can also jump over the plates and wait for the next set. Stand at the far left or far right side of the screen for the easiest time of dodging the plates.

Warlock Zone II: Statue of Cat

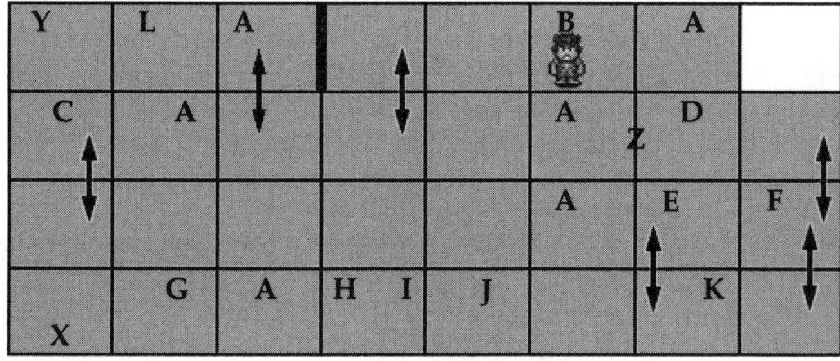

Map Legend

A. House.
B. Travel Agency.
C. Store. Straw Sandals ($30), Straw Coat ($50), Straw Hat ($50).
D. Candy Shop.
E. Jutsu School. No. 1 ($400), No. 3 ($800).
F. Game Center.
G. Lottery.
H. Store. Straw Sandals ($30), Straw Coat ($50), Bomb ($50).
I. Employment Office.
J. Travel Logbook Store.
K. Motel.
L. Sauna.
X. Passage to Side-View.
Y. Secret Area.
Z. River.

Top-View Tips

• The river (indicated as Z on the Map Legend) can't be crossed if you've only got one pair of Straw Sandals on. With two or more pairs of Sandals, you can jump over the river to the other side.

• Go to positionY on the map. Hit the door with your weapon to destroy it and reveal a passage to a secret area. You'll find a Gold Statue in this area, but you'll need three pairs of Sandals to jump over the rocks and collect it.

Side-View Tips

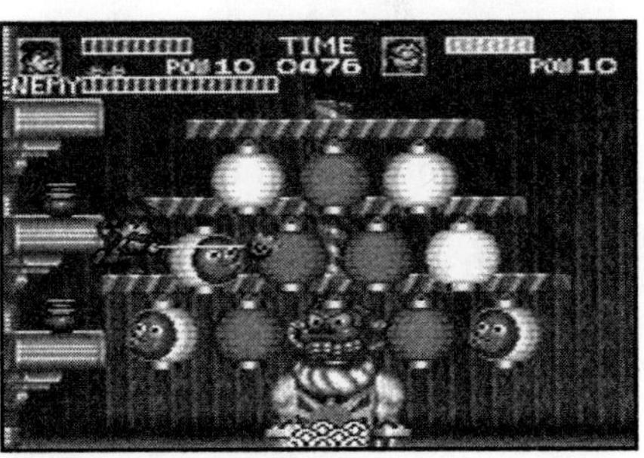

• Lantern Man is the Boss of this Zone. Your first goal is to destroy the lanterns above him. Go for the white lanterns first, then the red ones. You can stand on the lantern ledges without harm; you'll only take damage if you touch a lantern or get hit by a bullet. Once the lanterns are destroyed, hit Lantern Man in the head. Use Lethal Coins or Shooting Stars to hit him while you stand on one side of the screen.

Warlock Zone III: Amusement Park

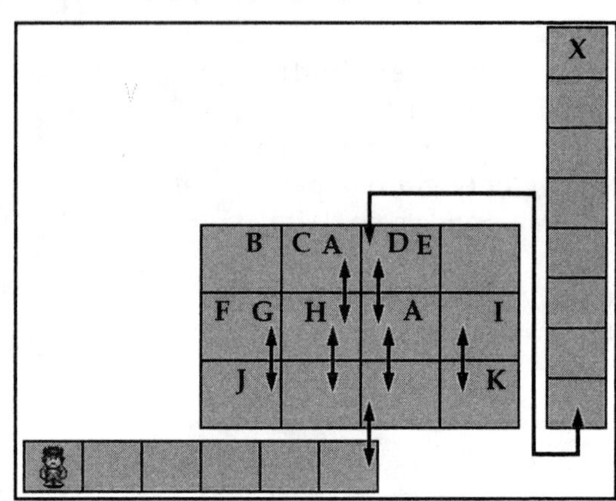

Map Legend

A. House.
B. Race Track.
C. Concentration Game.
D. Employment Office.
E. Casino.
F. Travel Logbook Shop.
G. Question Palace.
H. Game Center.
I. Store. Straw Sandals ($30), Clock ($50), Pizza ($60).
J. Sideshow.
K. Sushi Joint.
X. Passage to Next Zone.

Top-View Tips

• There is no Side-View in this Zone, just the Top-View. You can charge straight through the Zone without stopping, or you can take a moment to play some of the games.

• There's an Octopus on the second bridge near the end of the Zone. You can fight the Octopus, but it's easier to run past it without a battle. There's no reason to duke it out with a monster when you're so close to finishing the Zone!

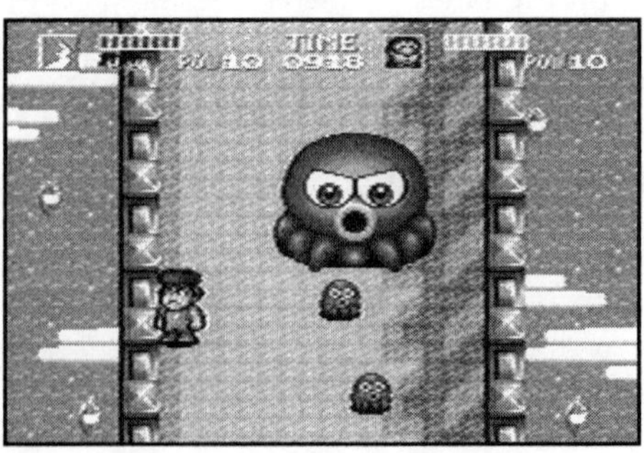

Warlock Zone IV: Defeat! Otafuku

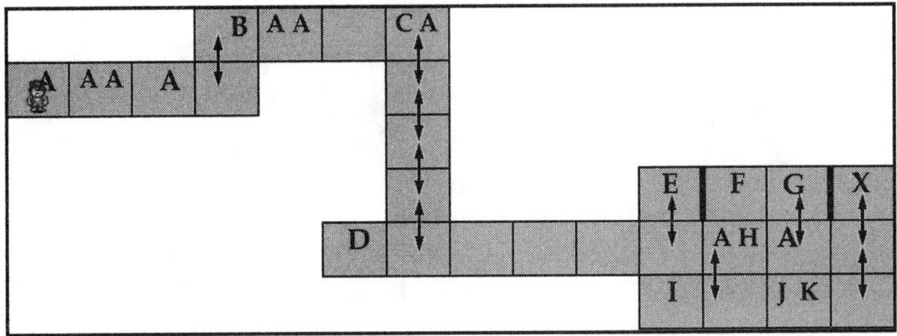

Map Legend

A. **House.**
B. **Store.** Straw Sandals ($30), Pizza ($120), 1-Up ($500).
C. **Motel.**
D. **Candy Shop.**
E. **Jutsu School.** No. 1 ($400), No. 2 ($800).
F. **Store.** Chain Armor ($150), Bomb ($100), 1-Up ($500).
G. **Travel Logbook Shop.**
H. **Employment Office.**
I. **Fortune Teller.**
J. **Hotel.**
K. **Concentration Game.**
X. **Passage to Side-View.**

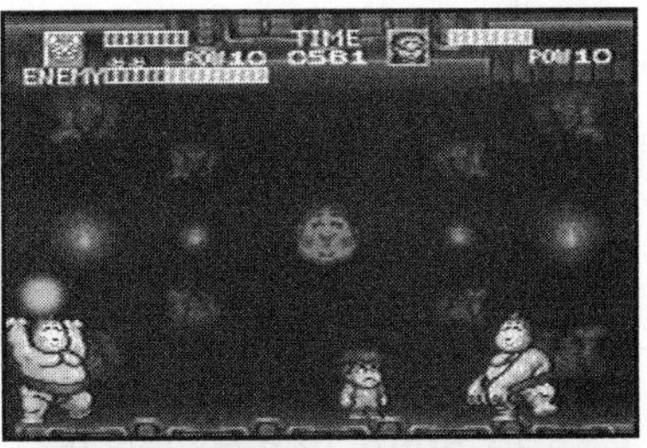

Top-View Tips

• The deer can hurt you, but don't hit them with a weapon or you'll lose $10.

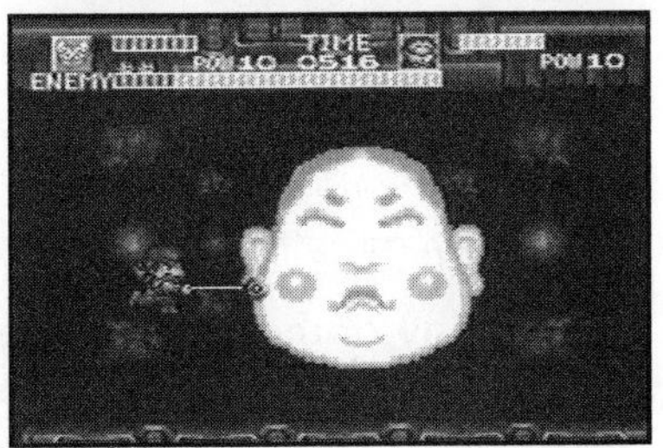

Side-View Tips

• Stomp onto the switches to rotate the room 90 degrees and create a pathway leading to the next section of the Zone.

• The two Sumo Wrestlers are simple to beat. Run underneath the fireball that they toss back and forth, then jump up and hit them in the face with your weapon.

• Otafuku is one Boss that's not ashamed to use graphic scaling! During the battle, Otafuku flies into the background, then flies back into the foreground and attacks with a different technique. Stand on the left side of the screen and hit him. During his final attack, stay on the extreme left edge of the screen and you'll be safe from his ballooning face.

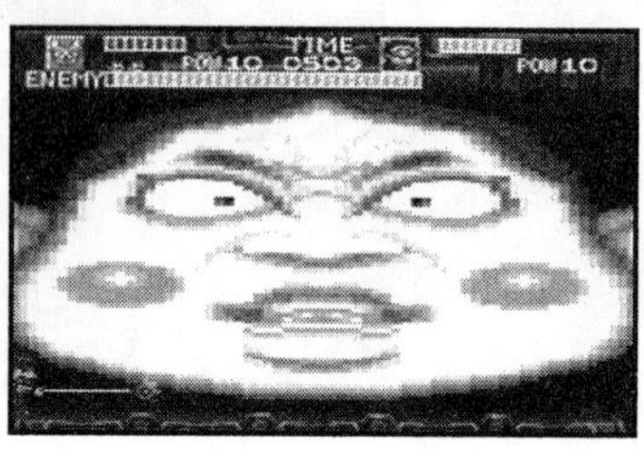

Warlock Zone V: Ninja Castle

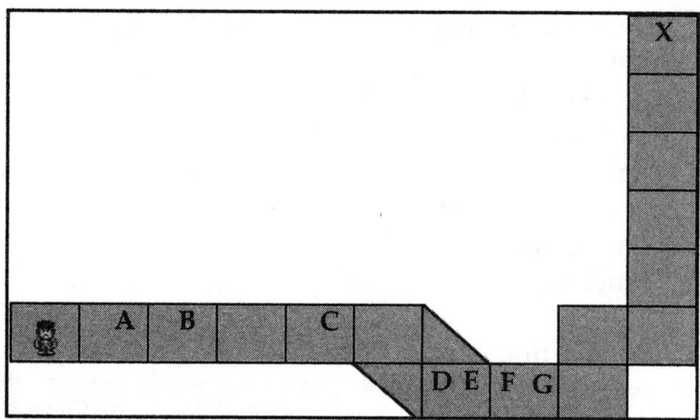

Map Legend

A. House.
B. Casino.
C. Motel.
D. Store. Straw Sandals ($40), Bomb ($220), Pizza ($120).
E. Jutsu School. No. 1 ($400), No. 3 ($800).
F. Store. Iron Helmet ($180), Chain Armor ($180), Pizza ($180).
G. Travel Logbook Shop.
X. Door to Side-View.

Top-View Tips

• Many of the caves in this Zone have hidden locations inside. Avoid the wild boars living inside the caves.

• Watch out for the Ninjas in the trees; they throw deadly Bombs with deadlier accuracy! Keep running and you shouldn't be hit by a Bomb.

Side-View Tips

• The Boss of this Zone is a group of Ninjas flying on a kite! The Ninjas attack in groups of two. Each group has a different attack, but they're easily avoided. Keep dodging and striking with your weapon, or use your missile weapon to strike from a distance.

• Once you've beaten the regular Ninjas, you'll get to fight the final Ninja on the kite. Use your missile weapon exclusively against the final Ninja. He hops up and down the three levels of the kite, but you should be able to defeat him easily.

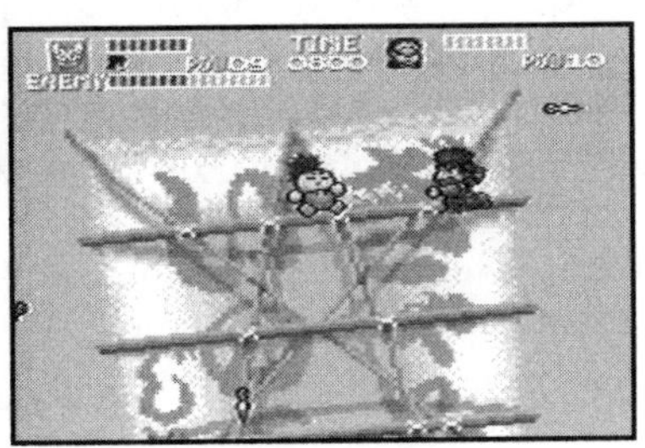

Warlock Zone VI

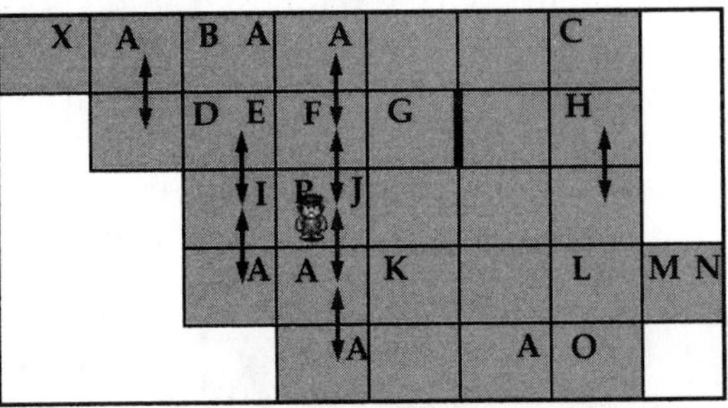

Map Legend

A. House.

B. Candy Shop.

C. Jutsu School. No. 1 ($400), No. 4 ($800).

D. Sauna.

E. Motel.

F. Employment Office.

G. Lottery.

H. Fortune Teller.

I. Store. Straw Sandals ($40), Chain Armor ($200), 1-Up ($800).

J. Secret Maze.

K. Sushi Joint.

L. Sideshow.

M. Race Track.

N. Game Center.

O. Travel Logbook Shop.

P. Store. Pass ($980), Bomb ($260), 1-Up ($800).

X. Door to Side-View.

Top-View Tips

• You can't enter the Side-View half of the Zone without buying a Pass from the Store at point P on the Map. With so many creeps walking around, you shouldn't have a problem collecting the money to buy it!

Side-View Tips

• The first Bosses you encounter are the old warrior dudes. Stay in the middle of the screen and strike the warriors with your weapon (or with Coins/Stars). The final warrior attacks with leaves; jump over each leaf and attack before he throws another leaf.

• The final Boss has two different forms. In his first form, he floats around the screen in a box, then lands on the ground and shoot leaves into the air. Whack the box with your weapon to cause damage, then hit the leaves falling down at you.

• Once you've destroyed the box, the Boss attacks on the ground, shooting his wig at you, or spitting out poisonous gas. Use your Coins/ Stars to hit the Boss, staying about a third of the screen away from him. From this distance, you can jump over the poison clouds. If you're too far away, the clouds will hit you no matter how high you jump.

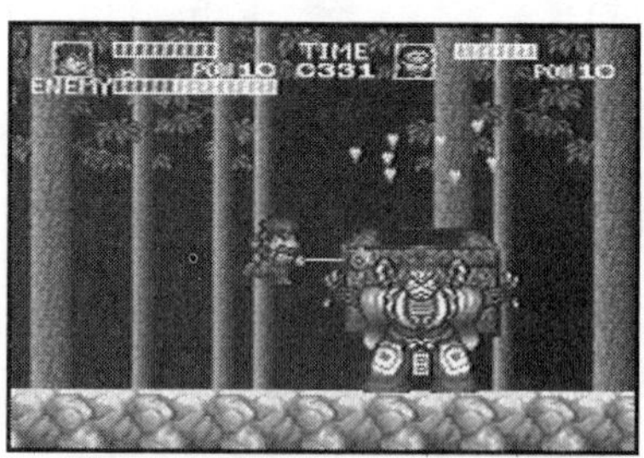

Warlock Zone VII: White Mirror

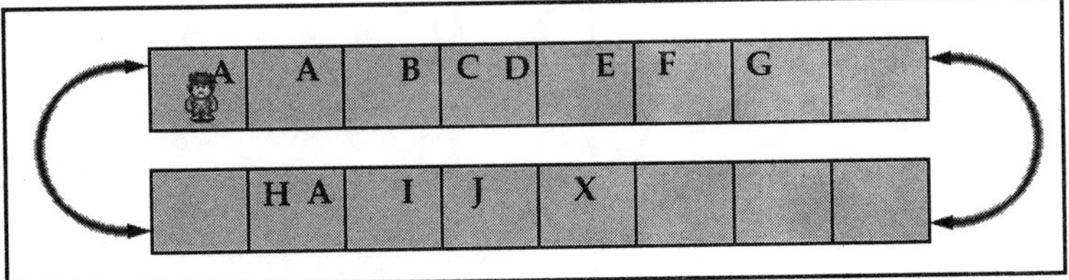

Map Legend

A. **House.**
B. **Store.** Straw Sandals ($40), Bomb ($220), Pizza ($120).
C. **Sushi Bar.**
D. **Jutsu School.** No. 2 ($1600), No. 3 ($1600).
E. **Casino.**
F. **Store.** Iron Helmet ($180), Chain Armor ($180), Pizza ($180).
G. **Concentration Game.**
H. **Sauna.**
I. **Jutsu School.** No. 1 ($400), No. 2 ($800).
J. **Travel Logbook Shop.**
X. **Passage to Side-View.**

Top-View Tips

• The first half of this Zone is one long horizontal strip of screens. Stock up on money, buy the required supplies, and go to the Side-View!

Side-View Tips

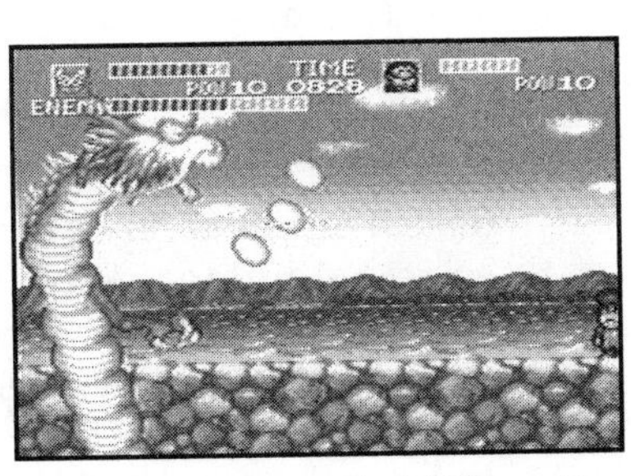

• Stay out of the water! Ying and Yang may be Jutsu masters, but they can't swim. (Kinda strange, considering they live on an island surrounded by water, but then this whole game is strange.)

• The Boss of this Zone is a huge sea snake! When the snake rises out of the water, run to the opposite side of the screen from the snake. Throw Coins/Stars at his head and dodge the fireballs he shoots at you. If you run out of Coins/Stars, you have to get macho and strike from extremely close range with your weapon.

Warlock Zone VIII: Save! Princess

Map Legend

A. House.

B. Jutsu School.
No. 1 ($600),
No. 4 ($2400).

C. Store.
Gold Helmet ($300),
Gold Armor ($380),
Text ($980).

D. Door to King.

E. Store.
Straw Sandals ($50),
Bomb ($260), Pizza ($240).

F. Sushi Bar.

G. Jutsu School. No. 2 ($1600), No. 3 ($1600).

H. Travel Logbook Shop.

Top-View Tips

• To learn about the hidden entrance to the Side-View, you've got to talk to the King. Unfortunately, you won't understand a word he says until you've purchased the Book at the Store (point C on the Map). There are also a few folks beside the King who you won't understand without the Book in your hand.

• Take a swing at all of the lion statues at the front of the castle to reveal hidden areas. (On the Map, the front of the Castle is the second row of screens from the top.) Remember to bring three pairs of Sandals here to collect all of the items in the areas.

Side-View Tips

• This Side-View section is definitely the hardest in the game. You'll have to make a bevy of tough jumps to reach the first of two Bosses. Our best advice: when you jump onto the moving platform, be ready to duck and jump!

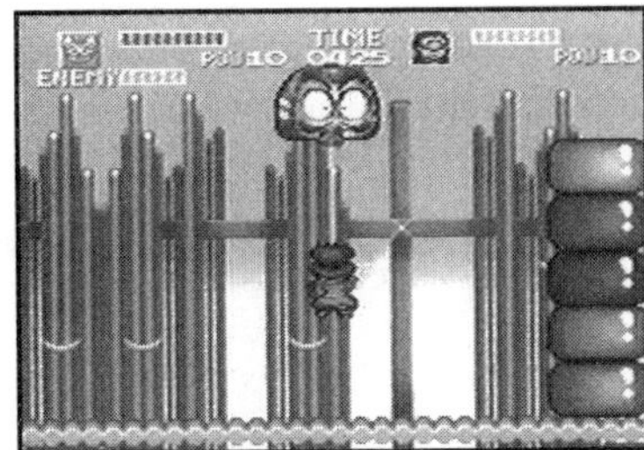

• The first Boss is a colorful guy! When he starts sliding across the screen, jump over the lowest body segment, then crouch down to avoid the high segments. When the Boss' head flies across the screen, whack it with your weapon. After you hit the head, you'll destroy it, and the next segment becomes the head.

When you destroy five heads, you'll drop into the next section of the Zone.

• The second Boss is guarding the Princess. Hit him rapidly in the head to make him zig-zag back and forth. Stay as close to his head as possible, walking back and forth on the ledge as it moves around the screen. Keep swinging until you gain access to the final Zone!

Warlock Zone IX: Final Story

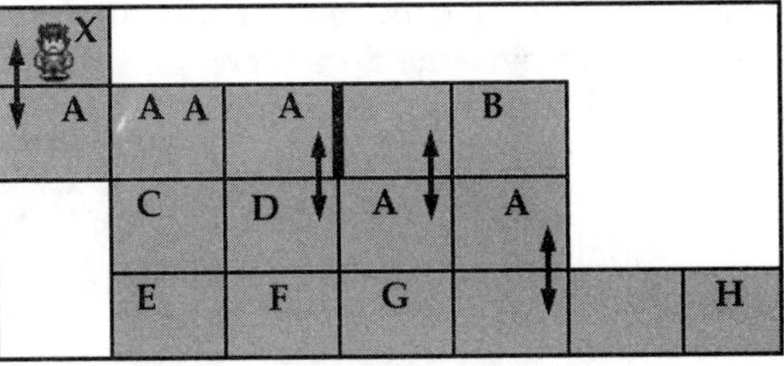

Map Legend

A. Prison.
B. Ruler of the Castle.
C. Jutsu School. No. 1 ($600), No. 4 ($2400).
D. Jutsu School. No. 2 ($1600), No. 3 ($1600).
E. Store. Gold Helmet ($320), Gold Armor ($500), Pizza ($300).
F. Candy Shop.
G. Store. Straw Sandals ($50), Bomb ($300), Clock ($100).
H. Travel Logbook Shop.
X. Door to Side-View.

Top-View Tips

• You'll be released from prison by the Ninja woman Yae, whom you helped back in Zone IV. Once you've been freed, head for the Ruler's Prison. The Ruler tells you about a secret door in your prison cell. You can't find the secret door until the Ruler mentions it.

Side-View Tips

• At the end of the Side-View, you'll have to fight three Bosses. The first two Bosses, Lantern Man and Otafuku, you already know how to beat. The third Boss is brand-new!

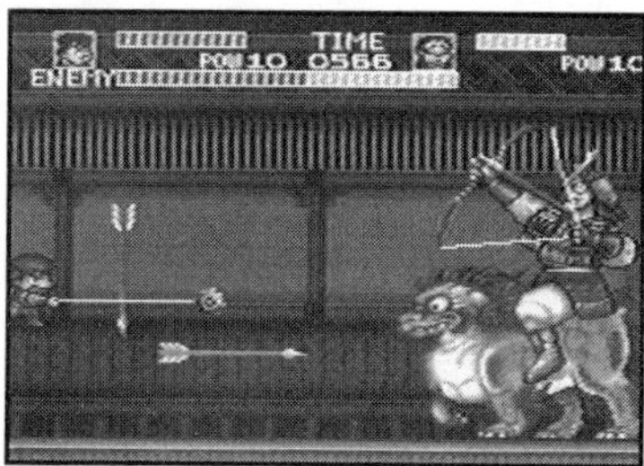

• When the third Boss fires his arrows, jump up and hit the arrows as they fall downward. Hit the arrows so they strike the creature that the Boss is riding. If you keep hitting the creature, you can stay at the left side of the screen. If the Boss moves too far to the left, you have to position yourself between the arrows and the Boss. This is a tight squeeze, so be careful!

• After you've defeated the Boss's mount (which turns out to be a fox—not a babe, but an animal), he starts using a rolling attack. Jump over the Boss when he's rolling along the ground, and crawl underneath him when he bounces. Strike the Boss when he's not rolled up to cause damage.

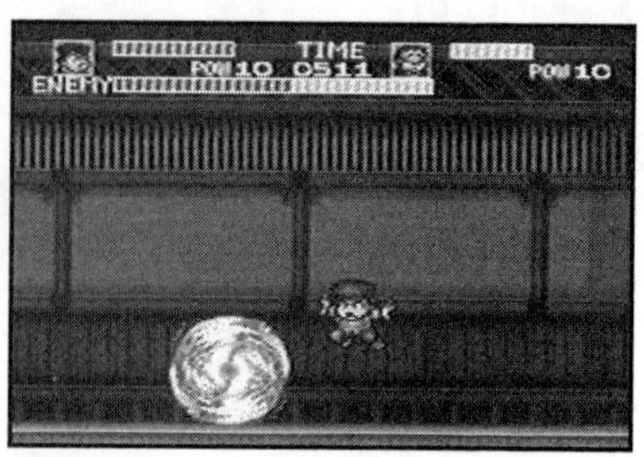

• When you defeat the third Boss, the Super NES takes over and guides you to the final encounter—and the ending sequence!

SHH . . . THE SECRETS

Passwords

Use these one-player (Kid Ying) Logbook passwords to start at any Zone from II through IX, with a decent wad of cash and the Yokohama Yo Yo.

Zone II	?Ldzn p<n69 J&Xl$!5nrr <kn$x n$q6x 3
Zone III	zrbG; Gm;Rh zJ5/9 VX;DD mL;9? ;9=RL P
Zone IV	-YK95 %P5;% H/;%y Bn5WW P$5yY 5y2;1 =
Zone V	kX6n$ m^$$@ BxLZn +y$00 -p$n& $ndzX w
Zone VI	BHzwq r>q3" M1Thd 82qpp >gqdt qdn3+ 6
Zone VII	>%5=" 4j""t q?v4= kH"NN bT"=J "=9Kz :
Zone VIII	K@@ll 18l&< G6N$Z ^%lvv :ylZz lZh&v t
Zone IX	zrPK; :R;Rh zJ5/9 VX;DD mL;9? ;9=R- X

CHAPTER 7

The Legend of Zelda: A Link to the Past

by Nintendo of America

WHAT'S GOING ON?

The Legend of Zelda game is the most popular adventure game for the 8-bit NES system, more than four years after its introduction. It has a perfect combination of combat, exploration, and secrets that keeps players coming back for more. Now you can experience a fabulous new adventure on the 16-bit Super NES!

The Legend of Zelda: A Link to the Past game isn't a sequel to the first two; it's a "prequel." The evil Ganon has broken free of an ancient spell and plans to throw the land of Hyrule into darkness. He's kidnaped the distant relatives of the Wise Men who cast the spell. You are Link, a valiant hero and all-around nice guy. Rescue the relatives, defeat Ganon, and save Hyrule!

PLAYERS

The Legend of Zelda: A Link to the Past game is for one player only. There are three save positions, so up to three people can "share" the game.

HEART CONTAINERS AND RUPEES

You start the game with three Heart Containers. As you play through the game, you'll earn more Heart Containers by defeating Dungeon Masters and by finding pieces of Containers hidden throughout the land. It's possible to have a total of twenty Heart Containers by the end of the adventure.

Rupees are the currency of choice in Hyrule. You'll find Rupees under bushes and pots, in trees and treasure chests, and even more places. You'll need Rupees to buy weapons and special items.

LIVES AND CONTINUES

You only have one life. Your strength is shown by the Heart Containers. These Containers become empty as you're hit by enemies. When all the Containers are empty, the game is over, and you're given a choice of three options: Save and Continue, Save and Quit, or Do Not Save and Continue.

Save and Continue saves your progress in the game and allows you to continue playing. Save and Quit saves your progress and returns the game to the title screen. Do Not Save and Continue allows you to continue playing without saving the progress you made in your last game.

You should use the Save and Continue option most of the time, particularly if you find a special item while exploring a dungeon. Think carefully before using the Do Not Save option!

WEAPONS

Your main weapon is the **Sword**. The Sword has four levels of power. When you first obtain the Sword from your Uncle, it's at Level 1. When the Sword reaches Level 2 or higher, you can shoot magical bolts from the end of the weapon (if your Heart Containers are filled).

CONTROLS

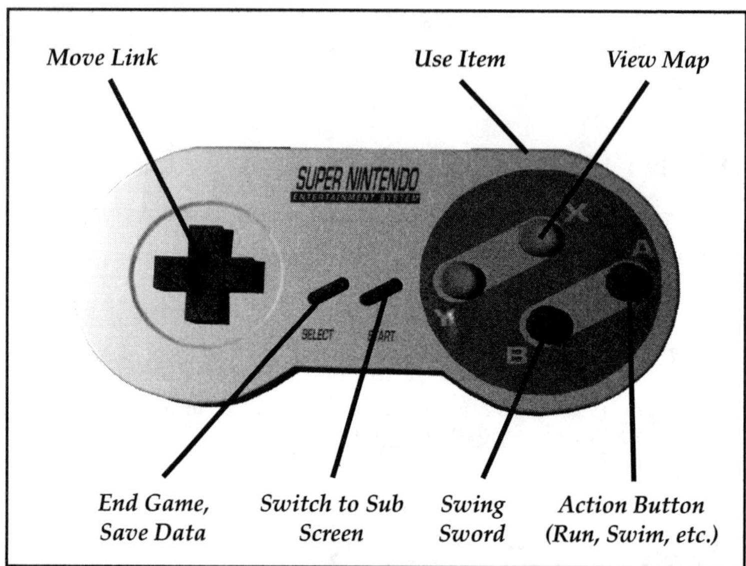

The **Boomerang** stuns your enemies for a few moments, giving you time to strike. The Boomerang can also collect Rupees and Hearts.

The **Bomb** damages enemies and blows holes in walls. It can also hurt you if you're too close when it explodes! You can drop up to two Bombs at once. You can even pick up a Bomb and throw it before it explodes, but this is a highly dangerous maneuver!

The **Bow** is a great weapon against some enemies. You need Arrows to use the Bow (of course). Arrows are found when you defeat certain enemies or look under certain pots. Near the end of the game, you'll find a Faerie who turns your Arrows into Silver Arrows, which you need to defeat Ganon.

The **Fire Rod** shoots a ball of fire that burns your enemies. Some enemies are more vulnerable to the Fire Rod than others. The Fire Rod can also be used to light torches.

The **Ice Rod** shoots a gust of freezing air. Weaker enemies will be destroyed outright, but stronger enemies might turn into blocks of ice.

ARMOR

You start the game wearing a suit of green cloth, which doesn't protect you against damage. For protection, you need the **Blue Mail** and **Red Mail**. Blue Mail reduces enemy damage by 25%, Red Mail by 50%.

When you find your Uncle, he'll give you the **Shield**. The Shield has three levels of protection. It starts at the lowest level of power (of course).

SPECIAL ITEMS

The **Book of Mudora** is needed to decipher the ancient Hylian hieroglyphics.

The **Bottle** is an all-purpose container that can hold potions, Faeries, and more. You can find four Bottles in the game, and you'll want all of them!

The **Bug-Catching Net** is used to swipe bugs and Faeries out of the air to put into Bottles.

The **Lamp** provides you with light in the dark areas of the dungeons. You can use the Lamp to light up torches in the dungeons, as well.

The **Moon Pearl** keeps you from transforming into a rabbit (!) when you enter the Dark World, by protecting you against the magical powers of the Triforce.

Pegasus Shoes help yoou run at incredible speed. You'll gain a new attack and several new skills with the Shoes.

The **Power Glove** and **Titan's Mitt** increase your strength, allowing you to lift heavy objects you normally couldn't budge.

Zora's Flippers allow you to swim. If you try swimming without the Flippers, you'll be dumped back onto the shore at the place where you jumped in. The Flippers are a must-have item; you can't finish the game without them.

FRIENDS

Link's gotta lotta friends, but two of them are most important: Princess Zelda and the elder Sahasrahla. Zelda is the key to preventing Ganon from taking over Hyrule, and Sahasrahla gives you hints and help about tricky puzzles in the dungeons.

ENEMIES

There are plenty of different enemies in the game, but they're just too numerous to mention! The most dangerous enemies in the game are the Dungeon Masters. You'll often need to use a special type of attack to damage a Dungeon Master. Each of the ten dungeons in the game has a Master to fight. You receive a complete Heart Container when you defeat a Master.

STRATEGY SESSION

This Strategy Session presents a guide to the secrets of the Light World, and takes you through the first three dungeons. When you finish the three dungeons, and defeat Ahagnim in Hyrule Castle, you'll be ready to explore the Dark World and begin the quest to find the seven Crystals. Read on!

The Light World

We've divided the Light World into 16 sections. Each section is made up of 16 screens. Under each section, we've listed interesting areas and secrets to discover. We haven't listed everything, so you'll need to find some secrets on your own!

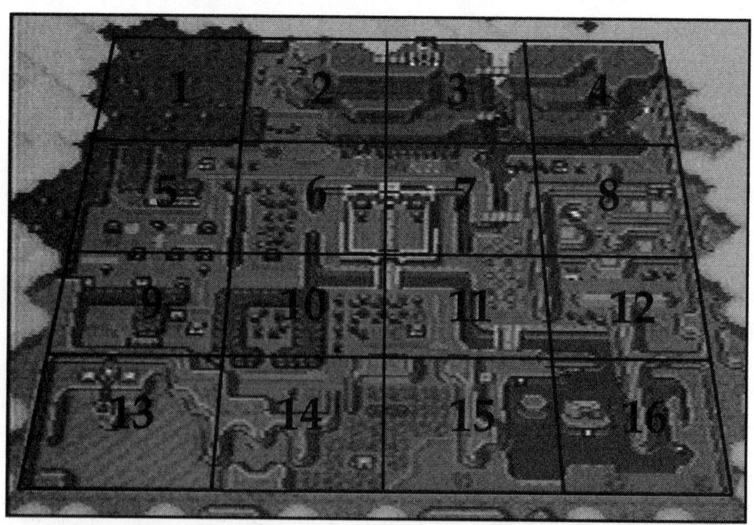

Section 1 (The Lost Woods)

Den of Thieves

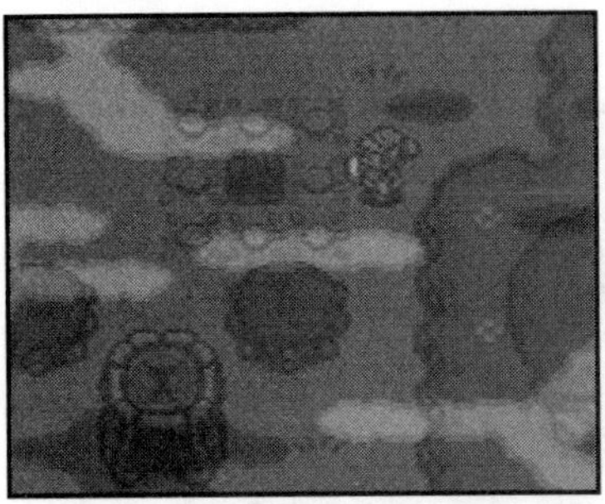

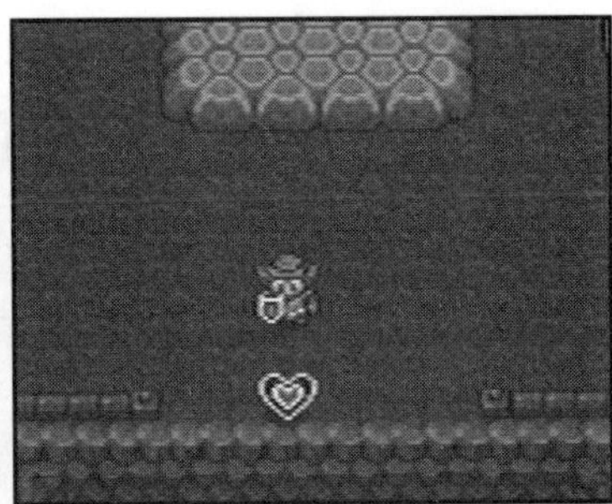

There's a Heart Container piece in the Den, but you can't get to it through the visible entrance. Chop down the bushes North of the entrance and you'll find a hole that drops you down to the Container Piece.

Master Sword

There are fake Master Swords scattered throughout the Lost Woods. The true Master Sword is in the Northwest corner of the Woods, and you won't be able to claim it until you've collected the three Pendants.

Section 2 (Outer Woodlands/Death Mountain)

Death Mountain Tunnel

Lumberjacks

The lumberjack twins are cutting down a tree. Come back here when you've got the Pegasus Shoes and run into the tree to shake off the leaves. You'll reveal a hidden passage.

You can't go into the tunnel unless you have the Power Glove. With the enhanced lifting strength of the Glove, you can lift the rock blocking your way.

Mountain Cave

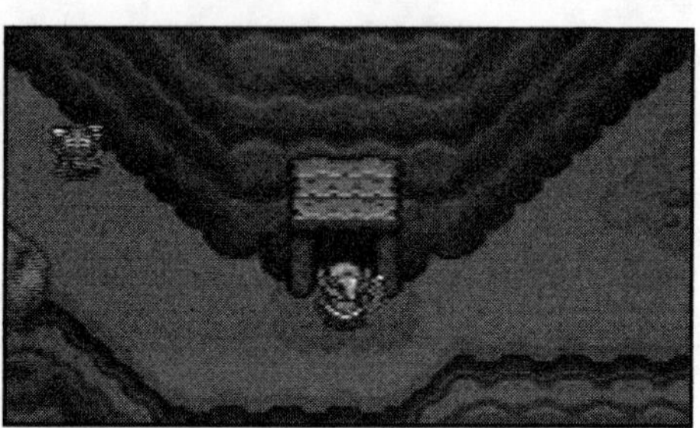

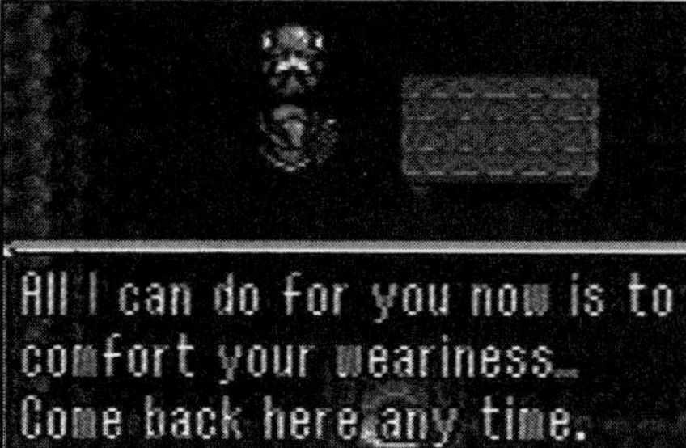

When you make your way through the tunnel, you'll come across an old man. Escort the old man to the Mountain Cave and he'll give you a useful special item. If you restart the game, you'll be able to restart from the Mountain Cave.

Section 3 (Death Mountain)

Broken Bridge

You can't cross this bridge until you have the Hookshot in your possession. Across the bridge, you'll find several caves (and a Dark World transport square).

Spectacle Rock

When you teleport into the Dark World, Spectacle Rock disappears, but you can still see the outline of where it used to be. Stand in the middle of the outline and use the Mirror to return to the Light World, then jump off Spectacle Rock to the North. Now you can walk to the Tower of Hera.

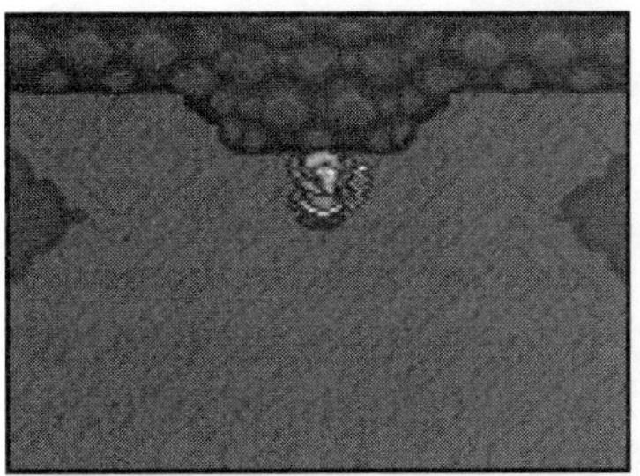

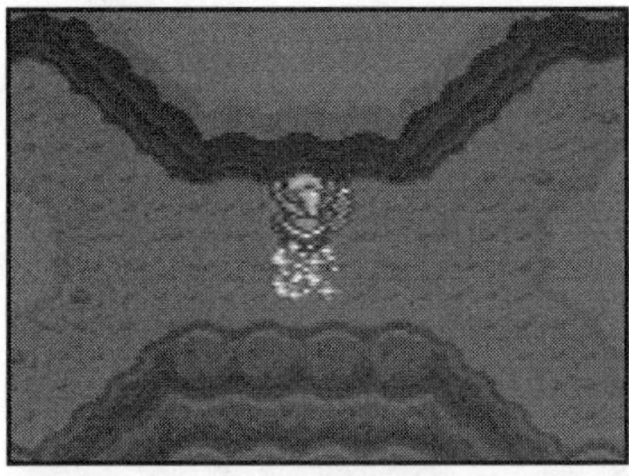

Section 4 (Death Mountain/Zora's Falls)

Waterfall of Wishing

Try throwing an empty Bottle into the Mysterious Pond underneath the Waterfall of Wishing. The Faerie will fill it up with Magic Medicine for free!

Zora's Falls

Zora will sell you his flippers for the hefty price of 500 Rupees. You have to have them to complete the game, so save up and come here to buy the Flippers as soon as you can.

Section 5 (Outer Village/Kakariko Village)

Bottle Merchant

This man sells one of the four Bottles available in the game, at the reasonable price of 100 Rupees. Buy it as soon as you can afford it.

Thieves' Hideout

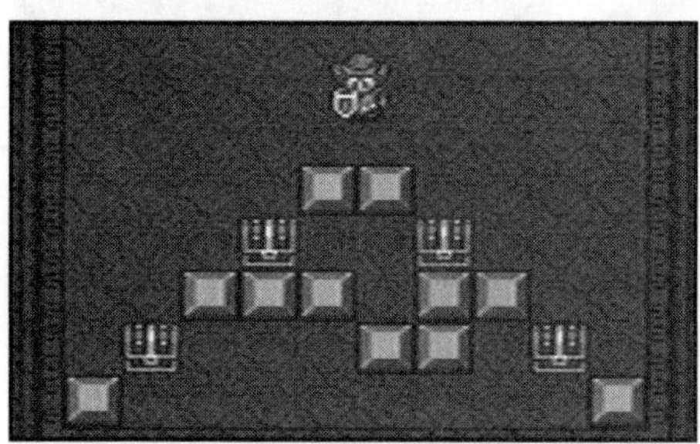

You'll find the hideout in the building to the left of Sahasrahla's House. Climb down the stairs and raid the chests for red Rupees, then plant a Bomb against the North wall and go into the hidden room for more Rupees and a Heart Container Piece.

Section 6 (Woodlands)

Sanctuary

This is the location that Princess Zelda directs you to after being rescued. You'll find a complete Heart Container in the chest. You can't re-enter Hyrule Castle from here, but there's a secret entrance in the Graveyard.

Section 7 (Woodlands)

Graveyard

Push the gravestones to see if there's anything underneath. You won't find anything interesting until you've got the Power Glove or Titan Mitt. This gives you the strength to lift the big rocks blocking access to a few of the gravestones. The gravestone in the Northeast corner of the Graveyard covers a secret entrance leading back into Hyrule Castle.

Section 8 (Eastern Palace)

Magic Shop

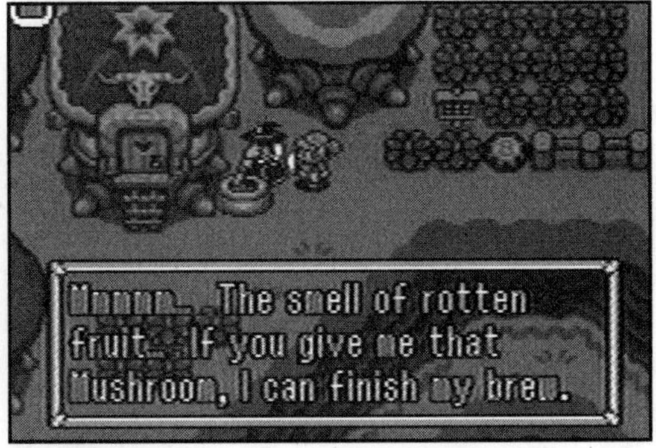

The good witch outside the shop needs a Mushroom. Bring her one from the Lost Woods, then visit the shop later and you'll be given the Magic Powder. Try the Powder on the cucumber creature walking around near the shop for a humorous effect.

Section 9 (Kakariko Village)

House of Books

Come to this location once you've got the Pegasus Shoes and run into the bookshelf. The book that falls to the ground is the Book of Mudora, which you'll need to translate some of the ancient Hylian language.

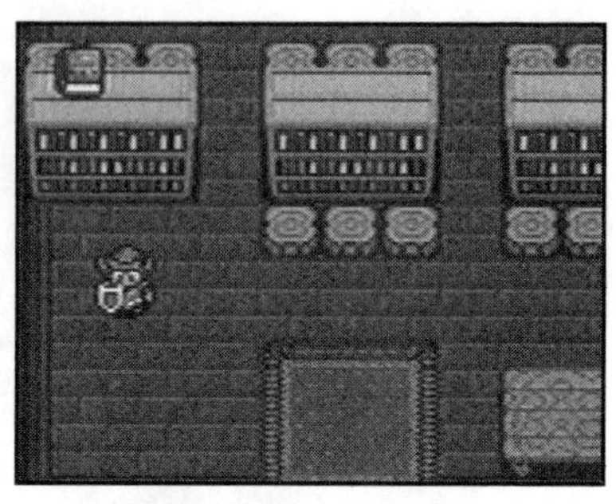

Inn

Talk to the men in the bottom half of the Inn for some information. Go through the door at the top of the Inn and open the chest for a Bottle.

Mysterious Hut

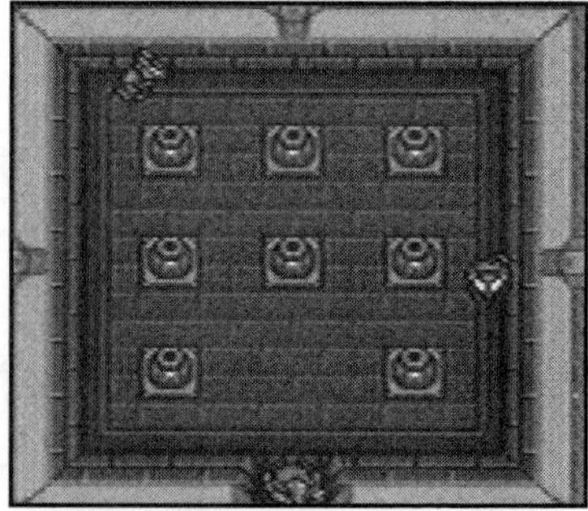

This hut doesn't seem to have any doors. Use a Bomb to blow it open. Inside, you'll find two rats guarding some eight jugs with the following items underneath: four Bombs, five Arrows, and two Rupees. You can go outside and come back to collect the items over and over again.

Quarreling Brothers

Blow up the wall separating the two brothers, then go outside and run a race through the maze. If you get through in 15 seconds or less, you'll earn a Heart Container Piece. There's a shortcut near the end of the maze where you won't have to chop down bushes in your way.

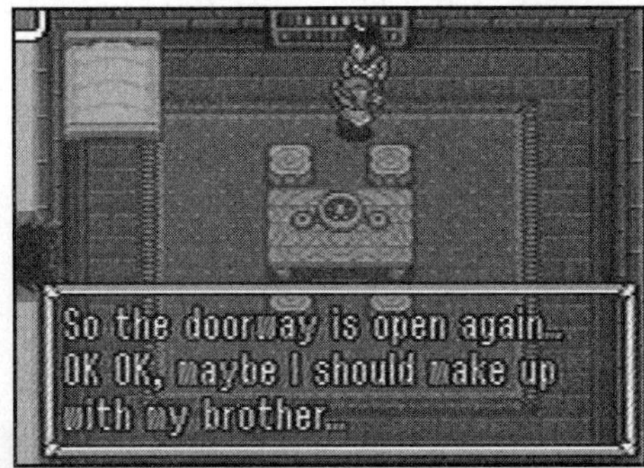

Sick Boy's House

Visit the Sick Boy when you've got a Bottle and he'll give you the Bug-Catching Net. You can use the Net to snag much more than bugs, however (see The Secrets on Faeries for more details).

Section 10 (Woodlands)

Haunted Grove

The Grove is the key to obtaining the Flute, an item that saves you lots of time in getting around the Light World. Visit the Grove when you're in the Dark World to get the shovel, then return to the Light World and dig around for the Flute. Return to the Dark World and play it for the kind person one final time. Then go to the weather vane in the center of Kakariko and play the Flute. Now you can use the Flute to travel to eight different locations in the Light World.

Smithy's House

Two brothers run this smithy, but one of the brothers is missing. Look for him in the Dark World and bring him back to the Smithy. The reunited brothers will offer to temper your Sword. Let them have the Sword, go outside and explore for a while, then return to obtain your new and improved weapon!

Section 11 (Woodlands)

Link's House

Your humble home is a great place to pop in when you need healing. The three jugs in the Northwest corner of the house have Small Hearts underneath. If you leave the house, then go back inside, the Small Hearts reappear.

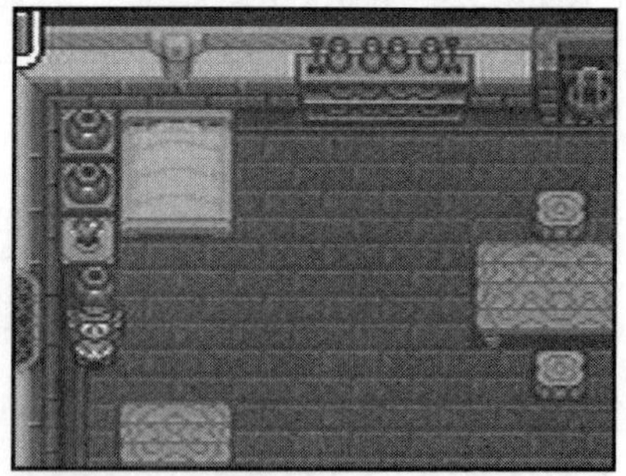

Section 12 (Eastern Palace)

Faerie Caves

There are two Faerie caves in this Section of the Light World. The Western cave has a Faerie queen who heals all your Heart

Containers, but she can't be captured with the Net. The Eastern cave has four small Faeries who can be captured with the Net and placed into Bottles (see The Secrets for more on Faeries).

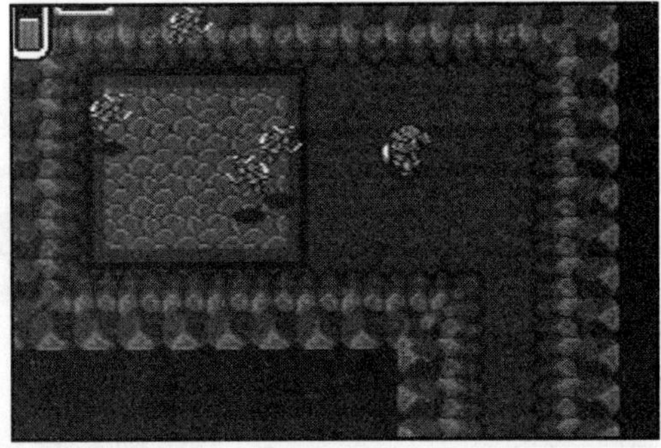

Section 13 (Desert of Mystery)

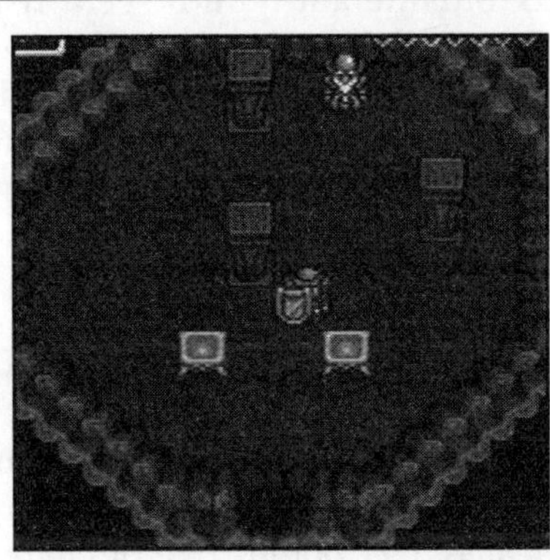

Desert Cave

The Cave leads to Aginah, a wise old man who advises you to obtain the Book of Mudora. Plant a Bomb against the wall South of Aginah and go through the hole to find a chest with a Heart Container Piece.

Section 14 (Great Swamp)

Middle-Aged Man

No, this isn't the character from Saturday Night Live. (You're lookin' at his gut, aren't ya?! He's working on it!) He's a thief who can open a locked chest that you find in the Dark World. Inside the chest is a Bottle.

Rupee-Rich Fish

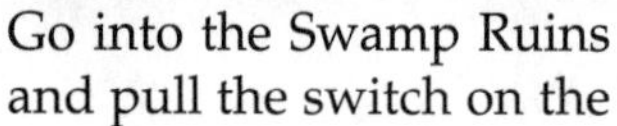

Go into the Swamp Ruins and pull the switch on the right to drain the water. Walk outside and you'll see a fish flopping around. Grab the fish and walk North one screen. Walk toward the circle of stones until the fish hops out of your hands and into the water. He'll give you 20 Rupees as thanks. You can repeat this trick over and over to build Rupees (although there are much easier ways to build your wealth).

Section 15 (Great Swamp)

Shop

You shouldn't have to buy anything here. Get Small Hearts from Link's House and other locations; some monsters even drop Small Hearts when they're defeated. Get Bombs free of charge from the Mysterious Hut in Kakariko Village. And buy the Red Potion at the Magic Shop.

Section 16 (Lake Hylia)

Fountain of Happiness

Happy happy, joy joy! Every time you throw Rupees into the Fountain, your Happiness increases. When your Happiness reaches maximum, a Faerie appears and offers to increase the total number of Bombs or Arrows that you can carry. Visit often to increase your carrying abilities.

Ice Cave

Plant a Bomb to the left of the door into the Ice Cave to reveal the door that leads to the chest. Inside the chest is the powerful Icerod.

The Dungeons

Here are guides for the first three dungeons in the game. We've provided maps of each dungeon, along with the locations of important items.

Eastern Palace

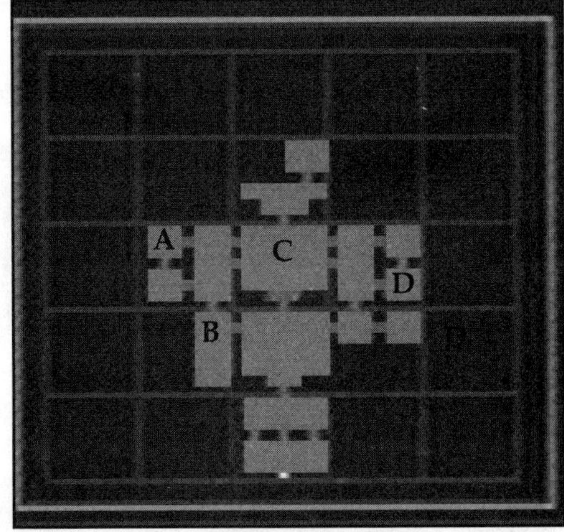

Eastern Palace
1st Floor

A. Compass
B. Big Key
C. Bow
D. Map

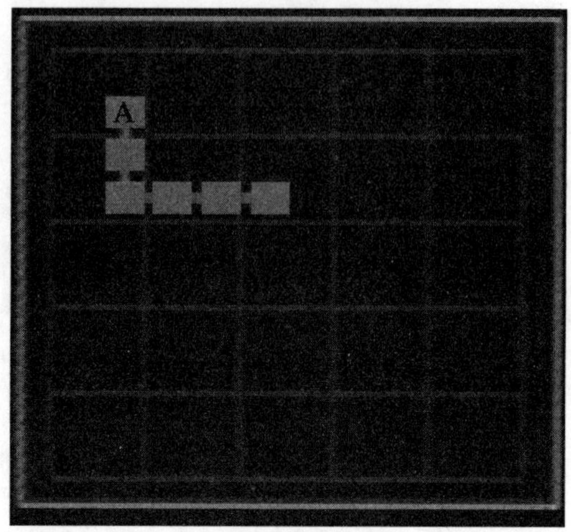

Eastern Palace
2nd Floor
A. Armos Knights (Dungeon Masters)

Desert Palace

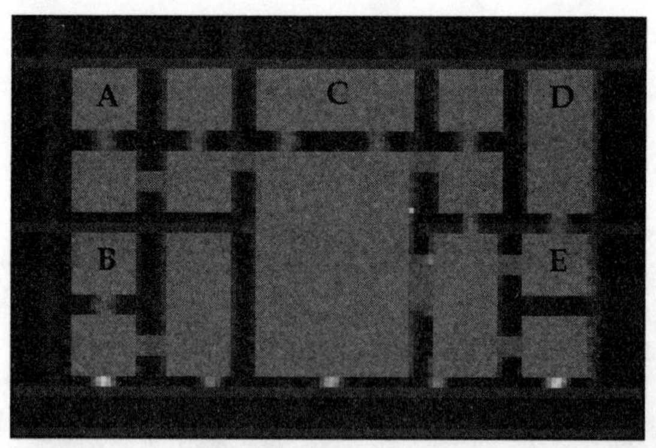

Desert Palace Basement
A. Power Glove
B. Faeries
C. Map
D. Big Key
E. Compass

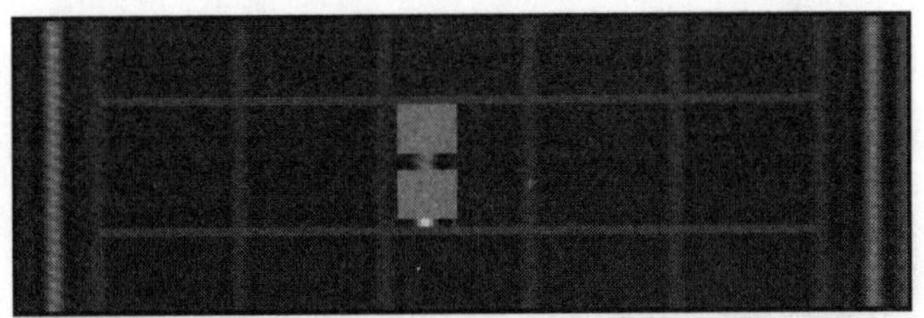

Desert Palace 1st Floor

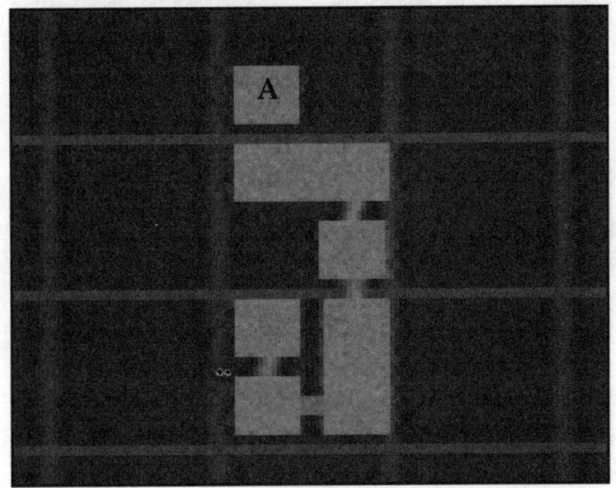

Desert Palace 2nd Floor
A. Sand Worms (Dungeon Masters)

Tower of Hera

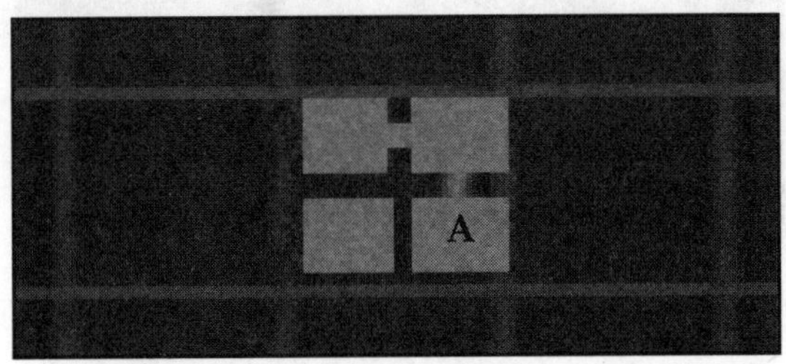

Tower of Hera 1st Floor
A. Big Key

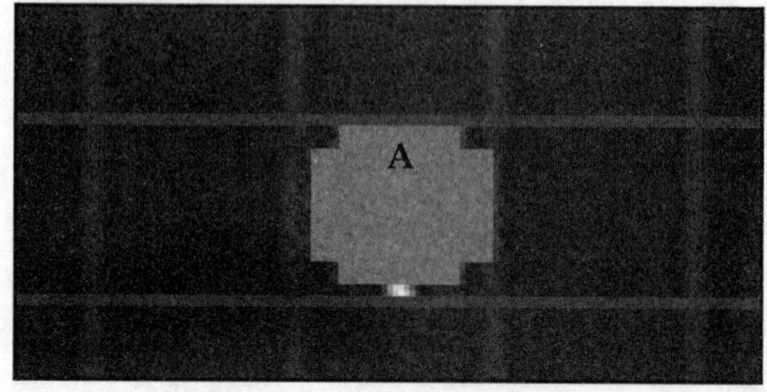

Tower of Hera 2nd Floor
A. Map

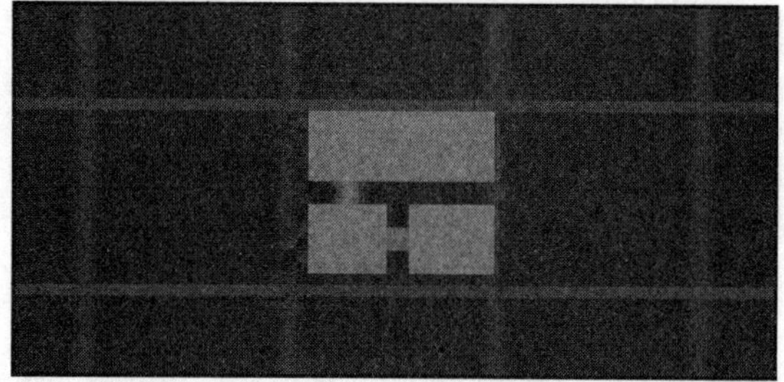

Tower of Hera 3rd Floor

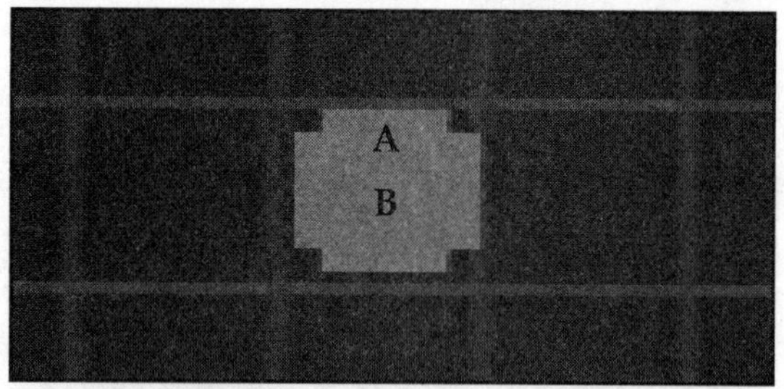

Tower of Hera 4th Floor
A. Moon Pearl
B. Compass

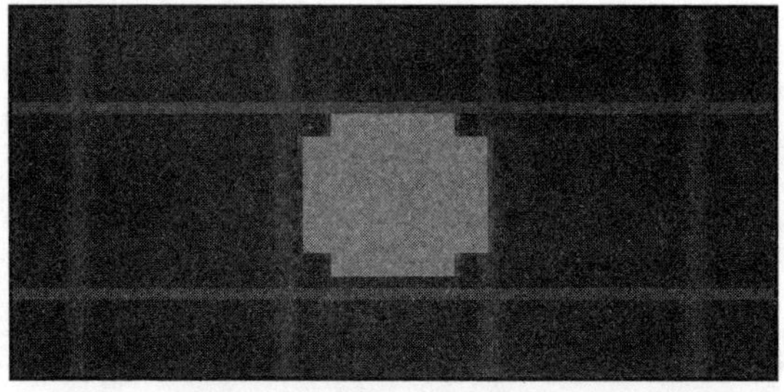

Tower of Hera 5th Floor

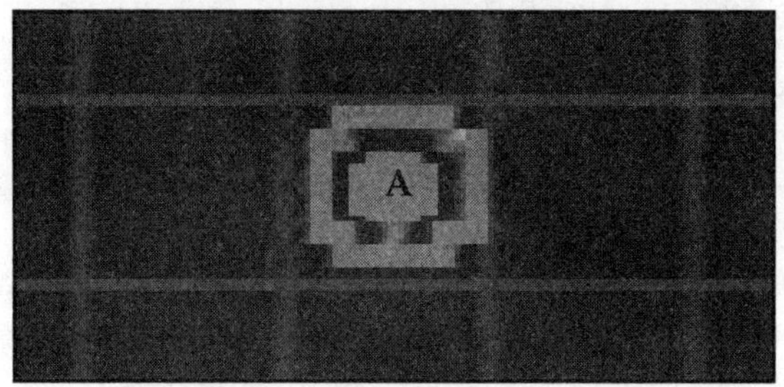

Tower of Hera 6th Floor
A. Giant Wurm (Dungeon Master)

SHH... THE SECRETS

Angry Chickens

Want a good laugh? Find a chicken in the Light World and thrash it with your sword. Keep thrashing away until a flock of chickens flies onto the screen to defend their brother! The chickens can hurt you, so watch out.

Faeries

Use the Bug-Catching Net to catch a Faerie, and put it into a Bottle. If your Heart Containers run out, the Faerie will come out of the bottle and resurrect you at the location where you perished. This is the most effective way to continue the game.

Trees

When you've obtained the Pegasus Shoes, use them to ram into every tree you find. Some trees hold Heart-restoring apples, Faeries, and other items. A few trees have bees inside, so "bee" careful. (Groan.)

MORE SECRETS . . . MORE SECRETS . . .

Do you want to know everything about The Legend of Zelda: A Link to the Past game? It's a huge adventure, and there are a lot of tricks, secrets, and hidden items. In fact, we had so much information that there's no way we could have put it all into this chapter. So we wrote an entire book about the game! It's called

The Legend of Zelda: A Link to the Past Game Secrets. This book is available from Prima Publishing.

The Legend of Zelda: A Link to the Past Game Secrets has all the information you'll ever need about The Legend of Zelda: A Link to the Past game—complete maps of the Light and Dark Worlds, where to find all of the Heart Containers, and other super secrets you won't find anywhere else! Look for *The Legend of Zelda: A Link to the Past Game Secrets* at your nearest bookstore, or use the order form at the end of this book!

CHAPTER 8

Might and Magic II

by American Sammy

WHAT'S GOING ON?

Might and Magic II for the Super NES is based on the computer game of the same name. It is a very, **very** large and complex game that includes a lot of quests and puzzles, plus more than 250 different monsters, hundreds of weapons and special items, and seemingly thousands of ways to die. In this chapter, we'll give you some secret ways to build your characters fast. You'll need very powerful adventurers if you hope to solve the mysteries of Cron.

We'll dispense with the usual format for this chapter in order to get right to the good stuff. You're still going to have to figure out most of the game, but we'll give you some of the most important information.

Warning: Even though we don't solve all the clues or provide all the maps, following these instructions will alter how the game plays. That's because you'll be so powerful by the time you're finished that most encounters will simply be toss-offs. You'll still have to figure out a lot of puzzles, and you'll be attacked by massive armies. There's still plenty of challenge. But you'll really kick butt most of the time. It's up to you whether to use our tricks or try things the hard way.

STRATEGY SESSION

The first thing you'll have to do is create and then build up your characters. Choose the following party for the best mixture, but remember that you can win this game with any party mix (cashews, almonds, peanuts . . . no, not that kind): Knight, Paladin, Robber (or Ninja), Cleric, Archer, Sorcerer. With this mix, you have good fighters, two magic users of each kind (Cleric and Sorcery), and someone to open the chests so you can get the good booty.

Remember, when you create your characters, you can use the Reroll option to get better statistics. Be patient. Eventually, you'll get a character with a really good roll. Later in the game, there are ways to increase even those stats.

Once the party is together, you'll need to introduce them very carefully to the world. If you take too many chances, you'll lose them. So here's what you can do:

The First Battle

When you wake up in the Inn at Middlegate, turn immediately to the left and walk to the end of the hall. Turn left again and walk through the wall. That's right, it's a fake wall. Now turn left and walk to the end of the hall. There will always be an encounter there. If you beat the enemy creatures, Search for a chest, choose Detect Magic, and then have your Robber/Ninja disarm any traps. Get anything good, equip any good weapons or armor you find, then walk back the way you came and walk back to the front desk of the Inn. Just before you turn to face the desk, choose the Rest command to recharge all your characters, then save the game by staying at the Inn. It's free.

Now you must be patient. Repeat this procedure again and again until you've built up some gold and some experience points. Be sure not to run out of food. For only 20 gold, you can get the Feeding Frenzy at the tavern just outside the Inn and to the left. The Weapon shop is also nearby.

Along the way, you may get some really useful weapons. Watch what happens when you equip new weapons or armor. Some of your statistics may change. For instance, a Chance Sword increases your Luck. A Quick Katana makes you faster.

Other items may have magic spells associated with them if you Use them. Also, try the Skeleton Closet nearby to gain more gold and experience, but be careful when opening the door.

When you've built up some good experience points, go to Turkov's Training by exiting the Inn and turning first right, then left. It costs gold to train, so be sure to bring all you can.

Keep up this procedure until your Sorcerer has learned the second- or third-level spells—in particular the Jump and Fly spells. Now you're ready to start gaining some real gold, if you're patient. If you want to try the next part earlier, that's all right. But you may get killed a few times along the way.

Lloyd's Beacon and the Middlegate Dungeon

Now you're ready to explore outside a little. Just a little, though. Go to the city gates (at city coordinates 5,15) and go out into the fresh air. Now you want to walk North along the path, past the sign leading to Castle Pinehurst and then one step past the sign pointing to Vulcania. Now turn West and walk until you see the sign pointing toward Tundara and Woodhaven. Turn South, walk four steps, then walk two steps East. Now go North until you reach Corak's Cave.

Immediately after you enter Corak's Cave, face South and walk two steps. You'll receive the Lloyd's Beacon spell. Before anything else happens, return to the exit and get back to Middlegate. If you get lost, cast the Fly spell and fly to area C2. The entrance to Middlegate is one step West and one step South of where you land.

Once you have saved your party at the Inn, go to the dungeon entrance and try to make it to the coordinates X(1),Y(0) in the southwest corner of the dungeon. Follow the path on the cavern map to get there safely and use the Jump spell where we've indicated it. You can also find the golden goblet for the magician at coordinates 0,7. Just before the doorway at 2,1 you'll face a group of Carnage Spirits and Zombies. Use a combination of the Lightning Bolt spell and the Turn Undead spell to get rid of Carnage Spirits. Any that are left should fall before your weapons, though some characters may not be able to affect them.

When you get to 1,0, Search and you'll find 1,000 gold (166 for each party member). Now cast the Lloyd's Beacon spell and set a new beacon. Return the way you came. Be sure to Rest if your spell points or hit points are too low.

Now, save at the Inn, then return and cast Lloyd's Beacon. Choose Teleport to Last and you'll be back at the money. Unless

To get to the treasure, follow the path marked with the dotted line. Jump at the letter J. You'll have to fight your way past the guardians at the doorway before entering the room with the treasure. Get the Treasure at the letter X.

Use a light spell or a torch to read the hints on the walls, and get the goblet at the eastern edge of the cavern.

you already have the Surface spell, you'll have to return by foot, getting by the Carnage Spirits again. Or, when you meet them, use the Run option. If it is successful, it will put you back at the stairs up.

Cuisinarts

Now that you have a sure method of getting money, gather up several thousand gold and then go to Edmund's Expeditions and get the Mountaineering skill twice for 4,000 gold. You need it twice (both with one character, or once each with two

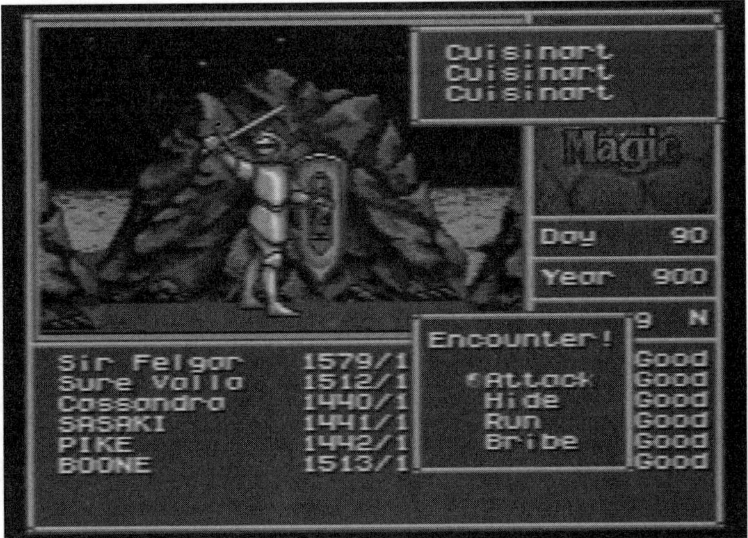

characters). Now you can climb directly over most mountains. While you're in the neighborhood, visit Otto Mapper, Esq. and get the Cartography skill for one of your members.

After saving the game at the Inn, head to the Poorman's Portal West of the Inn and take the passage to Sansobar. Find Sly's Opportunities at 0,5 and get the Pickpocket skill twice for your Robber/Ninja. It's more than worth it. Don't linger there, however, but find the Sirocco Portal (check the Portal chart for locations) and go to Tundara. Then head out via Polar Passage Portal to Vulcania. In Vulcania, visit the Bestway Blacksmith at 15,8 and buy two Herbal Patches for each character. They cost 400 each.

Portal Chart

Portal Name	City	X,Y	To:
Poorman's Portal	Middlegate	0,5	Sandsobar
Portal Dune	Sandsobar	8,1	Middlegate
Sirocco Portal	Sandsobar	4,15	Tundara
La Porte	Tundara	6,11	Sandsobar
Polar Passage Portal	Tundara	6,9	Vulcania
Vulcanian Transport	Vulcania	6,3	Tundara
Vulcanian Export Co.	Vulcania	8,3	Atlantium
Beautify Atlantium	Atlantium	3,0	Vulcania
The Mystic Portal	Atlantium	12,0	Middlegate

Return to Middlegate and save your characters at the inn. Or go on to Atlantium and purchase the Thief's Pick +4 at 4,000 gold each. If you can afford it, your Robber/Ninja will be much better at opening chests. If you can equip several of them, he'll become an ace lockpicker.

After returning to Middlegate and saving, go back outside and cast the Fly spell or walk North and take the first turn West. In any case, when you see the sign that mentions the Circus, walk another 12 steps until you reach B2 1,7. Turn North and walk two steps to meet the Cuisinarts.

These guys will really chop you up, but there's a way to beat them—let them beat themselves! What you do is keep using the Herbal Patches or healing spells to restore your unconscious characters. Don't bother trying to attack these things. Just keep restoring your characters each round. Eventually, the Cuisinarts will frenzy, then die. If you're lucky, you'll win. If something goes wrong with your plan, it's OK. Just try again until you "win."

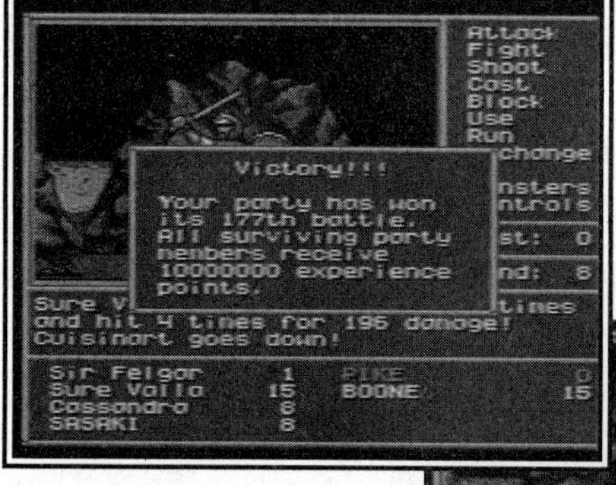

Why would you want to attack something so powerful? Maybe it's the experience points you gain if you survive—more than a million of them for each character!!!! And, if you Search and successfully open the chest, you'll get a rich reward as well.

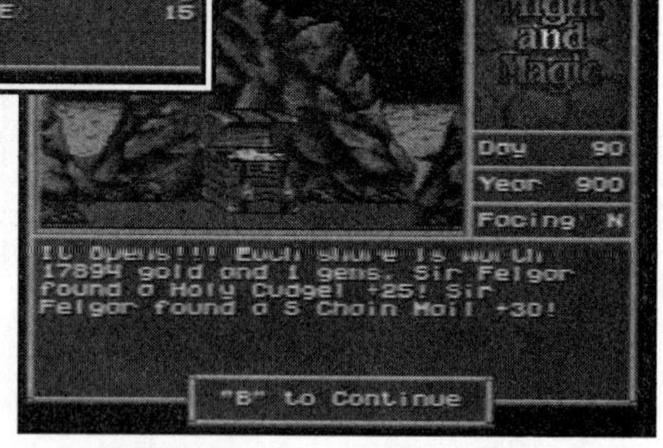

Dragons

Believe it or not, having killed the Cuisinarts and gotten all that good stuff, you're still not going to be the most powerful guys around. Cron is full of danger, and you'll need a lot more power in several categories. So the next place you may want to visit is the cave called Dragon's Dominion. But first, you'll go on a little adventure to the most dangerous area in Cron.

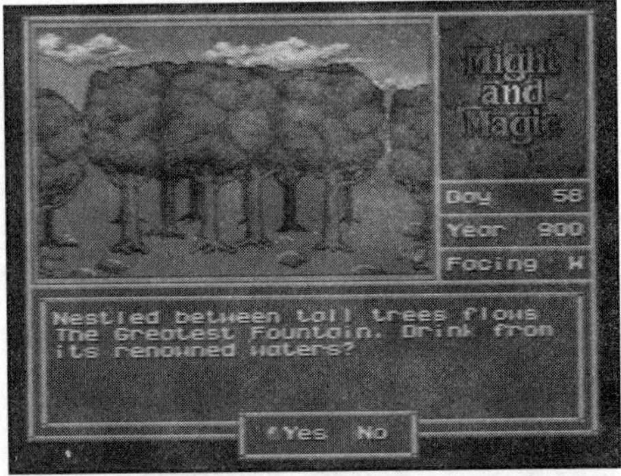

Use the Fly spell to go to area E2. You'll land at a special tree. Pick the fruit and all your food stores are replenished. If you're ever low on food, simply Fly here. But that's not why we had you Fly here this time. You want to get to 11,9 where there's an oasis. So first turn East and cast a Teleport spell 8 steps in that direction. Now you have to be a little lucky. Walk North one square and you'll be attacked. Use the Hide spell. If it doesn't work, you may want to use the Time Distortion spell to get back to the fruit tree and try again. If you Hide successfully, then walk one more step North to the fountain and drink. Set a Lloyd's Beacon here so you can come back. While you're doing that, check out your character's stats! 200 each! Not bad!

Now use the Fly spell to go to area D1. Getting to the Dragon's Dominion cave is tricky unless you are very powerful. There are numerous bandits in the hills waiting to attack you. So, we'll use a trick to get around them. Turn North and walk one step from the place you landed. Now turn East and walk directly through the mountains. Walk 8 steps East, turn North and walk 10 steps. Now turn West and walk 1 step; turn North and you're there!

Inside the cave, you'll have to walk very carefully. Some of your spells won't work, but one spell that will is the Jump spell. Look on the map we've provided to see where to Jump and where to walk. There are three locations of interest. The spot at 0,0 will give each party member 10 permanent hit points until they reach 200. The spot at 11,2 will give each member 25 hit points until they reach 65,000! And the spot at 7,14 gives each member 1,000 hit points (but only once). The trick is that each location is guarded by a dragon or group of dragons. If you use the fountain from E2 before you come here, you'll be strong enough to beat the guardian and get the reward. But remember, the effect of the fountain will disappear after the first encounter. So you'll only be able to do this once before returning to the fountain.

The 1,000-hit point location is guarded by the Ancient Dragon, a creature of immense power. There's no way you'll beat it now, so your best bet is to try to Hide when you meet it. If you fail, cast the Time Distortion spell and try again (Resting if necessary between tries). If you don't have the Time Distortion spell, you probably shouldn't try to take on the Ancient Dragon.

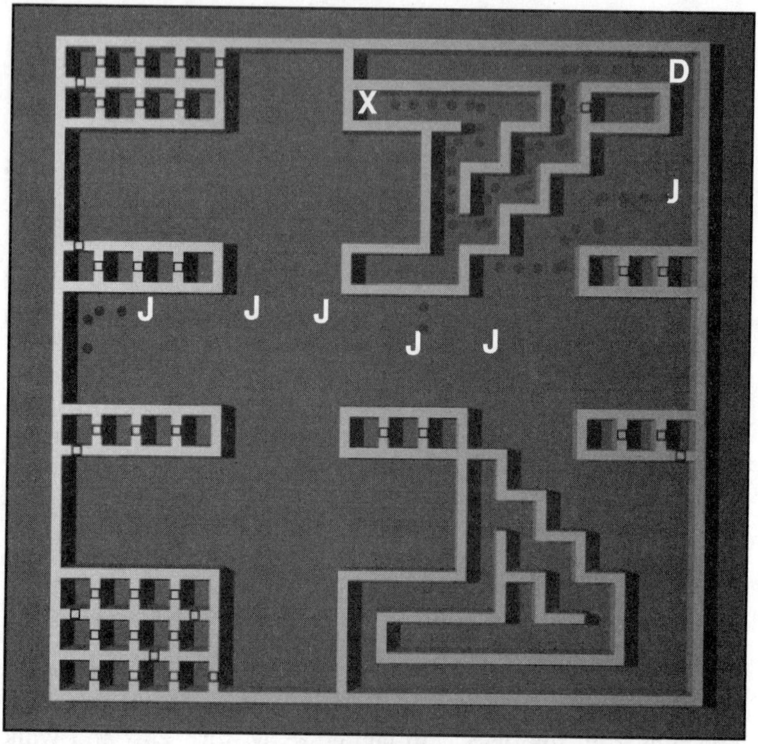

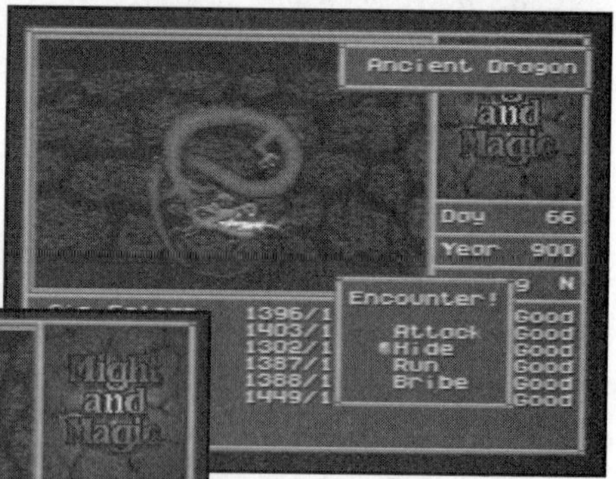

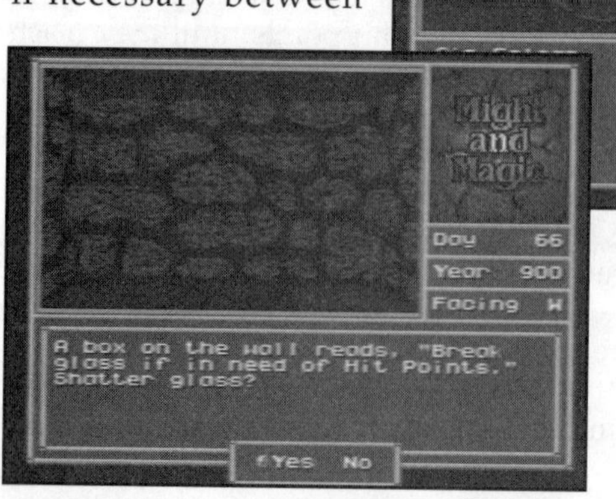

The area at 11,2 is the best area to recharge after you get the 1,000-hit point bonus. So you might want to set the Lloyd's Beacon there and continually charge up. Charge up, Rest, then Surface (with the Cleric's spell), return via the beacon, and so forth. If you do this, the beacon you set at the fountain will be gone, but you can get back there to set a new one if you wish.

Rounding Out Your Character

There are still many interesting things to try. If you have lots of hit points and the power of the Fountain on your side, you may be able to take on the Ancient Dragon. The reward is very rich—more than 3 million experience points, 1,666,666 gold each and 166 gems each.

Another place to get lots of points is to win the Black Ticket battle in the arena called the Colosseum in Atlantium. You'll win a lot of gold and experience. All you need is one Black Ticket for each battle. Get them in the weapon shop. With all your new hit points you should win, but you can use the fountain again to ensure victory.

Even with all this you may not be powerful enough, so there are places where you can enhance your other characteristics. See the chart for locations.

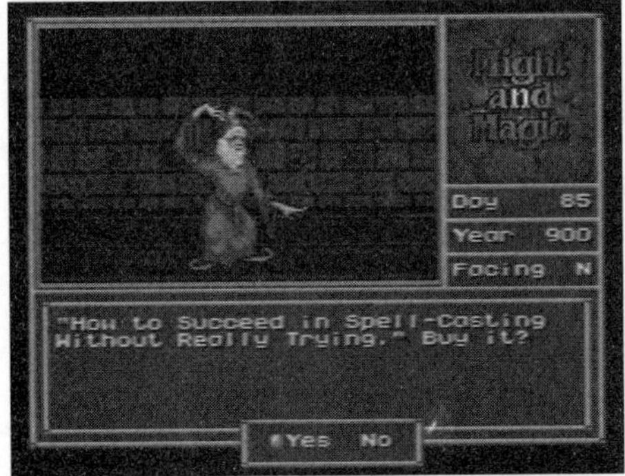

Finally, you can search for all the magic spells, but there is a character in the second level of Lord Peabody's dungeon under Castle Pinehurst who will sell all spells to all party members for a paltry one million gold. At this point, you shouldn't have trouble raising the cash. Here are the locations of the stairs: In Pinehurst go to 11,2. On the first level go to 1,2. On the second level go to 2,1 to buy the magic, but avoid the locations at 4,6; 0,3; and 1,7.

- There are also ways to change your alignment, sex, or age. You can even buy experience points in several places. However we'll let you find those on your own. At this point you should be ready to take on Cron. Just a few more hints . . .

Statistics Enhancement Chart

Statistic	Location	Area	X,Y
Accuracy	Pinehurst Dungeon	A2	14,13*
Speed	Nomad's Hideaway	E3	0,15
Might	Druid's Point Cavern^	C3	1,15
Intelligence	Atlantium Dungeon	A4	11,15
Personality	Ice Cave	B1	15,8 (M); 15,7 (F)
Endurance	Vulcania Dungeon	E1	15,14
Luck	Dawn's Mist	D4	12,7

*on Level One
^Figure out the password from the stones. Hint: Consider the name of the cavern.

- You need to win the Triple Crown in each color by purchasing a ticket and fighting in the arena in each town. Buy the different colored keys and use them to free the captive Bishops (they're in the castles).
- You need Mark's keys. Find him in the Beggar's Grove in C1. His keys are somewhere in A2.
- There are many quests to perform. You'll need to visit the mysterious Jurors in area D2.
- Each character class will have to complete a specific quest (see chart).
- There are three Lord's Quests. We'll give you some help with them:
- In Lord Slayer's Quest, find the Dragon Lord in area D1. The Queen Beetle is in area E2. The Serpent King is in area E3.
- In Lord Hoardall's Quest, the Sword of Valor is in area A2. The Sword of Nobility is in area D1. The Sword of Honor is in area D4.
- Lord Haart's Quest takes you through some specialized travel that only Lord Peabody can help you with. Once you figure out the secret to that, find Spaz Twit in area A1; The Long One is in area E2.

Character Class Quests

Class	Quest
Knight	Dread Knight in area B3.
Paladin	Defeat the Frost Dragon general in the Forbidden Forest Cavern in area C3.
Archer	Shoot Baron Wilfrey in area B2.
Cleric	Reunite Corak's Soul and Body. Soul is in area C1; bring it to Body in Corak's Cave in area C2.
Sorcerer	Free wizards Yekop and Ybmug (try reading those names backwards). Find Yekop in the Tower of Mercy in area B4. Ybmug is in the Dark Keep in area B3.
Barbarian	Defeat the Barbarian Chieftain in area C4.
Ninja	Kill Dawn in Dawn's Mist Cavern in area D4.
Robber	Accompany one or more others on their quest.

SUPER SECRETS

Ten Steps to Might and Magic

Only read these steps if you are stuck or confused as to how to complete the game.

1. At least one character must be the Chosen One. He or she gets to be that way by completing the Black Ticket triple crown (winning in each arena on the Black Ticket) and by completing the character quest for that character class. Then see Queen Lamanda in the Luxus Royal palace.
2. You must visit Lord Peabody. He'll send you to find his pal Sherman. (He's in area B2.) Hire Sherman at

Atlantium after you free him and take him with you to Lord Peabody.

3. Use the Time Machine to get the four discs from Castle Xabran (area C2 14,8) in the 9th century.
4. Travel to each Elemental Plane and use the disks to free the Talon in each one.
5. Find the four computer parts (Todilor, Fluxer, Capitor, and Radicon), one each found in the castles in the 10th century.
6. Take the four computer parts and at least one hireling to Dawn's Mist and get the Orb. There's a trick here. If you can't figure it out, the hireling can be dismissed. Maybe he can take something with him . . .
7. Return to the 9th Century with the Element Orb and the four Talons. Give them to King Kalhon so he can defeat the Mega Dragon, changing the course of history.
8. Return to Luxus Royal and talk to King Kalhon there. He'll give you the password WAFE and tell you how to get to Square Lake.
9. In Lake Geometrics Cavern, you have to fight your way through seemingly endless battles to get to Sheltem. Defeat him and enter the control room.
10. Figure out the cryptogram within the time limit to win the game and return to the inn to keep exploring if you wish. Hint: Be familiar with American history and the famous documents used to found our democracy.

There's still plenty of Cron to explore, so have fun.

CHAPTER 9

Out of this World

by Interplay

WHAT'S GOING ON?

Lester Knight Chaykin is a scientist with good taste in automobiles. One night, his particle acceleration experiment is struck by lightning. The experiment goes haywire, engulfing Lester in a strange light and transporting him to a place that's Out of this World!

PLAYERS

Out of this World is for one player only.

SCORING

There are no points in this game. You're just trying to play through the game, and check out the awesome graphics along the way.

LIVES AND CONTINUES

You've only got one life, and you'll lose it over and over again. Fortunately, you get a password every time you die. Out of this World isn't neatly broken up into levels, so you'll get passwords at many different points during the game.

CONTROLS

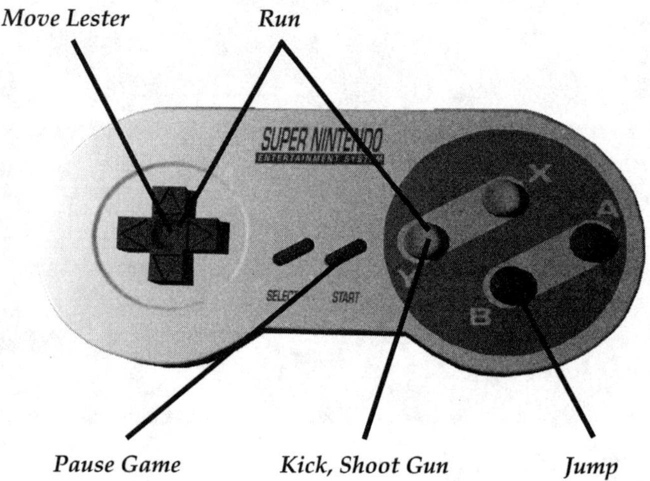

WEAPONS

At the start of the game, you're unarmed. Later on in the game, you'll equip yourself with a versatile laser gun. The gun can fire three different ways, depending on how long you press the Y button.

- A quick button-press fires a single Laser Beam. This beam is weak, but it'll do for shooting most enemies.
- Hold down the button for a short period of time to create a Force Field in front of you. Force Fields are worn down by enemy laser fire, and they slowly disintegrate over time, even if they're not being shot.
- Hold down the button for a longer period of time to fire a Super Shot. Super Shots blast through walls and destroy Force Fields.

The gun will run out of energy if you use too many Force Fields and Super Shots, so don't overdo it. You'll be able to recharge the gun twice during the game.

SPECIAL ITEMS

None.

FRIENDS

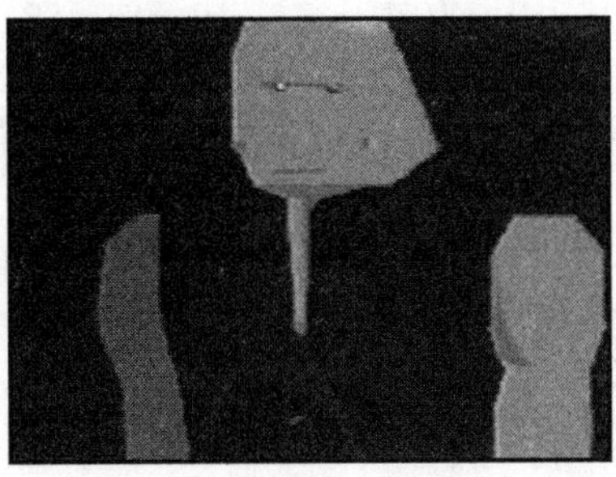

At the same time you find the gun, you'll make friends with an alien. He doesn't have a name, but he's an excellent friend who'll save your hide several times during the game. He's like Chewbacca to your Han Solo. Don't let your friend get killed, and don't leave him behind, or you're doomed!

ENEMIES

There are two types of aliens in the game: the good guys and the bad guys. Your friend is one of the good guys; everyone else is a bad guy. (The bad guys wear red belts; the good guys don't have any belts.)

STRATEGY SESSION

General Strategies

• We've divided the Strategy Session into different sections according to passwords. If you're stuck at a particular place in the game, look for the password of the area where you're located. Read on!

Password: LDKD

This section has a walkthrough in the Out of this World manual.

Password: HTDC

After being shot by the alien, you wake up in a cage with a fellow prisoner. (This alien is your buddy for the rest of the game.) After the guard takes off his black robe, swing the cage left and right with the controller. After a while, you'll get the guard's attention, and he'll fire some warning shots. Keep swinging until the cage falls down and squashes the guard flat!

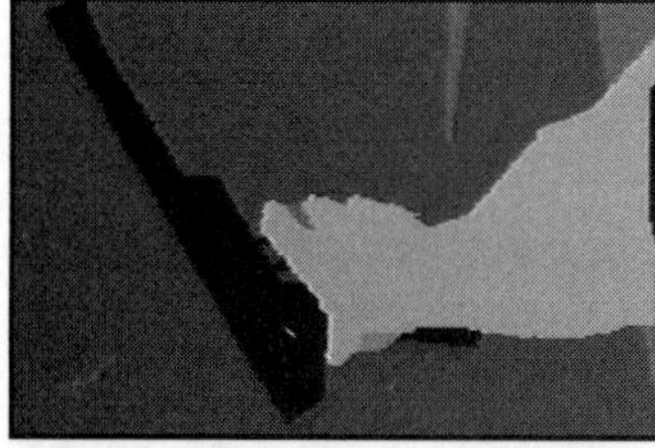

Your friend will put his hand on your shoulder and say something in an alien tongue. After he runs to the right, walk right and crouch down to pick up the squashed guard's gun. Witness the cool cut-scene, then run to the right. When your friend starts running to the left, duck down and blast the guard to the right. Another guard may or may not come from the left; shoot him if he shows up.

Run to the right until you see a small control panel. Your friend runs up to the panel and starts working on it. Put up a Force Field to the left of your friend, and keep putting them up until your friend has finished his work and walks to the right.

Follow your friend and walk onto the elevator. Push up and the elevator slides to the top level. Walk to the window on the right to see a neat (but completely unimportant) cut-scene. Return to the

elevator and go all the way down to the bottom level.

Once you reach the bottom, walk to the left and into the next screen. Start shooting as soon as you enter the next screen, to kill the guard before he kills you! Shoot the left wall with a laser beam to disable it. Return to the elevator and go up one level, then run to the left.

Your progress will be stopped by a door. Use a Super Shot to blast through the door, then run to the left until you're on top of what looks like a hole in the floor. Press Down and you'll shoot through the hole. Run left and stand underneath the next hole, then press Up to shoot upward. Run left into the next screen.

At this point, a guard comes after you and your friend from the left. Your friend pulls open a hatch in the floor; jump into the hole to escape the guard. Your friend will be captured, but you'll join up with him later.

Password: CLLD

You start this level at the top of a maze of ventilation shafts. Start by rolling to the left. Listen (and watch) for a steam vent. Wait for the steam to stop spewing out, then quickly roll past before it starts up again. Keep rolling to the left until you fall down to the next level.

Roll to the right. You'll hear and see a second steam vent. Get past the vent and keep rolling until you fall to the third level. There'll be steam vents on both sides of you! Roll past the vent to the right and keep rolling until you fall to the fourth level.

You won't encounter any more steam vents from here. Roll left until you fall to the fourth level, then roll right to fall out of the vents and finish this section of the game.

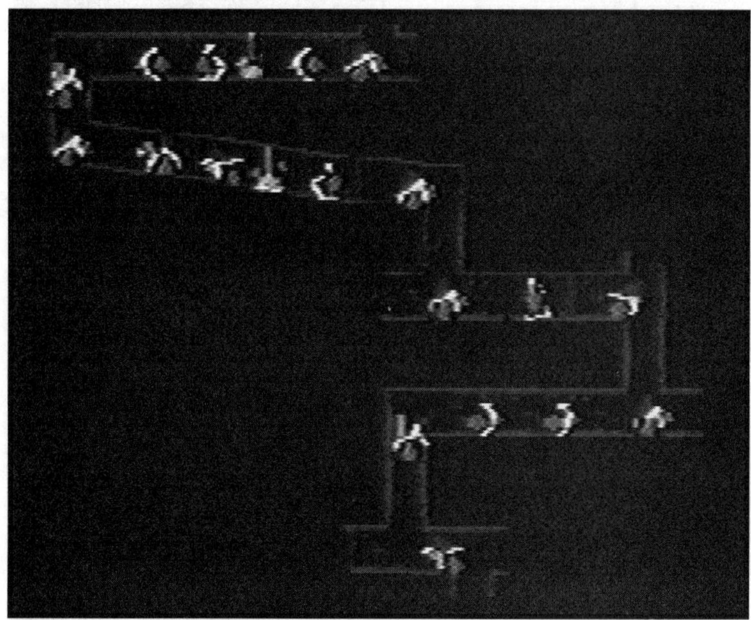

This picture shows the correct path through the ventilation shafts.

Password: LBKG

Walk left into the glowing room to recharge your gun, then walk to the right and use three Super Shots to blast through the walls. Run to the right two screens and you'll find yourself outside, with a guard in your way. Crouch

down and shoot the guard. Walk to the right and into the next screen. Tiptoe to the end of the ledge, then jump to the right. You'll fall and land on a small ledge. Walk to the right and use a Super Shot to blast through the rock, then walk through the hole.

Password: XDDJ

Run to the right and fall down the shaft. When you land, run to the right again and fall down the second shaft. You'll land on a strangely shaped rock. Run to the right and into the next screen.

Don't worry about the tentacle creature above you; do worry about the sharp spikes on the ground in the middle of the screen! Run to the right and leap over the spikes, then move right into the next screen.

Massive boulders start tumbling down at you. These rocks are hard to get past. Run to the right until three boulders fall to your left, then turn around and run to the left. Stop on the far left side of the screen and turn around.

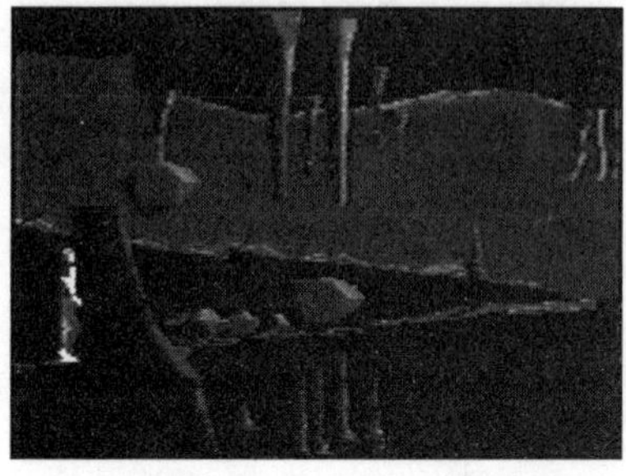

Run past the single boulder to the middle of the screen, then scamper to the right past the final two boulders.

There are more falling rocks on the next screen. Stand on the far left side and wait until the two boulders start falling at the same time. When this occurs, run past them to the middle of the screen. Wait a moment, then run past the final boulder. Continue walking to the right until you're just to the left of the tentacle creature.

Walk to the left, about halfway across the screen, then turn around and shoot the tentacle creature with a laser beam. The creature withdraws into the ceiling of the cave. Move right and into the next screen.

Run to the right (don't worry about the tentacle creature on this screen; he can't get you) and jump over the white creature in the cave floor (which eats you alive if you walk onto it). Walk to the right and jump over the next two creatures, then walk into the next screen.

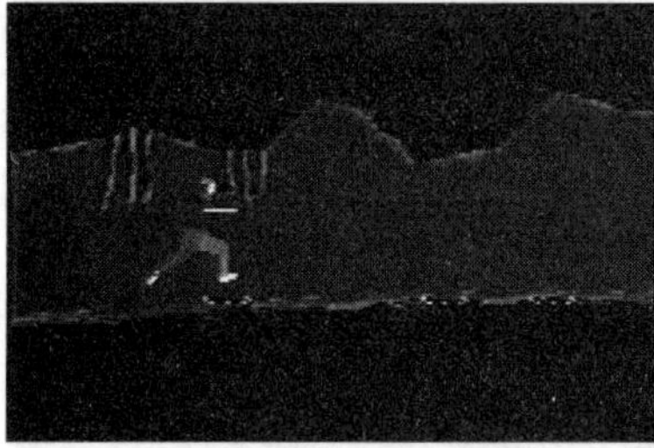

You'll see three tentacle creatures in the roof. Walk to the right until you're close to the tentacle creature on the left. Shoot three laser beams to hit all of the tentacles. Move back to the left, then run to the right and use two running leaps to get past the floor creatures.

Once you're past the creatures, walk to the right and into the next screen. Creep up to the edge and jump across the gap, then jump over the floor-beast. From here, run to the right until you find a small wall. Blast the wall with a Super Shot to destroy it. This doesn't seem important now, but you'll be glad you did it later!

Password: FXLC

Start running to the left. You don't have to worry about any tentacle creatures; just jump over the floor-beasts. Keep going to the left until you reach the first falling-rock screen. Look at the roof and you'll see a red bird perched on the roof. Run to the left, turn to the right, and shoot a laser beam at the bird. It'll fly off the roof. Move to the left and into the next screen.

Jump off the cliff and grab onto the stalactite on the roof. Climb to the top of the stalactite by pressing Up, then jump to the left until you're just to the right of the tentacle creature. Wait for the bird to fly into the tentacles, then jump to the left twice more. After the last leftward jump, you'll appear back on the strange rock.

Password: KRFK

Run to the left and fall off the top of the rock. Turn to the right, crouch down, and shoot the base of the rock with a Super Shot. The rock collapses to the left. Run up the rock and into the next screen.

Keep running to the right, leaping over the gaps, until you reach a screen with a huge basin of water. Use a Super Shot to destroy the pillar of rock at the

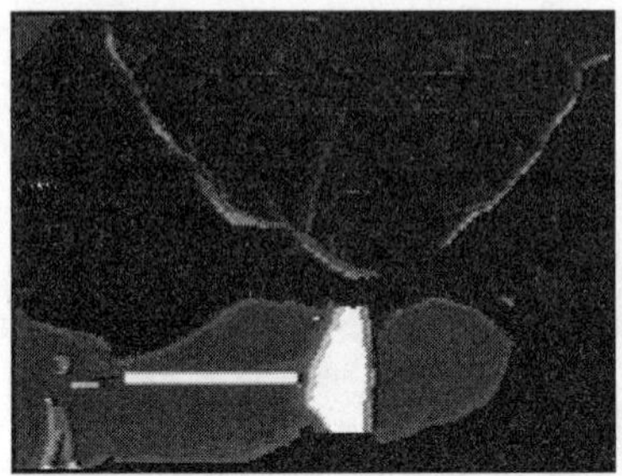

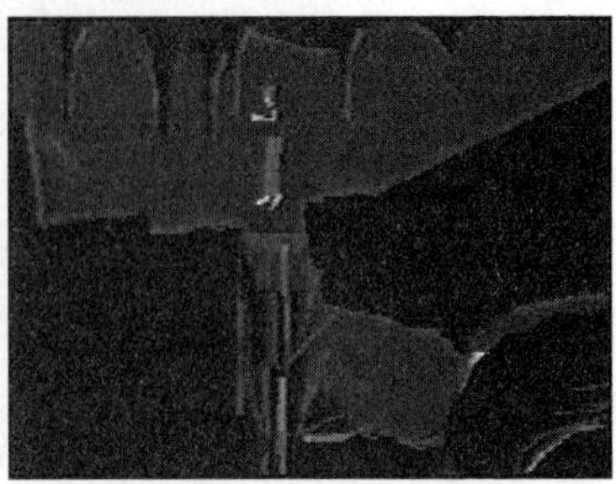

bottom of the basin and start running to the left. Jump over the gaps and keep going to the left until you hit a wall. The water blasts you upward to the top of the screen.

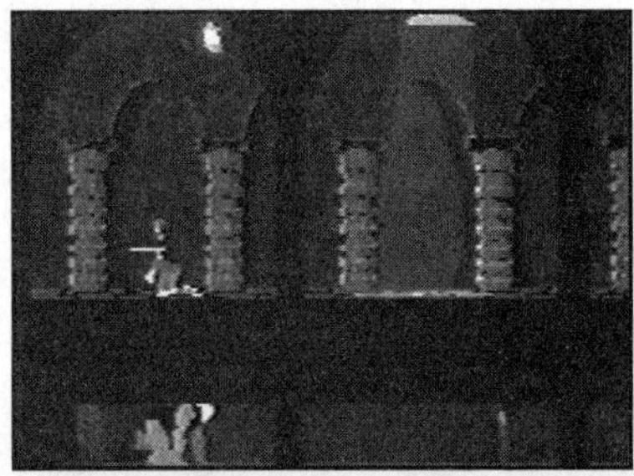

Run to the right until you reach a wall. Use a Super Shot to blast through. Run to the right until you reach some stairs. Climb up the stairs into the next screen, then go to the right, past the mossy waterfall, until you see your friend tossed into a tunnel beneath you.

Password: KLFB

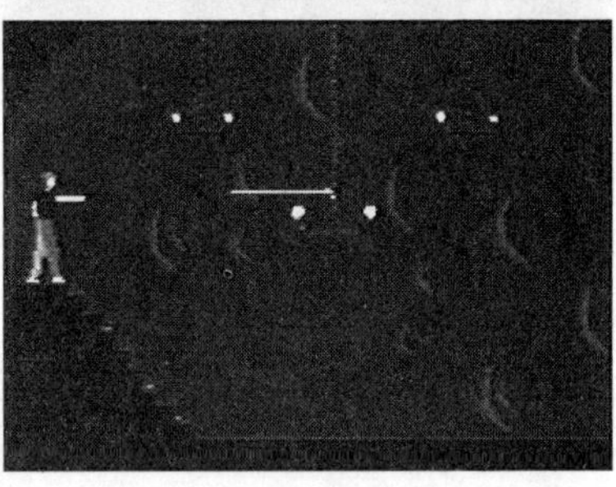

Return to the left until you reach the stairs. Climb down and run to the right until you enter a room with chandeliers on the ceiling. Walk down the stairs, crouch down, and fire a single laser beam. A guard charges onto the screen; fire another laser to fry him.

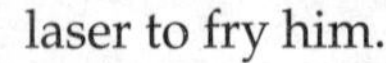

Climb back up the steps and turn to the right. Fire a laser to shoot the chandelier to the ground. Now your friend can escape the tunnel.

Run to the right for several screens, and keep going until an unseen guard punch-

es you to the ground and knocks the gun out of your hand. When he picks you up, hold Down on the control pad and press the Y button to kick him in the groin! When he drops you, run to the left and press Down to roll and pick up your gun. Shoot the guard before he blasts you.

Once you've toasted the guard, move to the right and into the next screen. Put up a Force Field on your right, then run past the Force Field so that it's on your left. Put up a second Field to your right. Two guards will come onto the screen, attacking from both sides. Concentrate on the guard to the right; as soon as you zap him, sprint to the right. The guard on the left follows you, but you can jump into the water before he catches you.

Password: DDRX

Swim down two screens, then swim left two screens. You'll see two passages leading upward; swim into the passage on the left. Swim to the top of the passage to get some much-needed oxygen from the air pocket. After you've had your fill, swim down two screens, then swim to the right. You'll climb out of the water and onto the ledge. Jump over the floor-beasts and into the next screen.

Shoot the power line with a laser beam, then return to the left. Use a running jump to clear the floor-beasts and jump back into the water. Return to the air pocket, then swim back to the right and upward until you reach the surface.

Password: HRTB

Climb out of the water onto the left ledge. Run to the left until you reach the room where you kicked the guard. Move underneath the elevator hole and press Up on the control pad to shoot upward. Climb up the stairs to the left.

When you enter the next room, shoot to the left to zap the guard. Climb to the top of the stairs, then jump over the gap and walk to the right, into the next room.

Walk a few steps to the right, then put up a Force Field. Walk to the right until the doors slide open and the guard releases a grenade. Run back to the left. The doors close, and the grenade bounces back and blows up the guard! Walk through the sliding doors, then use a Super Shot on the door to the far right. Move into the next room.

Move right and stand underneath the elevator hole, press Up, and then move left to recharge your gun. Take the elevator back down and run right into the next room.

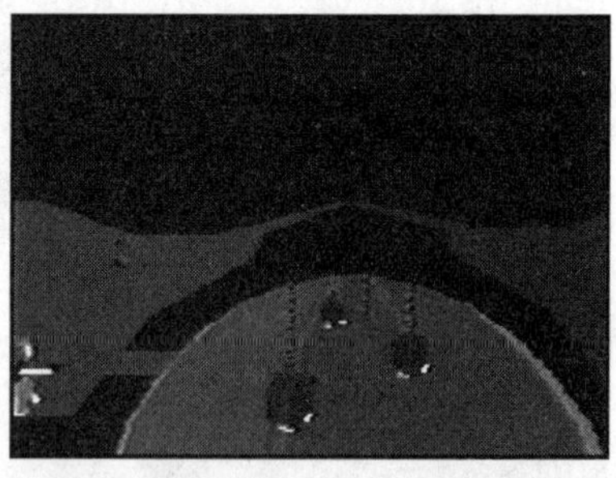

Duck down and watch the glass sphere in the middle of the screen. You'll see the reflection of a guard walking far below the sphere. Wait for the guard to stop underneath the ball, and quickly shoot a laser beam to drop the ball onto the guard. If the guard shoots up at you, you missed him, and you should start this section of the game over again.

Run back to the left, go down the stairs, go down the elevator, and run to the right until you reach the water. Swim across and climb out onto the right ledge, then move into the next room. See the guard you wasted? Ick!

Password: BRTD

Run to the right and fall down the shaft. As soon as you land, use a Super Shot to blast through the wall on the right. Now run like crazy to the right! The guards will shoot a fusillade of lasers at you, but as long as you keep running, they'll miss.

Eventually, you'll reach a dead end. Turn around and put up Force Fields to your left. Fight off the attacking guards until your friend pops open the hatch in the ceiling! After a moment, he'll stick his arm through the hatch and pull you to safety!

Password: TFBB

Your friend will run into the building to the right, but don't follow him. Walk a bit to the left until you walk onto the ledge in the background. Now run to the right into the next screen.

You'll see your friend being held at gunpoint by two guards. Keep running to the right until you're on the right side of the building, then run through the door and back into the building.

When the guards turn around, crouch down and shoot the one on the right. Your friend will take care of the other guard. Once both guards are history, follow your friend as he runs to the right.

You'll arrive at a gap, and your friend will wave at you. Run into his arms and he'll toss you across the gap. Your friend will try to make the jump himself, but he'll just miss. You have to help him out!

Walk to the edge and jump to the left. You'll fall down the shaft and swing into a tunnel on the left. Move to the right a few steps, then quickly turn around and put up Force Fields on your left. Several guards will attack you. Keep shooting 'em until they stop coming, then run to the left until you reach some stairs.

Password: TXHF

Run to the left. You'll see a group of guards running outside. Don't shoot at them! One of the guards will get trapped inside the building. Walk to the left until the door pops open. Crouch down so that you point your gun at the guard, but don't shoot! The guard holds up his hands, then hits a button that slams the doors shut.

Run back to the right, and go up the stairs. You'll see a guard hiding behind a wall. Jump across the gap and walk to the far right side of the room. Turn to the left and put up a Force Field, then blast a Super Shot to the left to destroy the wall. The guard starts rolling grenades down the stairs. Let him roll five grenades down the stairs, then shoot him with a laser beam.

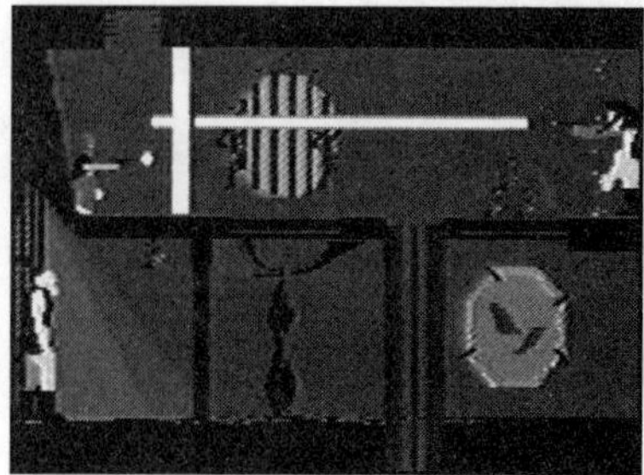

Move to the left, past where the grenade guard was,

and go down the elevator hole. Turn to the right and hold down the button to charge up for a Super Shot. The guard on the right uses a Super Shot to blast through the door. As soon as he does, use your Super Shot to destroy his Force Field, then fire a few laser beams to toast him.

Move to the middle of the screen and go down the elevator shaft. At the bottom of the elevator, shoot the power line, then go back up. Return to the room where the grenade guard was located, then walk down the stairs. You'll see a hole in the floor. Jump into the hole to fall into an underground chamber.

Start running to the right. You'll enter a pitch-black room. Some guards will fire at you from below, but keep running until they stop firing. As soon as the laser fire stops, stop running! Tap the controller to the right to move slowly in that direction. You'll eventually enter the next room, standing on the left side of a pit.

Jump over the pit and run to the lever. Lester automatically pulls it down. Return to the left and fall into the pit to see the havoc you've created! While the monsters chow down on the guards, start running to the right. Keep running and the laser fire won't hit you.

Go up the elevator hole as soon as you reach it, then walk to the left. Wait a moment and a ledge appears underneath your friend. He'll drop down to the ledge and run to the right. Follow him until you reach a strange black vehicle. Run into the vehicle and be prepared for a bizarre sequence!

Password: CKJL

Your friend steers the vehicle into the middle of a gladiatorial arena, with combat going on all around you. You won't last long with all the firepower being directed at the vehicle, so act fast!

When the control panel appears, press the lower button. Some more buttons will appear. Press the lowest, leftmost button and even more buttons will pop up!

Press the button just to the right of the green light. The whole control panel lights up! You can fool around at this point, pressing the buttons to use the various weapon systems of the vehicle, or you can finish pressing the buttons and get the heck outta here.

Press the four buttons in the upper-left corner of the control panel (the buttons will light up as you hit them). When all four buttons have been pressed, a white button starts flashing. Press the white button to rocket your way to the final stage of the game.

Password: LFCK

Your escape pod lands in a bath-house for the female aliens of this world. As soon as you jump out of the pod, run to the right and into the next room. Crouch down and put up Force Fields to the right. Laser fire will come from your left, but if you stay down, it won't hit you.

Keep blasting the guards to the right until they stop coming onto the screen, then run to the right. Keep running until your friend busts through the wall to join you. Follow him to the right. Eventually, you'll have the floor shot out from under you. There's nothing you can do about this, so just get ready to fall.

It will seem as if it's over, but you'll be caught by an alien. Unfortunately, he's not your friend. In fact, this jerk is the leader of the bad guys. He'll kick you to the right and into the final room.

As soon as you appear in the next room, hold the controller to the right to crawl toward the panel of switches. Your friend and the boss alien will get into a scuffle, giving you time to reach the switches. Wait until the boss alien defeats your friend and starts walking toward you.

When he reaches the middle of the screen, push Up and the Y button to pull a switch and disintegrate the boss. Immediately press Up and Y again to throw a second lever. Crawl back to the left before the guards blast you. If you're fast enough, you'll enter the elevator beam and shoot upward. Sit back and watch the cool ending sequence! (If this ending's not a setup for a sequel, we don't know WHAT is.)

CHAPTER 10

The Rocketeer

by IGS

WHAT'S GOING ON?

Cliff Secord is an ace GeeBee pilot in a traveling airshow. One day, he finds a weird-looking gizmo in the cockpit of his plane. The gizmo turns out to be the Cirrus X-3 Rocketpack, and the Nefarious Villain and his Invasion Force want it. They'll even kidnap Jenny Blake, Cliff's lady love, to get Cliff's attention. Help Cliff to save Jenny—and the world!

PLAYERS

The Rocketeer is for one or two players. The two-player mode is alternating, not simultaneous.

SCORING

The Rocketeer is broken up into seven arcade sequences. A different scoring system is used in each sequence.

At The Races: 200 points for every lap you complete. 10,000 points for winning the race.
Invasion: 100 to 250 points for each enemy you hit (the score varies according to how fast you hit the enemy).
Rocket Race: 200 points for each lap completed. 10,000 points for winning the race.
The Hangar: 100 to 250 points for each enemy you hit (the score varies according to how fast you hit the enemy). 10,000 points for defeating the Armored Flying Tanks.
Pursuit: There are eight different targets and point values, the lowest being 100 points (parachute bombs) and the highest 500 points (enemy Rocketmen and AFTs). 10,000 points for completing the round.
Aboard The Locust: Same point values as in Pursuit.
Final Fight: 75 points for every punch you land. 350 points for knocking out an Enemy Rocketman. 500 points for knocking out the Nefarious Villain. 10,000 points for completing the round.

LIVES AND CONTINUES

You start the game with three chances. You'll lose a chance if you crash your plane, lose all of your energy, or crash the Rocketpack. When you lose all of your chances, the game is over. There are no continues, so you've got to make every chance count!

CONTROLS

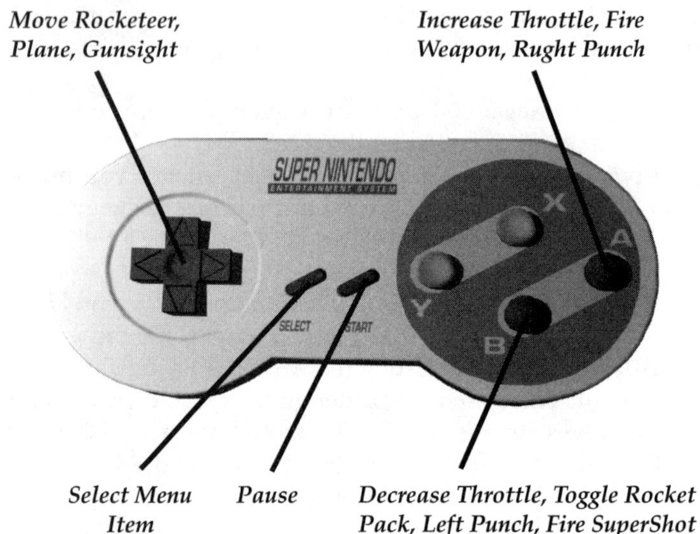

WEAPONS

Whether the Rocketeer is armed with a weapon or not depends on the sequence you're playing. The Rocketeer has a weapon during these sequences: Invasion, The Hangar, Pursuit, and Aboard the Locust. Learn more about the weapons in the Strategy Session.

SPECIAL ITEMS

In two sequences, Pursuit and Aboard the Locust, you can capture SuperShots. SuperShots wreak much more destructive power than normal shots.

FRIENDS

Jenny Blake is Cliff's girlfriend. You'll have to rescue her during the final stage of the game.

Peevy is an ace mechanic who works on Cliff's GeeBee. He'll appear during the comic-book intermissions, but never during an action sequence.

ENEMIES

The Nefarious Villain and his Rocketmen soldiers will attack you during most of the sequences. Defeat the Villain to save the world!

STRATEGY SESSION

General Strategies

The Rocketeer is a very nice-looking game, but even average players will blow through it quickly. We recommend this game to younger players and beginners, who will find it to be more of a challenge.

If you've got the asciiPad, or any controller with a slow-motion feature, you'll find it extremely handy during the Pursuit and Aboard the Locust sequences. It will slow your attackers to a crawl and allow you plenty of time to react to enemy fire.

At the Races

Peevy offers to show you the Cirrus X-3, but first he wants you to win two races in the GeeBee. You'll fly against two other planes: the Blue Caudron (which has excellent speed) and the Red Wedell Williams (which has excellent maneuverability).

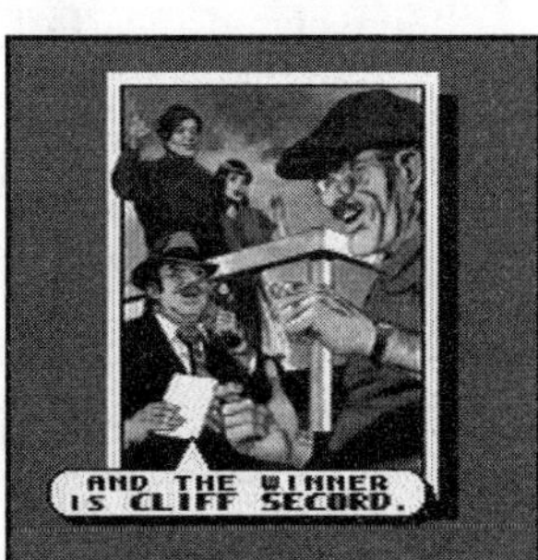

The best advice for this sequence is to completely ignore the side view of the race (which takes up most of the screen). Focus your attention on the small window at the bottom of the screen. Steer your plane to the left side of the course. When you fly around a pylon, the GeeBee swings out to the right; push the controller Left to make a tight turn. The competing planes will stay close to you, but don't worry about 'em. Just concentrate on staying to the left and taking the turns hard.

Invasion

Stay on one side of the Hangar! If you keep darting back and forth across the entire Hangar, you'll have too many gunmen to deal with. By staying on one side, you limit the number of targets you have to deal with. Use the Rocket Pack to zoom upward and downward to make yourself a tough target to hit.

Your gun has infinite ammo, so keep shooting. If you shoot fast enough, you can literally slow the game down with your rapid rate of fire.

Rocket Race

This is basically the same as At the Races, except instead of flying a plane, you're strapped into the lightning-fast Cirrus X-3. Don't worry about hugging the curves—as long as you move a bit to the left while you swing around the pylons, you'll stay way ahead of the competition.

The Hangar

This is similar to the Invasion sequence, except that the enemies are armed with grenades as well as guns. You can shoot the grenades out of the air, or you can just dodge them. Either method works fine.

Once you've destroyed enough gunmen, the Armored Flying Tank will appear. Aim for the engines, and fire away. If you see the enemy damage bar start dropping, you know you're hitting the right spot. When the Tank crashes to the ground, aim for the hatch on top of the Tank. Once you've destroyed the Tank, you've finished the sequence.

Pursuit

Stay to the far left side of the screen and shoot your gun as rapidly as possible. The more enemies you shoot, the closer you get to the Locust. Stay high in the air to avoid being hit by the rockets.

The only tricky enemies in this sequence are the enemy Rocketmen. These guys take a lot of shots. Use the SuperShots to blast through them, and be ready to fly to the right side of the screen to maneuver around the Rocketmen.

Aboard the Locust

Again, you should stay on the far left side of the screen, staying high on the screen and blasting the enemy weapons. There are more weapons to avoid, with the deadliest ones being the V-1 Rockets. These babies can fly all the way to the top of the screen, so shoot them immediately. Watch for the red tool boxes to fix the damage to the Locust.

Final Fight

As soon as you appear on the wing of the zeppelin, start walking to the right. When the first Rocketman lands in front of

you, start punching him rapidly. There's no need to mix up your punches; just use one hand repeatedly. As soon as you knock the Rocketman out, walk to the right before the next one appears.

The Nefarious Villain throws grenades at you from above. If he throws a grenade that strikes you, move to the left to avoid being hit again. Sometimes, the brainless Villain will throw grenades at his own Rocketmen and help you to defeat them!

Once you make it far enough to the right, you'll automatically climb up the ladder and pursue the Villain. He'll climb with Jenny to the top of the zeppelin, then throw her over the side and challenge you to a fight.

Knocking out the Villain is as easy as knocking out one of the Rocketmen. Just keep throwing one type of punch. Stay to the right, because the zeppelin will start to explode behind you! When you've knocked out the Villain, walk to the right until you're standing over Jenny. The game will take over and show you a brief ending sequence. You can choose to play the game again at a harder level of difficulty; the strategies we've given here still apply. Good luck!

CHAPTER 11

Smash TV

by Acclaim

WHAT'S GOING ON?

The year is 1999. Kindler, gentler TV programs are long gone. The most popular show on television is Smash TV! Contestants fight their way through a series of arenas, gunning down foes while picking up big money and big prizes. The biggest prize of all is survival. Get ready for the toughest battle of your life!

PLAYERS

Smash TV is for one or two players. It's easier to win with two players, because you'll have more firepower to destroy your enemies.

SCORING

You score points in Smash TV by shooting enemies and picking up cash and prizes. When you manage to get through an entire Arena, your cash and prizes are tallied up and you'll score big bonus points.

LIVES AND CONTINUES

You start the game with five lives. Every time you're hit by an enemy or a bullet, you lose a life. When all five lives are gone, the game is over.

You also start the game with four continues. When you lose all your lives, you have the opportunity to continue the game. If you continue, you'll start from the same arena you lost your last life in, and at the exact moment when you died. Your score will be carried over when you continue, along with all the Keys you have collected (see The Secrets at the end of this chapter for more details).

CONTROLS

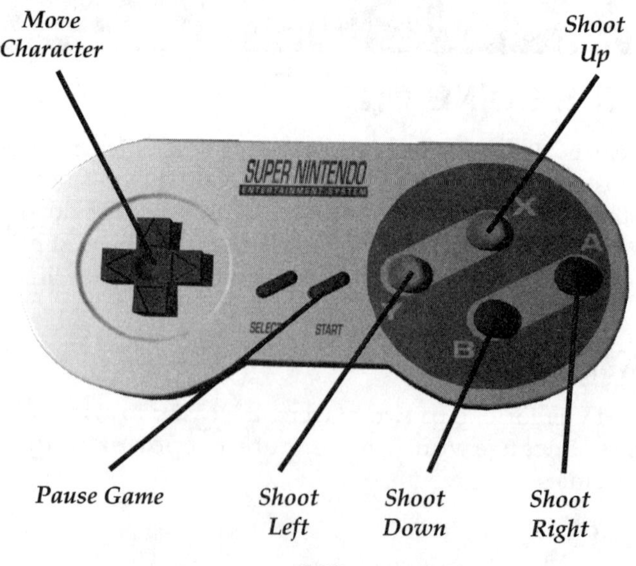

WEAPONS

You start the game armed with a machine gun. This weapon has an infinite supply of ammo. During the game, power-up weapons (with ridiculously long names) appear on the floor of the arena. Pick them up to equip yourself with better blasting ability. Special weapons have a limited amount of ammo, indicated by the six bars underneath your score. The bars turn from green to red as your ammo supply runs out. When all the bars turn red, the weapon is empty and you'll return to using the machine gun.

The **Discus Defense** is a group of five spinning stars. These stars will fly off, one by one, as they are struck by enemies.

The **High-Power Missile Launcher** has an awesome range and blasts through enemies with a single hit.

The **Machine Gun Firing Remote** is a small sphere that spins around you and fires whatever weapon you're currently using. The Remote will stay around you until it is touched by an enemy.

The **Mobile Forcefield** protects you from enemy damage for a limited time. When you've got the Forcefield, ram into as many opponents as you can—they'll be destroyed instantly!

The **Multi-Direction Photon Gun** is a powerful three-way weapon with good range and high power.

The **Rapid-Fire Grenade Launcher** is powerful, but its ammo runs out very quickly and the weapon has a dangerously short range.

The **Rapid-Fire High-Power Grenade Launcher** only appears during battles with the Bosses. It has a long range and lots of ammo.

The **Smart Bomb** destroys all the enemies on the screen.

SPECIAL ITEMS

These appear on the arena floor in the same way as weapons do.

The **Bonus Life** adds one life to your total. You can have a maximum of nine lives in reserve.

The **Key** is required (actually, 10 Keys are required) to enter the Pleasure Dome near the end of the game.

The **Speed Boost** makes you run faster. You'll only receive one dose of extra speed, even if you pick up multiple Boosts.

FRIENDS

There are no friends in this game. If someone runs into the arena, he's trying to bash in your skull or blow you up. If it moves, shoot it!

ENEMIES

Here's a list of the most common foes you will encounter, along with their point values.

Floating Robots are mechanical versions of the Hulk Clubbers, programmed to head straight for you. 1050 points each.

Hulk Clubbers are brainless dudes that walk straight at you—and straight into your machine gun fire. 500 points each.

Laser Orbs are nasty floating objects that stop moving to shoot laser streams vertically and horizontally. 2500 points each.

The **Orb-Train** is a one-way ticket to losing a life! These enemies take many shots to destroy, and crawl into the corners to get you. 2000 points per train segment.

Red Swarmers are small spinning pods that come in two types: Followers and Leaders. Followers are worth 2050 points each, while Leaders are worth a whopping 20,000 points each!

Shrapnel Bombs (also known as Mr. Shrapnel) walk around the edge of the screen, then stop and blow up into a spray of deadly shrapnel shards. Destroy them before they explode! 2350 points each.

Single Blue Orbs bounce slowly around the arena, so they're easy to dodge. 2000 points each.

Snakes are small blue reptiles that appear in the third and final Arena. 1000 points each.

Spear Men are primitive versions of the Hulk Clubber. 1000 points each.

Tanks roll around the room, stopping and pausing to shoot a spray of bullets before moving again. Watch out! 7500 points each.

Wall Gun Men fire at you from wall-mounted cannons. They take several hits to destroy. 5500 points each.

The final room in each Arena holds the Super-Star Opponents. These Bosses have stopped many Smash TV contestants—can you get past them?

Mutoid Man is the Boss of Arena 1. He's a massively muscled hybrid of flesh and steel, armed with deadly laser beams.

Scarface is the Boss of Arena 2. This guy is surrounded by a ring of armor that you've got to blast through, one segment at a time.

Cobra Head is the Boss of Arena 3. It's a pair of huge robotic snakes. Watch out for the electric beams that shoot from the snakes' mouths.

The **Game Show Host** with the Most is the Boss of Arena 4. Defeat him and you'll escape the Smash TV arena!

STRATEGY SESSION

General Strategies

One strategy stands out over all others. Stay in a corner! If you stay in the middle of the arena and try to fight off opponents on four sides, you're going to die often. By moving into a corner, your enemies will only be able to attack from two sides. You should move out of the corner only to grab a Weapon or Special Item, especially Keys.

The corner strategy works even better when you have a Machine Gun Firing Remote. The Remote doubles your firepower and makes it even easier to blast away the enemy hordes.

Arena 1

1. Collect 10 Keys!

The name of this room refers to one of the major goals of the game. If you collect 10 Keys, you'll be able to enter a secret room near the end of the game called the Pleasure Dome.

This room is pretty ordinary, with wimpy Hulk Clubbers and Shrapnel Bombs attacking you. The Wall Gun Men are dangerous, so destroy them immediately.

2. Meet Mr. Shrapnel

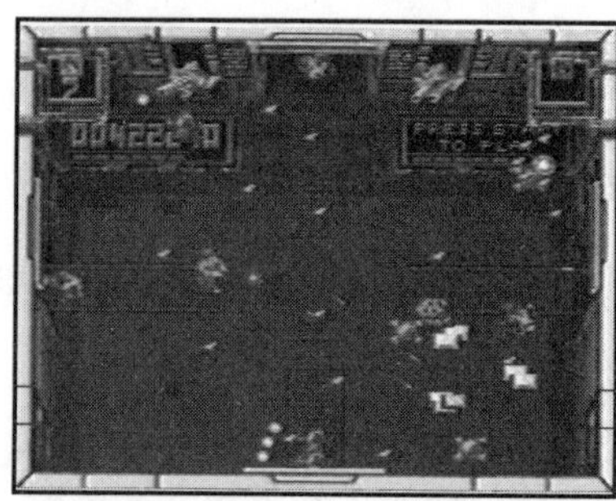

This room is your formal introduction to the Shrapnel Bombs, but you've already seen them in Room 1 (Collect 10 Keys!) and Room 5 (Collect Powerups!). The only difference is that there will be many more Shrapnel Bombs to destroy in this room. Don't get caught in a crossfire of deadly shrapnel!

3. Bonus Prizes!

This is Arena 1's Bonus Prize room. Large piles of cash and prizes appear for you to scoop up before your enemies start to attack. It helps if you collected a Speed Boost in the previous room. The extra speed helps you to collect the goodies faster.

You'll notice that a large amount of Bonus Lives and Keys appear in this room. This is the case for all of the Bonus Prize rooms, which is why you should try to enter them whenever possible.

4. Arena 1

This is the first room in the entire game, so it's totally easy. A few Hulk Clubbers attack, and a few power-ups appear, and that's about it.

5. Collect Powerups!

The action starts to heat up in this room. You'll see Shrapnel Bombs for the first time, along with floor mines.

When you see a Shrapnel Bomb stop walking and start to vibrate, it's about to explode. Get away from the Bomb and dodge any pieces of shrapnel that head your way.

The floor mines are only dangerous when cash and prizes appear in massive quantities and cover them up. Look closely whenever you're picking up prizes.

6. Crowd Control

This room features two Wall Gun Men. Take them out as soon as possible. The less gunfire you have flying through the air, the safer you'll be. You'll also have to destroy several Tanks before you can exit this room.

7. Tank Trouble

The title of this room says it all! Tanks will attack you from the first enemy wave to the last. Keep shooting them as soon as they appear. When there are multiple Tanks shooting bullets at you, survival becomes a matter of luck.

8. Mutoid Man!

A single Red Swarmer will attack just before Mutoid Man rolls onto the screen. Stay near the bottom of the screen as Mutie emerges from the large hole in the wall. What an ugly mug!

Start your attack by destroying the two Gun Men

mounted on Mutie's tank treads. You can damage them with the machine gun, so you won't need a power-up weapon. Once the Gun Men are gone, you can concentrate on Mutie.

Stay above Mutoid Man when you're attacking him. He can't turn his head toward the top of the screen, so when you strike from above, he can't counter-attack. It's even better to stay at a diagonal angle from Mutie, because he can quickly roll straight up the screen, but can't roll diagonally.

The occasional Shrapnel Bomb walks onto the screen, so don't get too close to the doors in the walls. Don't waste power-up weapons on destroying the Shrapnel Bombs, but don't ignore them, either.

Mutie can't be harmed by the machine gun, so you must attack him with power-up weapons. Some of these weapons are better than others. Avoid the Rapid-Fire Grenade Launcher, because its range is too short. The Rapid-Fire High-Power Grenade Launcher is the best weapon against Mutie, because it does so much damage.

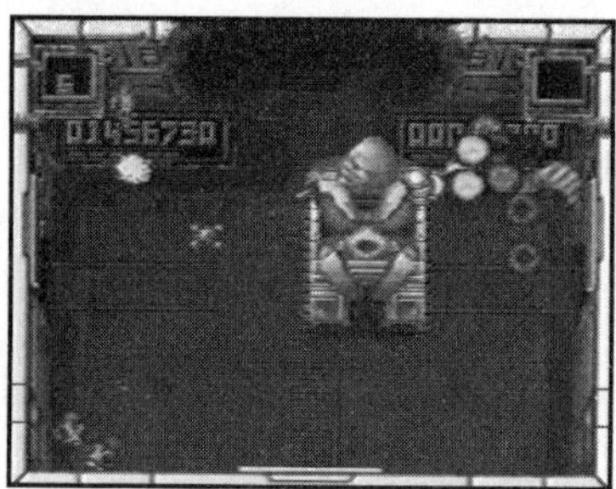

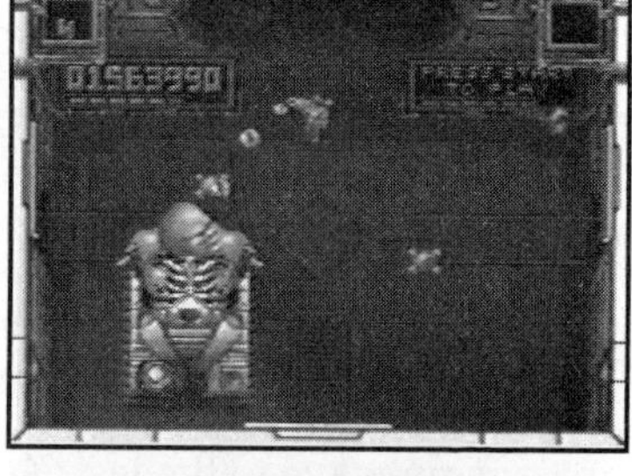

Mutie goes through several stages of damage. His left arm blows up, then his right arm. His chest blows up up to reveal his massive rib cage. After doing more damage, Mutie's head explodes! The headless Mutoid Man is the most harmless of all his forms. Continue to shoot until Mutie becomes a tank with a head! When you destroy the tank, you've destroyed Mutoid Man for good. Run to the lower-right corner of the screen, because Mutie rolls into the upper-left corner of the screen as he blows up.

When Mutie is gone, run through the exit and your cash and prizes will be counted up. You've completed the first of the four Arenas!

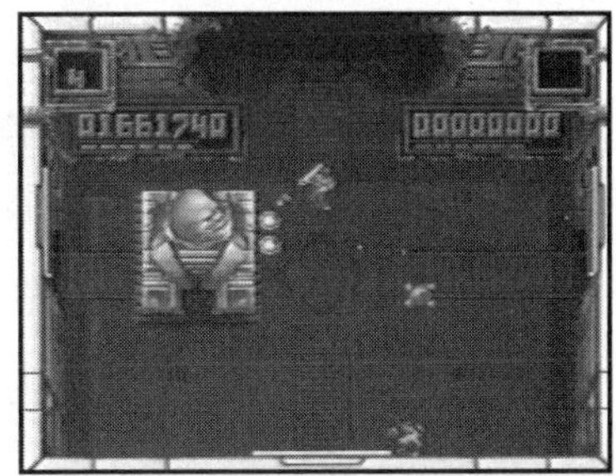

9. Eat My Shrapnel

You start this room in the center of a ring of Hulk Clubbers. Blast your way out before they start moving! You may see a Red Swarmer in this room, along with the Clubbers and Shrapnel Bombs.

10. Total Carnage

Like in Room 9 (Eat My Shrapnel), you start the room surrounded by Hulk Clubbers. There's nothing exciting here, just more Clubbers and Shrapnel Bombs.

Arena 2

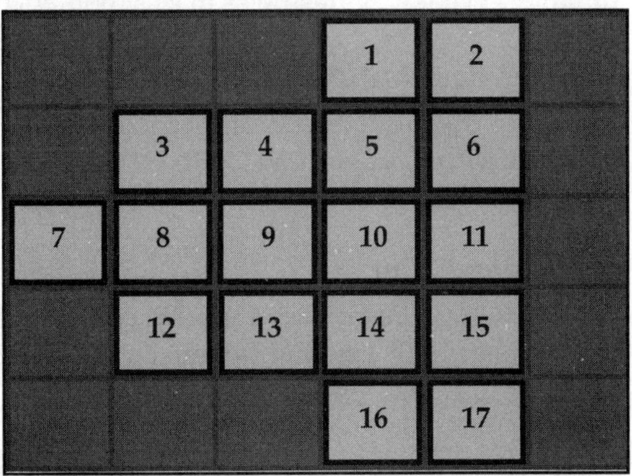

1. Metal Death

This room is filled with Orb-Trains and Floating Robots. It's gonna be a long battle—do you have the stamina to survive?

2. Watch Your Step

This Bonus Prize room is patrolled by Floating Robots and (near the end of the attack) Shrapnel Bombs. You should get through here with no problems.

3. Rowdy Droids

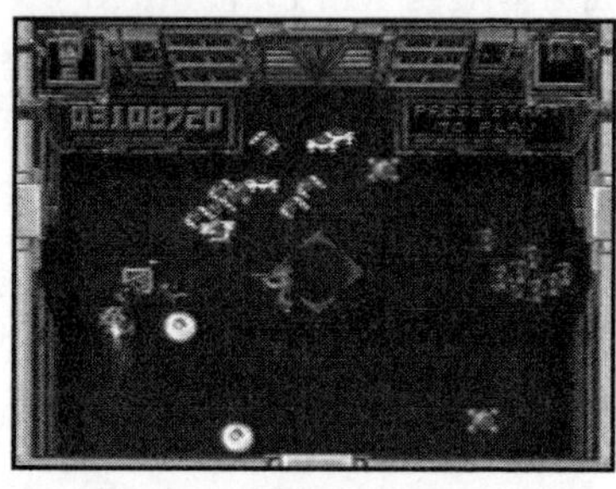

The first attackers in this room are the Orb-Trains. They're tough to destroy without a power-up weapon, but keep shooting at them. Don't get trapped in the corner, because the Orb-Trains will close in on you.

After the Trains attack, the Floating Robots come onto the screen. They're small and fast, so shoot accurately.

4. Vacuum Clean

This is a basic room, with Floating Robots and Red Swarmers. You may get a few Bonus Lives in this room if you're lucky.

5. Fire Power Is Needed!

The name of this room is an understatement! You'll want as many power-ups as you can get to blast through the Single Blue Orbs and Floating Robots. Fire away!

6. Slaughter 'Em

This room starts out with Single Blue Orbs and Red Swarmers, and ends up with Floating Robots and Tanks. Stay in a corner and destroy anything that comes your way.

7. Orbs!

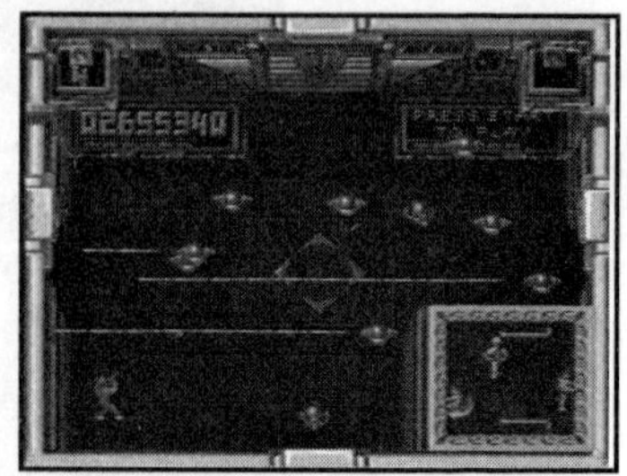

This room is filled with Laser Orbs. Move into the lower-left corner of the room and shoot upward, diagonally, and to the right. This will take out most of the Laser Orbs before they get close to you.

8. Meet My Twin

Stay at the top of the screen as you fight off the attacking waves of Floating Robots. This is one tough room!

9. Smash 'Em

This is a fully mechanical room, with Orb-Trains and Floating Robots. Shoot 'til you can't!

10. Lazer Death Zone

Lazer Death, in this case, refers to the hordes of attacking Laser Orbs and Tanks. Scurry into a corner and stay there as you shoot the Orbs.

11. Meet Scarface!

If you're shooting at Scarface with your girlie-man machine gun, he'll charge at you and squash you. If you're blasting him with a powered-up weapon, you'll drive him away. The moral of the story? Keep grabbing power-ups and blasting Scarface from long range.

Scarface is protected by twelve shield segments. You've got to destroy all of these segments before you can do damage to Scarface himself. The Multi-Direction Photon Gun is an excellent weapon because it allows you to shoot more than one segment at once.

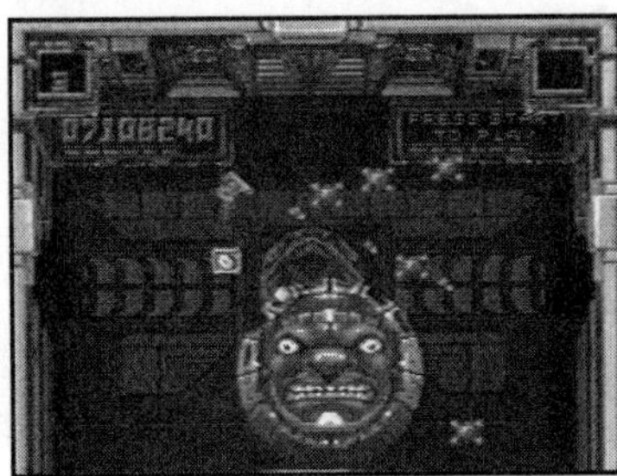

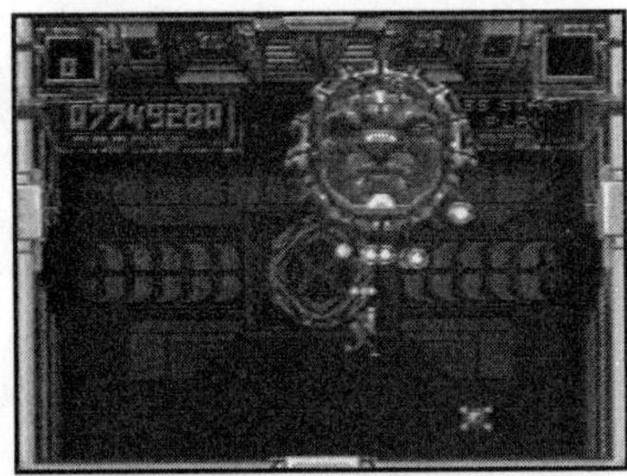

The Rapid-Fire High-Power Grenade Launcher is very helpful in this room because it creates a Mobile Forcefield around you (something it usually doesn't do). Unfortunately, Scarface is annoyed by the whining noise the Launcher makes, and he'll come straight at you, staying underneath the long-

range shots of the Launcher. Bounce the shots off the walls to hit Scarface.

When you destroy Scarface's first form, he moves to the center of the room, explodes, and mutates into a skull! Once again, you've got to destroy the shield segments around Scarface, then go for the kill. Keep snagging the power-ups and blasting away.

The skull Scarface can't kill you with his spark attack if you stay at the bottom of the screen and dodge, so this is a good place to attack from (once you've destroyed all of the shield segments). Keep shooting until Scarface is a memory!

12. Film At 11

The Single Blue Orbs attack first, followed by the Floating Robots. This is about as boring a room as you'll find in Arena 2!

13. Defend Me

This Bonus Prize room is defended by Floating Robots and Orb Trains, with Tanks and Shrapnel Bombs joining the fight later on. You're almost guaranteed to pick up at least one Key in this room; we've managed to pick up as many as four!

14. Turtles Nearby

This simple room is guarded by Laser Orbs and Tanks. Stay in a corner and fire away at the Orbs. The Tanks will usually roll right into your line of fire.

15. Chunks Galore!

This tough room is populated with Red Swarmers, Shrapnel Bombs, and Floating Robots. Keep up the fight!

16. These Are Fast!

This room is guaranteed to take a few of your lives, unless you're a superb player. There are just too many enemies, coming at you too quickly, to be avoided. Stay on the right side of the room, since that's where you have more room to maneuver. Pick up a Speed Boost if one appears.

17. Buffalo Herd Nearby!

Your first attackers are Red Swarmers. After four or five of these, the Orb-Trains start coming onto the screen, followed by a few waves of Single Blue Orbs. Your final foes are a large group of red Floating Robots.

Arena 3

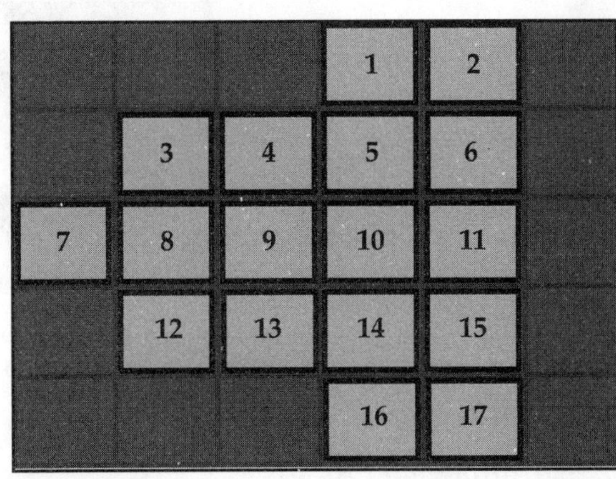

1. Secret Rooms Nearby!

The title of the room is totally bogus. There is a Secret Room, but it's at the opposite end of the Arena! Your enemies in this room are Tanks and Hulk Clubbers.

2. Enjoy My Wealth

A nice Bonus Prize room. You'll need to battle through a lot of Hulk Clubbers, but the cash and prizes are worth the trouble.

3. Turtles Beware!

The title of this room is a bit strange. There are no Turtles here, just lots of Hulk Clubbers.

4. Extra Sauce Action!

Another strange room name. Hulk Clubbers are the biggest problem in this room.

5. Cobra Just Ahead!

The name of this room isn't quite right. The Boss isn't just ahead, he's five rooms ahead! Blast through the Spear Men to get one room closer.

6. Walls Of Pain

A tough room with robotic foes—and nothing else worth mentioning.

7. No Dice

This room is filled with Spear Men. They're just as dangerous as the Hulk Clubbers, so blast 'em!

8. Temple Alert

This room is filled with Spear Men, Snakes and Orb-Trains, but there aren't many of them and you should finish the room quickly.

9. Scorpion Fever

After destroying the large wave of purple Hulk Clubbers, you'll have to destroy a few Shrapnel Bombs. Snakes attack from the top of the screen in this room.

10. Last Arena?

This room is the last one before the Boss. Orb-Trains (in the form of centipedes) and Red Swarmers are the major enemies here.

11. Cobra Death!

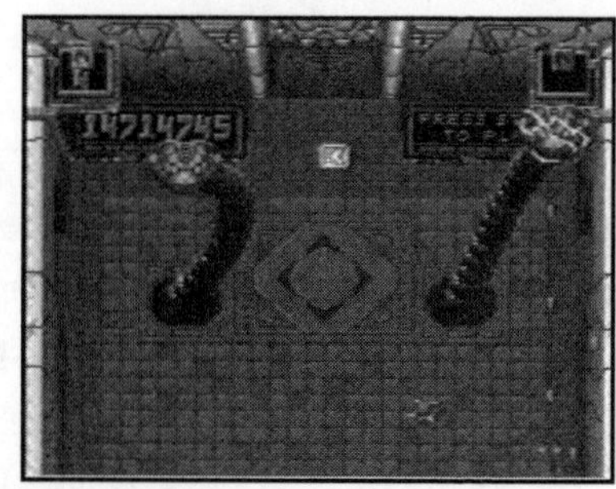

Compared to the first two Bosses, beating the Cobras is very easy. Stay in the lower-right corner of the room. Fire your machine gun upward to hit the heads of the two Cobras. If a Cobra's head sparks, your shot did damage. The

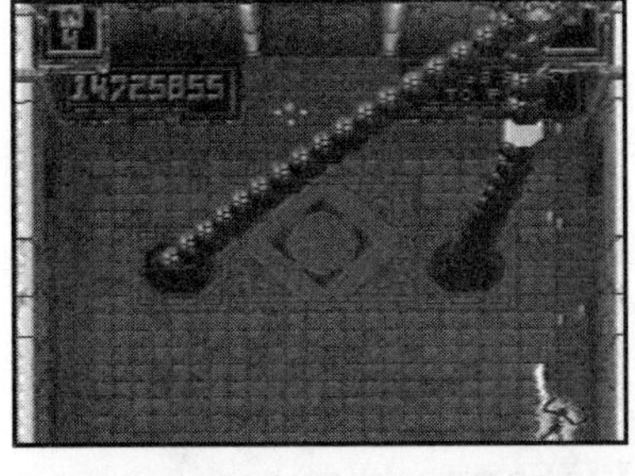

spike wheels that come from the Cobras won't hit you if you stay in the lower-right corner. You may have to dart out of the corner to avoid an electric blast from a Cobra Head, but otherwise, you'll be safe. Don't bother going for power-ups, except the Firing Remote, which gives you two streams of machine gun fire.

It takes a long time to wear down the Cobra Heads, but the Cobras will eventually blow up. Run to the right and you'll enter the fourth and final Arena!

12. No Turtles Allowed!

Snakes pour out of the heads on the wall, so stay at the bottom of the screen and shoot them.

13. Turtle Chunks Needed

An easy-to-survive Bonus Prize room. Hulk Clubbers, Shrapnel Bombs and Tanks are the only enemies you'll face.

14. Dynamite Cobra Boss

This room is a test of patience. Snakes will pour constantly from the heads on the wall, and Floating Robots will emerge from the doors in what seems like a never-ending stream. Keep shooting and be patient—the attacks will end eventually!

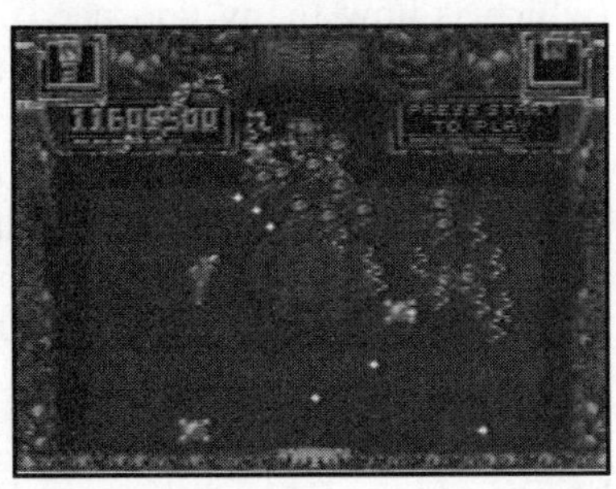

15. Use The Buffalo Gun

"Buffalo" refers to the large red Floating Robots. The "buffalo gun" is the Multi-Direction Photon Gun, which appears more than usual in this room. It takes about five minutes before the Robots stop coming, so keep firing away!

16. Witness Total Carnage

This simple room throws a ton of Hulk Clubbers and Snakes your way. Compared to some of the dangers you've faced before, getting through here is a piece of cake.

17. Secret Room Nearby!

Yep, there's a Secret Room next to this one (see The Secrets for more details). Otherwise, there's nothing special in this room, just lots of Hulk Clubbers and a few Shrapnel Bombs.

Arena 4

1. Almost Enough Keys!

This room's name is somewhat misleading; if you have 10 Keys (which is how many you need), you've got enough, no matter what the name says. If you don't have 10 Keys, this is your last chance to pick some up. Two or three Keys will usually appear in this room. Your attackers are mostly Laser Orbs, so stay in a corner, darting out only to pick up the Keys.

2. You Have Enough Keys! or Not Enough Keys!

If you enter this room with 10 Keys or more, the name will be "You Have Enough Keys!" If you haven't got 10 Keys, the name will be "Not Enough Keys!" and you won't be able to enter the Pleasure Dome.

Expect the longest battle of the entire game in this

room against the hordes of Hulk Clubbers. It will take everything you've got to destroy them all.

When you've fought through all of the Clubbers, one exit (if you have under 10 Keys) or two exits (if you've got 10 Keys or more) will appear. If two exits appear, go through the south exit. Otherwise, go to the east.

3. Eat My Eyeballs!

Get ready to battle the Game Show Host with the Most! The Host is very similar to Mutoid Man. Use the same attack strategies against the Host that you did against Mutoid Man, because they'll work just as well.

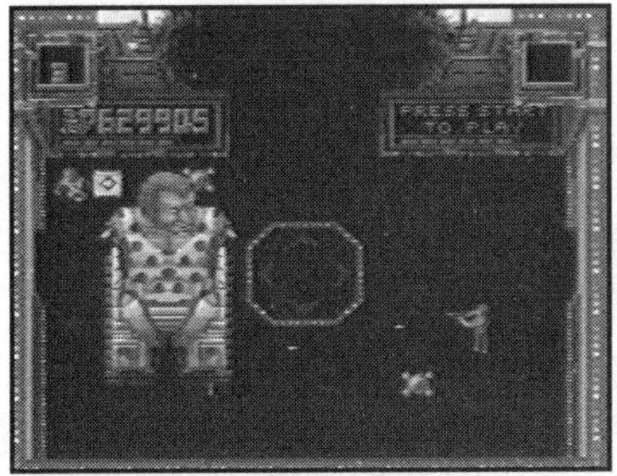

The Host with the Most takes damage a lot like Mutoid Man as well, with his arms, then his chest, exploding. The final form of the Host is a tank with a head; destroy it and you'll be a true champion.

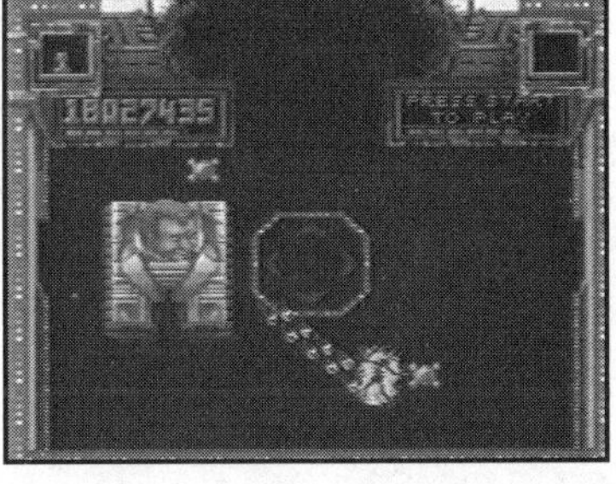

Before the exit appears, you'll have the opportunity to pick up some cash and prizes. Congratulations! You've joined the ranks of the Smash TV survivors!

4. Pleasure Dome

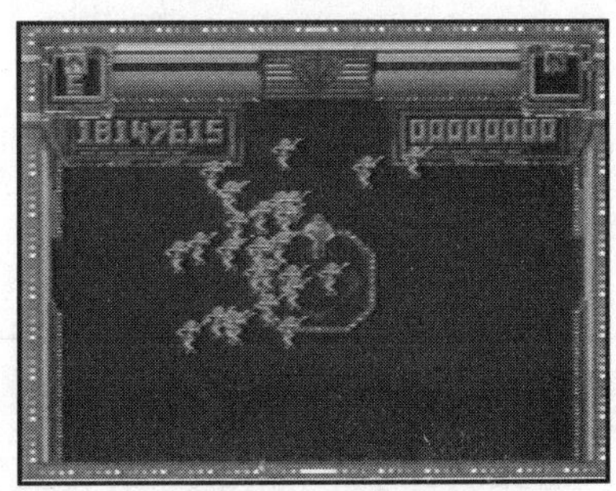

This room is the reason why you picked up all those Keys. Pick up the Game Show Hostesses and your score will soar.

A small group of Hulk Clubbers comes from one of the doors just before a Mystery Pickup appears in the lower-right corner. Don't get killed by the Clubbers, or you won't be able to pick up the Pickup before it disappears. (See The Secrets for more details on Secret Rooms and Mystery Pickups.) There's only one exit out of this room, which leads to Room 3 (Eat My Eyeballs!).

SHH... THE SECRETS

The Pleasure Dome

To enter the Pleasure Dome, you must collect 10 Keys. If you lose all your lives and continue the game, all the Keys you've collected to that point will be carried over.

Extra Lives and Continues

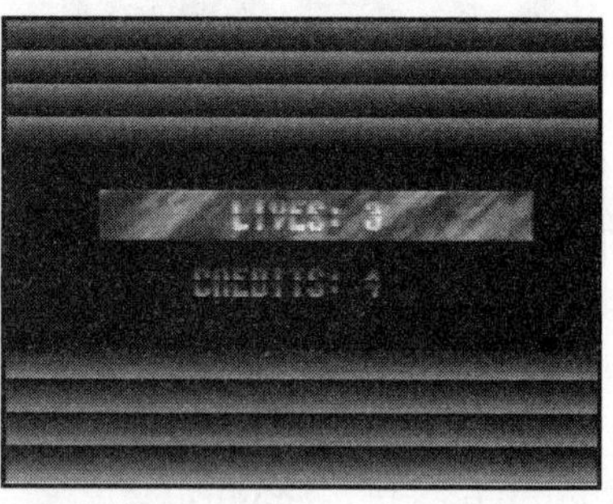

When the One Player/Two Player Select screen appears, press Down, L, R, and Up. You'll hear the sound "Bingo!" and be taken to a screen where you can select the number of lives and continues you begin the game with. The fewest lives you can have is three; the fewest continues you can have is four; the most lives or continues you can have is seven.

Secret Rooms

In each level of the game, there is a Secret Room. Secret Rooms aren't shown on the map that appears at the beginning of the level, and the Exit lights that go on after you've completed a room won't show the way to Secret Rooms.

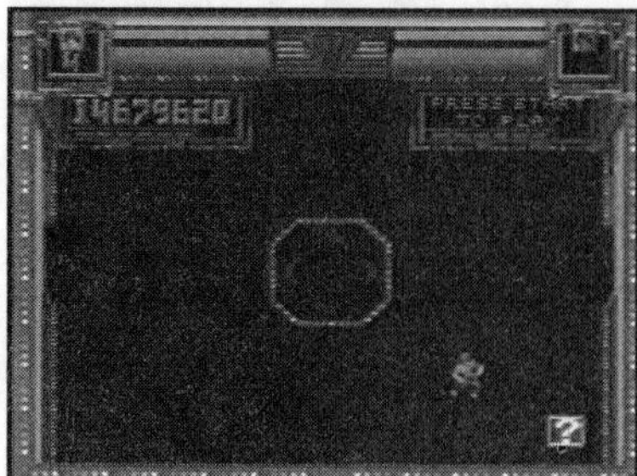

Secret Rooms are filled with bonus cash and prizes. More importantly, a Mystery Pickup appears in the lower-right corner of each Secret

Room. These Pickups are the key to activating a radical feature called the Turbo Mode (see below). The Pickups are similar to power-up weapons in that they only stay on the screen for a short time before blinking and disappearing. Grab them quickly.

There are three Mystery Pickups in the three Secret Rooms. The fourth Pickup is in the Pleasure Dome. The fifth Pickup appears after you defeat the Game Show Host with the Most.

Each Secret Room has multiple Exits. Some Exits lead to the Boss (or the room just before the Boss). Others lead to rooms early in the level. The lists below indicate where the Exits take you. It's not always wise to skip straight to the Boss unless you've collected a lot of Keys in the current Arena.

Secret Room 1: Up Exit to Room 7, Down Exit to Room 2.

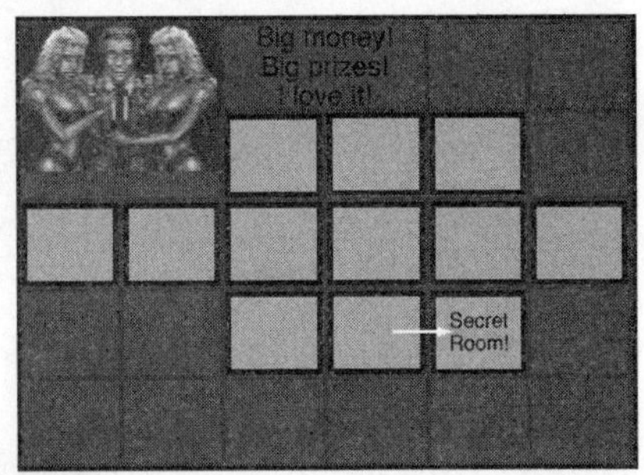

Secret Room 2: Up Exit to Room 15, Right Exit to Room 11, Down Exit to Room 1.

Secret Room 3: Up Exit to Room 15, Right Exit to Room 11, Down Exit to Room 1.

Circuit Warp

When the One/Two Player Select screen appears, press Right, Right, Up, Down, R, L. You'll hear the sound "Bingo!" Select one or two players and press Start. The Circuit Warp screen will appear, allowing you to pick your starting point.

Sound Test

When the One/Two Player Select screen appears, press the buttons on top of Controller One in this sequence: L, R, L, L, R. You'll hear the sound "Bingo!" and the Sound Test screen will appear. Press Start to return to the Player Select screen.

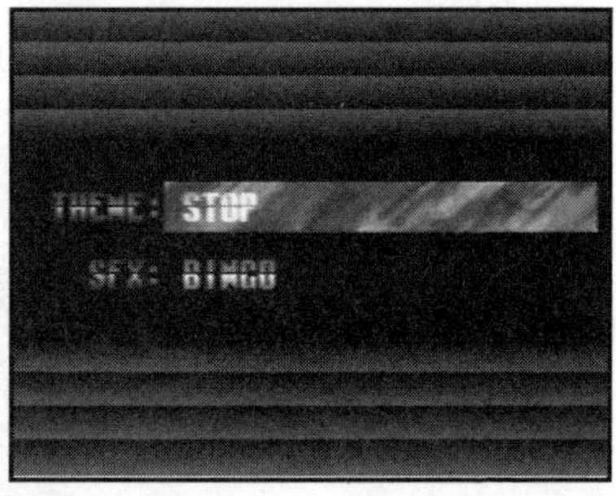

Turbo Mode

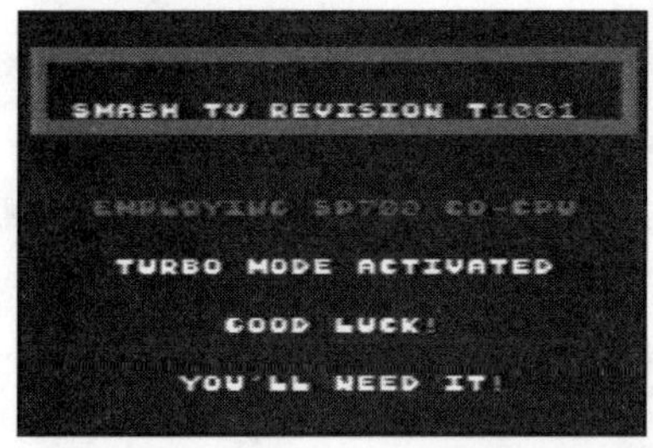

Only the best players will activate the Turbo Mode. To do it, you have to defeat the game on the Normal or Hard level of difficulty, and you must collect all five Mystery Pickups. After you destroy the Game Show Host with the Most, and have your prizes counted up, you'll see a neat little graphic sequence, and the game will inform you that Turbo Mode is activated.

The game will start all over again (and you'll keep your remaining lives and credits), but this time, everything will move much faster—about five times faster! (And to think other Super NES games experience slowdown?) If you defeat the game a second time, you're truly the Ultimate Champion!

CHAPTER 12

Street Fighter II

by Capcom

WHAT'S GOING ON?

It's the hottest arcade game since Pac-Man, and it's arrived on the Super NES! Street Fighter II turns you into one of eight different World Warriors, each with a variety of special attack moves. Fight your way through eleven opponents in the one-player mode, or have some real fun and take on another player in the Vs. Mode. Either way you play, you're in for some awesome fighting action!

PLAYERS

Street Fighter II is for one or two players. In the one-player mode, you fight through the other seven World Warriors, then battle four more characters before you win the game. In the two-player Vs. Mode, each player chooses a character and fights in a best-of-three match.

LIVES AND CONTINUES

In the one-player mode, you have only one life, but you also have an unlimited number of continues. In the two-player mode, it's a simple best-of-three match. The first guy to win two rounds is the champion!

CONTROLS

Street Fighter II uses six of the buttons on your Super NES controller, four on the front (A, B, X, and Y) and two on the top (L and R). This setup simulates the six buttons of the Street Fighter II arcade game (Short, Forward, Roundhouse, Jab, Strong, and Fierce). In this version, the buttons have been renamed.

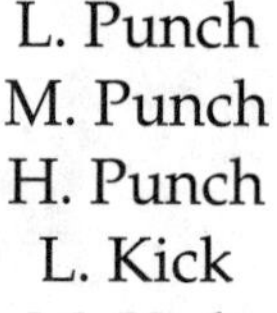

ARCADE	SUPER NES
Jab	L. Punch
Strong	M. Punch
Fierce	H. Punch
Short	L. Kick
Forward	M. Kick
Roundhouse	H. Kick

CapCom plans to release the Competition Joystick in July of 1992. This infrared controller is specifically designed for use with Street Fighter II, but it can also be used with all other games for the Super NES. The Competition Joystick will even work with the 8-bit NES! We'll have coverage of this hot controller in *Super NES Games Secrets 3*.

WEAPONS

No weapons in this game, just fists and feet. Check out the Strategy Session for detailed profiles of each World Warrior.

FRIENDS

See the Strategy Session for details on all eight World Warriors.

ENEMIES

In addition to the eight World Warriors, there are four opponents you'll fight in the one-player mode: Balrog, Vega, Sagat, and M. Bison. You've gotta whip them all to win the game. Check out their profiles in the Strategy Session.

STRATEGY SESSION

General Strategies

• All of the strategies in this chapter apply to both the arcade and home versions of Street Fighter II. You'll be able to kick butt equally in both versions!
• Defense plays a major role. You just can't be on the attack all the time. Learn how to block quickly and easily. Once you can block attacks, you can learn how to counterattack!
• Most people who play the arcade version of Street Fighter II love to be Guile, for two reasons. He's got great special attacks, and he recovers quickly after using them. A poor player using Guile can beat a good player using a lesser character. Once you master Guile, try the weaker Warriors.

World Warrior Profiles

In the Warrior Profiles that follow, we give you instructions on how to execute special moves. Each bolded word in the instructions indicates a joystick move.

• **Left, Right, Up, Down**: Left, Right, Up, or Down on the controller.
• **Punch**: Any Punch button.
• **Kick**: Any Kick button.
• **Back**: Press in the opposite direction of your opponent.
• **Towards**: Press in the direction of your opponent.

Any controller movement from Up or Down to Left or Right has to be a circular motion. For example, Chun Li's Cyclone Kick is Down, Back, Kick. You start the move by pressing the controller Down, then circle the controller Back (either Left or Right, depending on your position), then press any Kick button. Got it? Good! Let's fight!

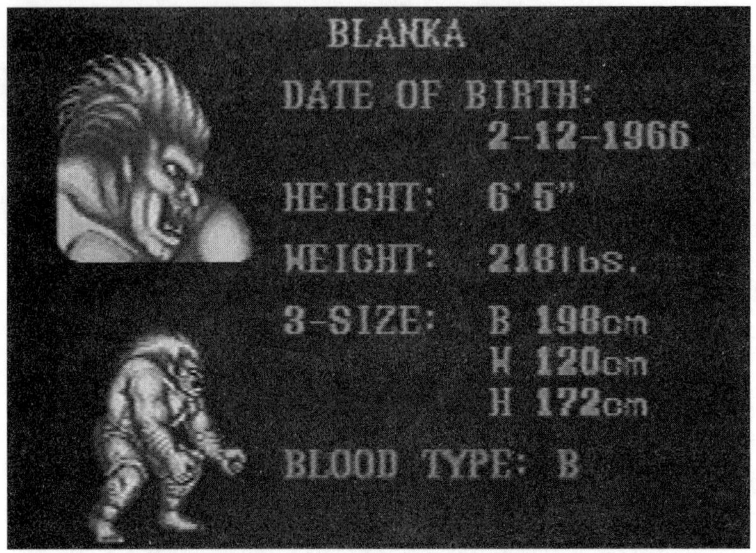

As a baby, **Blanka** *was one of the passengers of a plane that got caught in a thunderstorm over Brazil. The storm caused the plane to crash and gave Blanka amazing electrical powers. Blanka's mother has been searching for him since the crash.*

Electricity

Blanka's electrical powers are put to good use with this special move, which turns your opponent into an X-ray! Move Blanka into close range and press any **Punch** button rapidly. The Punch button used determines the electric power of the Shock.

Face Bite

Get close to your opponent and press the **H. Punch** button rapidly to chow down on his ugly mug! The first Face Bite does a lot of damage, but subsequent nibbles are weaker. Zangief has an easy time defending against this special move.

Rolling Attack

Definitely the most powerful of Blanka's attacks. The only problem is that Blanka takes massive damage if his opponent counterattacks. Don't overuse it! Press **Back two seconds, Towards**, and any **Punch** button. The Punch button used determines the speed of the attack.

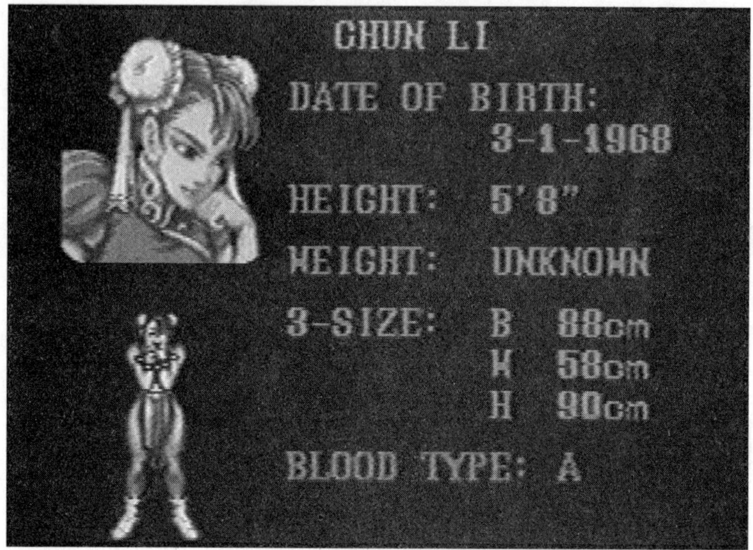

***Chun Li** is a foxy lady who's been following the trail of the Shadoloo smuggling organization. The trail has led her to M. Bison, who was the man responsible for the death of her father. Chun Li is the fastest of the World Warriors.*

Head Stomp

The most devastating of Chun Li's close attacks. She leaps into the air and mashes her opponent's head with her heel. This move is an excellent set-up for other attacks. Jump **Towards** the opponent, then press **Down** and the **M. Kick** button.

Lightning Kick

Chun Li shows off her amazing foot speed with this awesome move, which does tremendous damage at close range. This is a great move against a cornered opponent. Press the **L. Kick or M. Kick** button rapidly, then press both buttons to keep the Lightning Kick going.

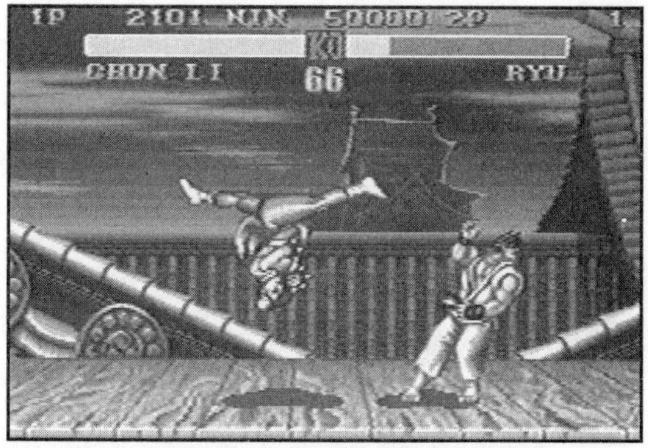

Whirlwind Kick

Chun Li spins upside-down to execute this kick. which strikes opponents with multiple hits if done correctly. Press **Down two seconds**, **Up**, and any **Kick** button. The Kick button used changes the speed and distance of the Whirlwind Kick.

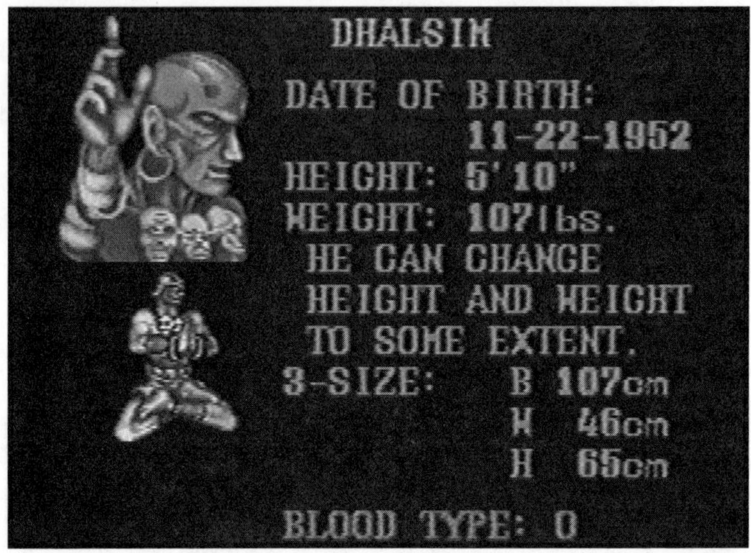

***Dhalsim** is an Indian guru and a master of Yoga. He can stretch his limbs to extraordinary lengths to strike an opponent! He's entered the Street Fighter tournament to test his skills and raise himself to a higher state of consciousness (or unconsciousness, if he loses).*

Yoga Fire

Dhalsim's got a severe case of halitosis. He can spit fireballs from his mouth! Press **Down, Towards,** and any **Punch** button. The Punch button used determines the speed (but not the power) of the fireball. To use the **Yoga Flame** instead, press **Back, Down, Towards,** and any **Punch** button.

Yoga Nugie

Dhalsim must've been on the receiving end of a few nugies as a kid, because he sure knows how to dish them out. Press **Towards** and the **M. Punch** button. To use the Yoga Throw instead, press **Towards** and the **H. Punch** button.

Yoga Spear

This maneuver is very effective as a setup for the Yoga Throw or Yoga Nugie. It's tough to defend against because of the wicked angle of attack. Jump into the air and press the **H. Kick** button **at the top of the jump**. To use the Yoga Mummy instead, press the **H. Punch** button **at the top of the jump**.

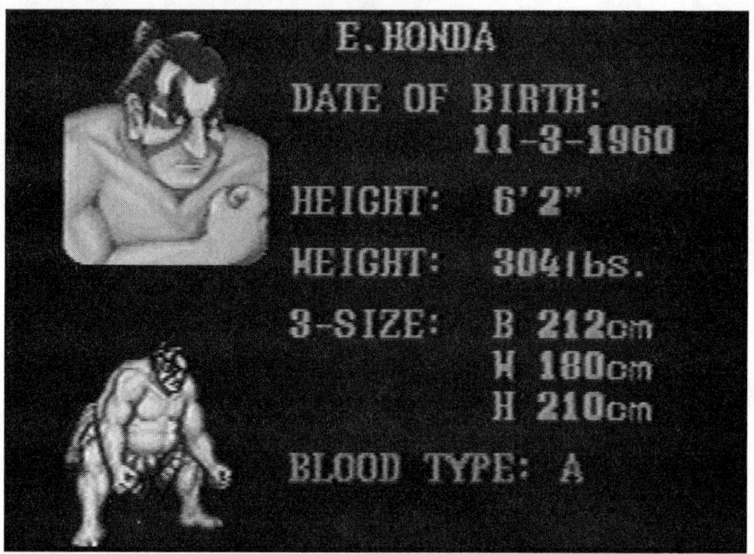

***E. Honda** lives in Japan and is a teacher of sumo wrestling. His students are beginning to think that sumo wrestling isn't the best of the martial arts, so he's entered the Street Fighter Tournament to show them the superiority of sumo.*

Bear Hug

Honda's got a crush on you, and he'll prove it with this crushing maneuver. You can set up the Bear Hug with a Flying Kick or Short Kick. Press **Towards** and the **H. Punch** button. To use the **Sumo Throw** instead, press **Towards** and the **M. Punch** button.

Hundred Hand Slap

E. Honda's Hundred Hand Slap is very similar to Chun Li's Lightning Kick. This move works great when your opponent is cornered on the side of the screen. Press the **L. Punch** or **M. Punch** rapidly to start the Slap, then press the button rapidly to keep it going.

Sumo Head Butt

When used at close range, the Head Butt can strike the opponent twice. Press **Back two seconds, Towards**, and any **Punch** button. The Punch button used determines the speed of the Sumo Head Butt.

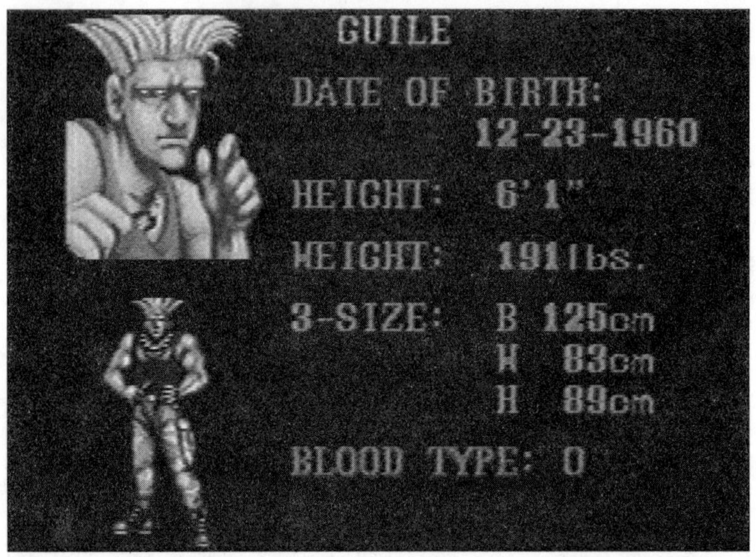

Guile *is a former member of a Special Forces unit. Six years ago, he and his friend were captured and tortured. Guile escaped, but his friend died, and now he wants revenge on M. Bison, the man who captured him. Guile has a wicked assortment of special moves.*

Back Breaker

You can only use this move when your opponent jumps into the air. Jump **Towards** your opponent and press **Down**, then press the **M. Kick** or **H. Kick** button. To use the **Air Punch** instead, jump **Towards** your opponent, press **Down** and any **Punch** button.

Flash Kick

This counterattack move is practically unstoppable. Only the Dragon Punch and a few jump kick moves can get through it. Press **Down two seconds**, **Up**, and any **Kick** button. The Kick button used determines the height (but not the power) of the Flash Kick.

Sonic Boom

This move is equal to Ken or Ryu's Fire Ball. Guile recovers quickly after using the Boom. Press **Back two seconds, Towards**, and any **Punch** button. The Punch button used determines the speed (but not the power) of the Sonic Boom.

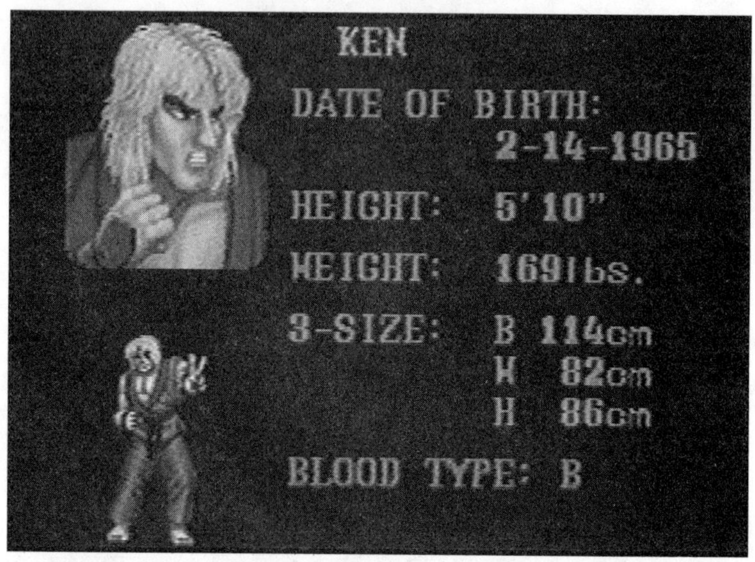

***Ken** is one of the two disciples of Master Sheng Long (Ryu is the other). Ken is a great fighter, but his fighting skills have gone downhill in the past year (he's been making time with his girlfriend). Ken's ego is even bigger than his muscles.*

Dragon Punch

This move, also known as Sheng Long (see The Secrets for more on Sheng Long), can counter any attack. Press **Towards, Down** (go from Towards to Down without circling the controller), **Towards** (this time, circle the controller from Down to Towards), and any **Punch** button.

Fireball

Ken wouldn't last long without this deadly flaming sphere. It takes a few moments for Ken to recover after he uses the Fireball (it, like, drains his karmic energy, y'know?). Press **Down**, **Towards**, and any **Punch** button. The Punch button used determines the speed of the Fireball.

Hurricane Kick

This spinning jump kick will strike for multiple hits if you use it correctly. Press **Down**, **Left**, and any **Kick** button. The Kick button used determines the speed, and distance, of the Hurricane Kick.

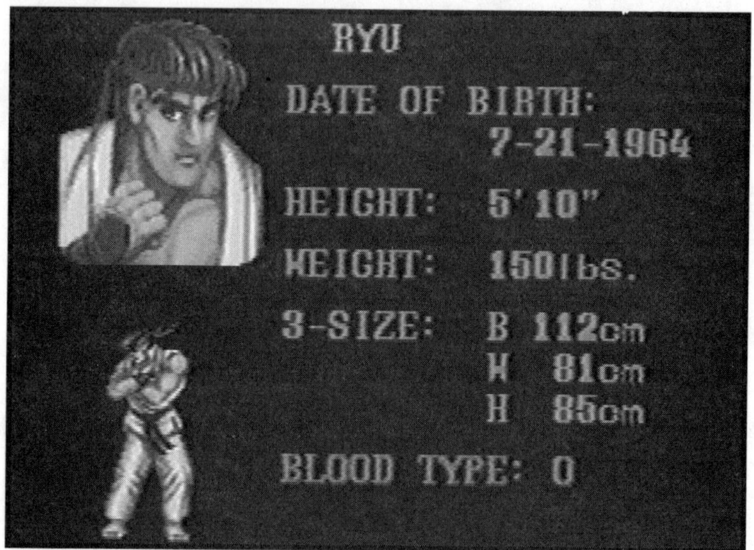

***Ryu** is a fighter from the original Street Fighter arcade game (which never made it to the Super NES, but appeared as a TurboGrafx-16 game called Fighting Street). He trained with Ken in Japan, and his special moves are practically identical to Ken's.*

Dragon Punch

The Dragon Punch is a great defensive and offensive move. Press **Towards**, **Down** (go from Towards to Down without circling the controller), **Towards** (this time, circle the controller from Down to Towards), and any **Punch** button.

Fireball

The Fireball is an excellent missile weapon. It takes a few moments for Ryu to recover after using the Fireball. Press **Down**, **Towards**, and any **Punch** button. The Punch button used determines the speed of the Fireball.

Hurricane Kick

This spinning jump kick will strike for multiple hits when you use it correctly. Press **Down**, **Back**, and any **Kick** button. The Kick button used determines the speed and distance of the Hurricane Kick.

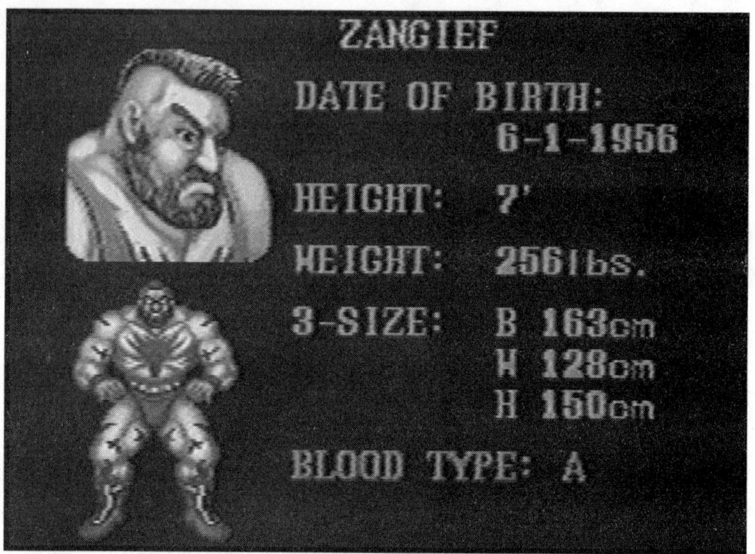

***Zangief** is a burly wrestler from the former Soviet Union. He's got two weaknesses: he has no missile attacks, and he's slower than a broke-kneed turtle. He makes up for his flaws with some devastating wrestling moves.*

Head Slam

This move is a perfect example of Zangief's brute strength: he picks up his opponent, turns him upside-down, and slams him head-first into the ground! (Who says the art of conversation is dead?) Press **Towards** and the **H. Kick** button.

Spinning Clothesline

This move deflects missile attacks like the Fire Ball and Sonic Boom. Zangief can still be hit with a low attack while spinning, and he can't move forward. Use the Clothesline for defense only. Press **all three Punch buttons** to spin.

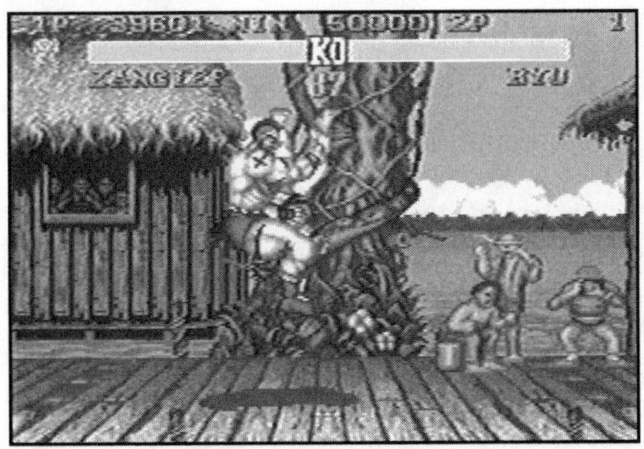

Spinning Pile Driver

Zangief grabs opponents from long range to execute this move, even when they're attacking him. **Spin the controller 360 degrees** and press any **Punch** button. The Punch button used determines the speed (but not the power) of the spin.

***Balrog** used to be the Heavyweight Champion of the World, but he lost the title, and has since spent his time sulking in Las Vegas. He's joined the Street Fighter Tournament to see if he's still got what it takes as a boxer.*

Super Backfist

Balrog has a deadly array of punching attacks, with the Super Backfist being the most powerful. Balrog is susceptible to missile attacks (particularly the Fire Ball) and jump kick attacks. Balrog will attack with low blows, so watch out!

Vega is a "glamour boy" who wears a mask when he fights to protect his good looks. He can climb on the fence in the background of an area, and then leap off to attack with a jump kick! He's also got wild moves like the Cartwheel and Air Throw.

Wall Climb

Vega has a weakness against a slow Fire Ball (press the **S. Punch** button for a slow Ball). He's also vulnerable to Uppercuts when he gets off the ground after being knocked down. It takes him a moment to get his guard up, giving you a great opportunity to strike!

***Sagat** got his butt kicked by Ryu in Street Fighter I, and he's been training hard ever since, looking to get revenge. He's added a slew of new attacks to his repertoire, and he plans for Ryu to find out about them all, the hard way!*

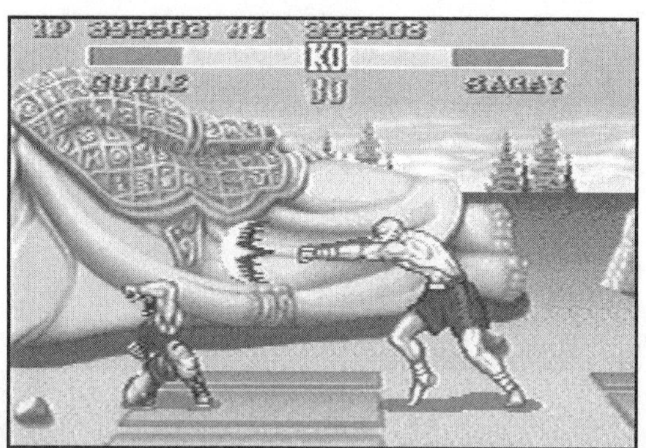

High Tiger Ball

Sagat can fire High and Low Tiger Balls, similar to Fire Balls. His favorite move is the Tiger Uppercut, which does more damage than the Dragon Punch. However, it leaves Sagat wide open for a counterattack, and any blows that strike him after a Tiger Uppercut do twice as much damage.

M. Bison *is the final boss of Street Fighter II. Two of the World Warriors have scores to settle with him (he killed Chun Li's parents, and tortured Guile's friend during the VietnamWar). He can channel energy through his body to attack.*

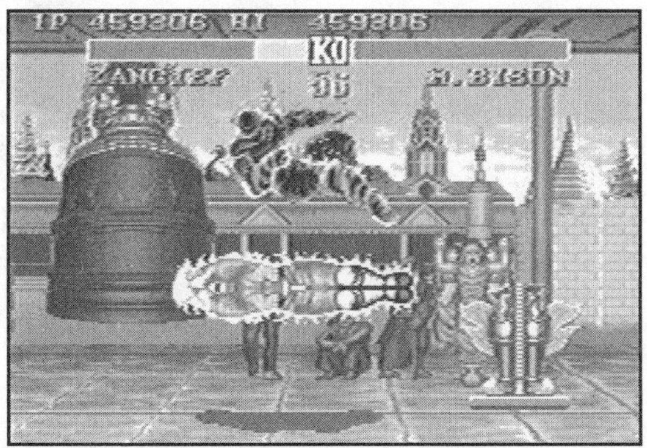

Flaming Torpedo

The Flaming Torpedo is only dangerous when you're dizzy. Otherwise, you can knock Bison out of the air with a straight punch. Ken and Ryu have a hard time against Bison, but more powerful Warriors will rip through him, especially Guile (with his Jack-Knife) and Blanka (with his Roll Attack).

Combinations

The key to victory in Street Fighter II is to master attack combinations. Nothing's more satisfying than striking your opponent with a flurry of unanswered blows. Listed below are the most effective combinations we've discovered, along with a few other miscellaneous strategies. Combos are hard to execute, so keep practicing.

Blanka

Try this combination: a jumping ***H. Punch****, a nM.* ***Punch*** *once you land, and a low* ***L. Kick****.*

Chun Li

Jump kick or jump punch toward your opponent. If he blocks, grab and throw by pressing ***M. Punch*** *or* ***H. Punch*** *and* ***Towards*** *your opponent. This is extremely cheap, but it works great and it's almost impossible to hit Chun Li before she grabs.*

Dhalsim

Try this combo to score two solid hits. Use the ***Yoga Nugie,*** *walk toward your opponent, and then head-butt with the* ***H. Punch*** *button. Another strategy is to keep shooting* ***Yoga Fire****. If your opponent jumps over the Fire, use any* ***Kick*** *button to knock him backward. A final note: Dhalsim can slide underneath missile attacks.*

E. Honda

Use the jump-grab-throw strategy that Chun Li uses for some excellent results. If you're fighting an opponent without a missile attack, hold the controller ***Back*** *and press the* ***S. Punch*** *button rapidly (but not fast enough to start the Hundred Hand Slap). If your opponent jumps over your fist, press* ***Towards*** *and any* ***Punch*** *button to execute the* ***Sumo Head Butt****.*

Guile

Guile's the only World Warrior with a four-hit combination. This combo is guaranteed to dizzy your opponent. Strike with a chop, punch, Sonic Boom, and backhand punch in rapid succession. Use the ***H. Punch*** *button to throw all of these blows, and move the controller appropriately to execute the Sonic Boom. (By the way, if you're hit while you're in the air, hold the joystick back to charge up for a Flash Kick, which you can use as you land.)*

Ken

Ken has three combos: ***H. Punch*** *followed by* ***Fireball, H. Punch*** *followed by* ***Hurricane Kick****, and* ***S. Punch*** *followed by the* ***Dragon Punch****.*

Ryu

Ryu has three combos: ***H. Punch*** *followed by* ***Fireball, H. Punch*** *followed by* ***Hurricane Kick****, and* ***S. Punch*** *followed by the* ***Dragon Punch****. (Deja vu?)*

Zangief

*Here's one of Zangief's more powerful moves, the not-so-graceful Swan Dive. Press **Up two seconds, Down**, and the **H. Punch** button.*

SHH . . . THE SECRETS

Different Endings

There are eight different endings programmed into the game, one for each of the eight World Warriors. You won't get an ending if you don't play at a high level of difficulty. Here's one of the endings, showing Blanka reunited with his mom. We'll leave it to you to fight your way to the other seven!

Same Character vs. Same Character

Street Fighter II has an awesome hidden feature: Same Character fights! Turn on your Super NES and enter the following code when the Capcom logo appears: Down, R, Up, L, Y, B. You'll hear a noise if you enter the code correctly. (R means R button, not Right; L means L button, not Left.) Now you can have Same Character battles, with Player Two's character having different colors so you can tell your fighters apart.

CHAPTER 13

Super Adventure Island

by Hudson Soft

WHAT'S GOING ON?

Master Higgins was snuggling under the stars with his honey, Jeanie Jungle, when the evil Dark Cloak flew onto the scene. He turned Jeanie to stone and dared Higgins to come to his castle on Ice Mountain. Higgins tugged on his baseball cap, adjusted his grass skirt, and got ready for his greatest adventure ever!

PLAYERS

Super Adventure Island is for one player only.

SCORING

You score points by picking up weapons, shooting bad guys, and clearing Areas. There are five Areas, separated into three Rounds each, The higher your Energy Bar when you finish a Round, the more bonus points you'll receive.

LIVES AND CONTINUES

You start the game with three lives. You can have a maximum of six extra Higgins (shown at the bottom of the screen). Your strength is shown by the Energy Bar along the top of the screen. The Energy Bar will slowly decrease as time goes by. You've got to keep the Energy Bar at full strength by eating fruit and drinking milk. You'll find fruit scattered throughout the game; you'll only find milk in the Star Bonus Rounds.

You also start the game with two continues. If you lose your last life, you can use a continue to keep going from the last Round you reached. There's no way to earn extra continues, so if you run out of lives and continues, the game is over.

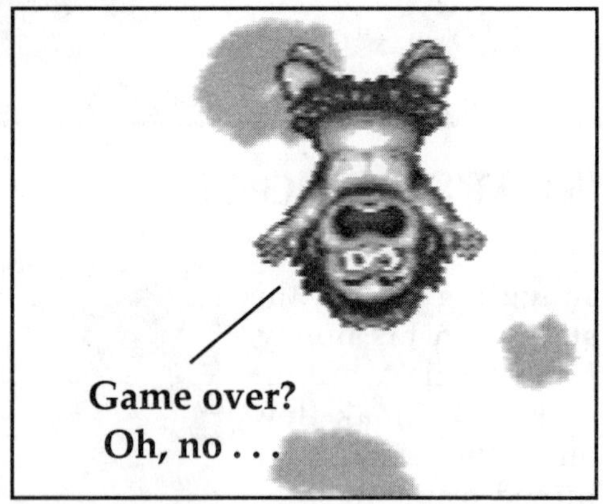

Game over? Oh, no . . .

CONTROLS

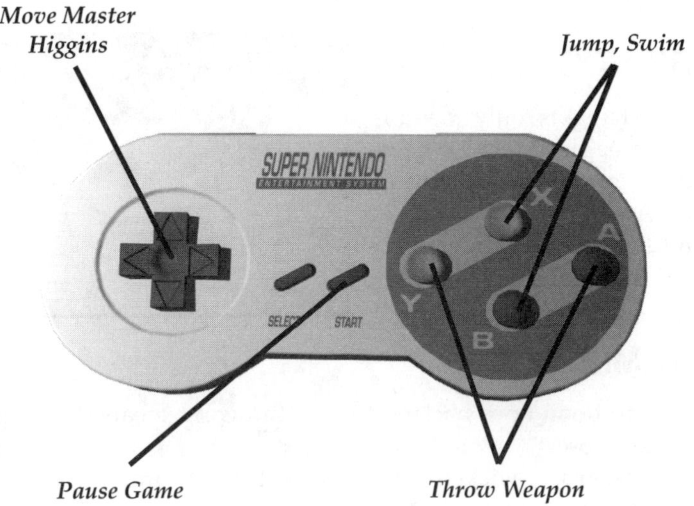

WEAPONS

There are two weapons on Adventure Island: Boomerangs and Axes. You can aim Boomerangs with the Control Pad, but you can only throw Axes in an arc in front of you. You can collect up to four Boomerangs or Axes, but you can't collect both. If you have one weapon and pick up the other type, you'll switch weapons. When you collect the fourth Boomerang or Axe, they will become Fire Weapons. Fire Weapons are twice as strong as normal weapons, and they can even destroy rocks (but not rolling boulders).

SPECIAL ITEMS

You'll find Skateboards in some Rounds. When you hop onto a board, you'll be able to really zoom through your enemies. If you're hit while riding a Skateboard, the Board will disappear, but you won't suffer any damage.

In the Star Bonus Round, you have to bounce from spring to spring, collecting bonus items and trying not to fall. If you can collect all of the bonus items, the word PERFECT will appear on the screen and a 1-Up Item will appear. Try to grab the 1-Up Item as you fall!

FRIENDS

Master Higgins' only friend is a huge eagle that will drop him off at the first Round of each Area. Too bad the eagle can't help Higgins fight Dark Cloak's minions!

ENEMIES

Bamboon hops back and forth, throwing spears if you get too close.

Beezer is a wicked wasp that will fly toward you as soon as it sees you.

Bloobs are minuscule black blobs that are tough to hit. Don't get too close to them!

Blue Reptilly uses a balloon to float down from the top of the screen. If he lands on the ground, he'll attack by breathing fire.

Flounder is a flying fish that spins around in the air.

Lectron appears in the swimming Rounds. It shoots four lightning bolts diagonally from his body. Stay above or below Lectron and you'll be safe.

Peppy is a nasty penguin that will dash straight at you. If Peppy appears from behind you, get ready to jump!

Shelly is a pointy shell creature that crawls slowly along. Duck down and throw your weapon to hit her.

Skizzer is a massive blue flying dog that looks more like a ghost. Skizzer will never actually touch you, but he'll come very close.

Skullfoot is a strong guy who takes two hits from your weapons to be destroyed. (If you're using the Fire Weapon, you'll only need one hit.)

Smokestack Sammy is a walking candle, and a real hothead. Don't try to jump over Sammy or you will get burned!

Wally is an over-inflated walrus. Pop him with a well-thrown weapon.
Bamboozal is the Boss Master of Area 1. It shoots pillars of fire at you.
Kraken is the Boss Master of Area 2. It's protected by sea urchins and shoots small attack fish into the water.
Lavaslither is the Boss Master of Area 3. It lives deep within a volcano. Watch out for the lava flows!
King Reptilian is the Boss Master of Area 4. He's armed with a giant laser sword.
Dark Cloak is the Boss Master of Area 5. Defeat him and Jeanie will return to normal!

STRATEGY SESSION

General Strategies

• The Boomerang is the better weapon to have. It's got a longer range than the Axe, and you can aim it by using the Control Pad. The only time you need the Axe is against certain Bosses.
• The Super Jump is only useful when you need to jump. It's almost impossible to Super Jump while moving. Instead, use the High Jump by holding the Control Pad Up. If Higgins gets a running start, he'll automatically High Jump when you press the Jump button.

Round 1-1

Enemies: Blue Reptilly, Shelly

This level is a real cinch. You'll only encounter one group of Blue Reptillys, and the Shellys are very easy to hit with the Axe or the Boomerang. Practice the Super Jump move while running (a difficult maneuver that will come in handy during the final battle with Dark Cloak).

You'll find the Skateboard near the start of the Round (you'll pass three Shellys before you find it). There are two areas that are tricky to get through with the Board.

The first area is a group of two rocks, spaced apart so that you must use two small jumps to pass them instead of a Super Jump (if you Super Jump, you'll strike the second rock and lose the Board).
The second area is the large hill near the end of the Round. Hit the Shelly on the top of the hill, then strike the Reptilly floating down at you. If you don't do this just right, you'll lose the Board for sure!

Round 1-2

Enemies: Bamboon, Beezer, Shelly

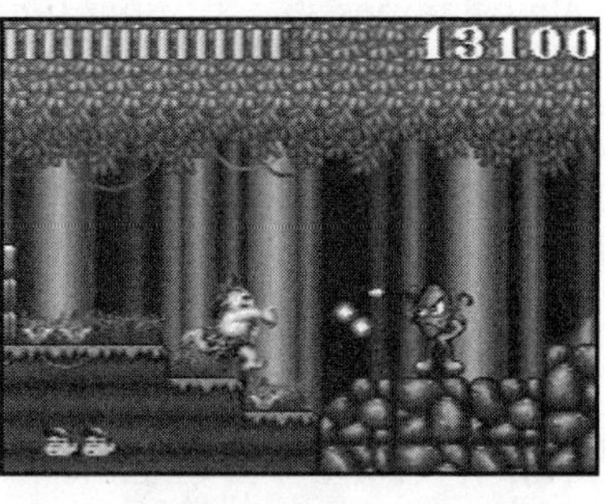

This is another simple Round. The Bamboons are the toughest enemies to defeat. Stay at a distance and strike them with Boomerangs. Be ready to leap a spear whenever you're attacking a Bamboon!

About halfway through the Round, you'll come to an Axe positioned so that you'll take it when you jump onto a moving platform. To avoid taking the Axe, Super Jump or High Jump over the Axe when the moving platform is all the way to the right. You'll land on the right side of the platform, still armed with the Boomerang weapon.

Round 1-3

Enemies: Bloob, Smokestack Sammy

It's possible to leap over the Axe at the start of the Round by using a Super Jump, but you really don't need to. Just continue to the right until you start going downhill. When the boulder appears behind you, keep going until you reach the bottom of the hill. Leap over the lava pit and you'll grab the Boomerang before landing safely.

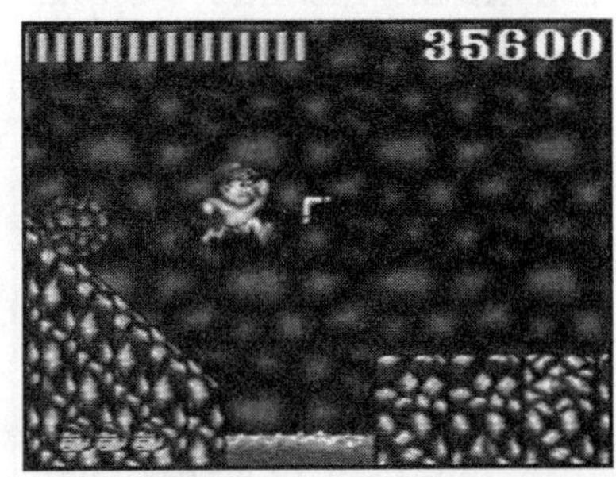

It's possible to jump over the Smokestack Sammys by using the Super Jump, but the wiser strategy is simply to attack with your weapons. The Sammys move slowly and are easy targets to hit.

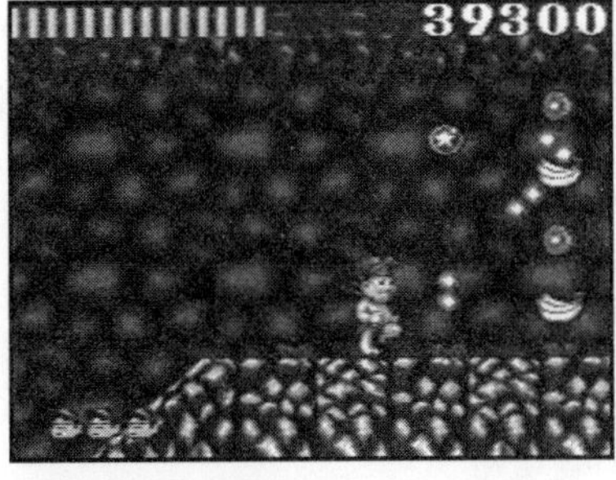

When you reach the Starball at the end of the Round, throw your weapons at the right side of the screen to reveal four hidden fruits. Snatch up the yummy stuff and touch the Starball to head toward your first Boss Master.

Round 1-4

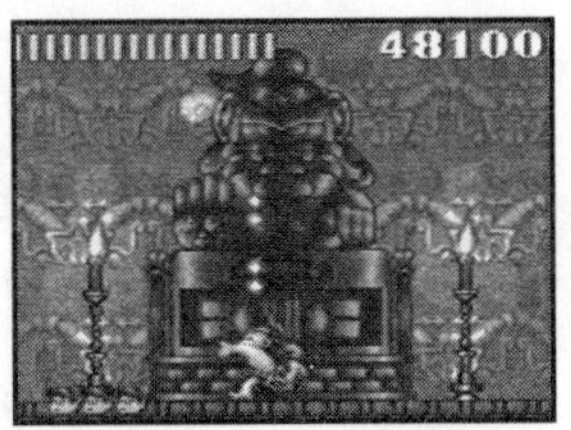

If you have the Boomerang, beating Bamboozal is a breeze. Stand underneath his head and throw the Boomerang straight up nine times for a quick victory.

If you've got the Axe, fighting Bamboozal is tricky. Stay to one side of the screen, leap into the air, and throw the Axes at Bamboozal's head. Leap over the fire that Bamboozal sends your way. Don't jump straight up;

jump up and over the fire. Keep throwing Axes until Bamboozal falls apart!

Round 2-1

Enemies: Flounder, Peppy

The Peppys are nasty little buggers. Be ready to strike the Peppys as they appear on the right side of the screen. If a Peppy appears on the left side of the screen, behind you, jump over him. If you've got the Boomerangs, you can strike the Peppys as they fly underneath you.

Halfway through the Round, you'll meet up with someone holding a shield. If you've got the Boomerang, you can beat him by throwing a Boomerang behind him. The Boomerang will hit him from behind as it returns to you. With the Axe, you'll have to hit him as he lowers his shield to throw his spear.

Round 2-2

Enemies: Peppy, Shelly, Wally

There are only two areas in this Round worth mentioning. The first is the hidden Star Bonus Round; check The Secrets to find out its location (or look for it yourself). The second area is a tricky jump near the end of the Round. A Peppy will appear behind you when you leap onto a

ledge in the water. Sometimes the Peppy will just hop harmlessly into the water, but other times the Peppy will soar across the screen and hit you in the air.

What's the secret? Jump onto the right side of the ledge. If you land on the right side, the Peppy will jump into the water. If you land on the left side of the ledge, the Peppy will take off and nail you.

Round 2-3

Enemies: Flounder, Lectron

You'll be taken to this Round after a Jonah-esque encounter with a giant breaching whale! Use Boomerangs to strike the Flounders and Lectrons as they swim by. Keep throwing the Boomerangs up and down as you swim along to reveal hidden fruits. Don't float off the bottom of the screen or you'll drown!

There's an Axe next to the Starball. Take the Axe, because it's a better weapon to use against the Boss Master. Throw a few Axes into the lower-right corner of the screen, below the Starball, to reveal a few hidden fruits. Take the fruits and touch the Starball to face off against the Boss Master.

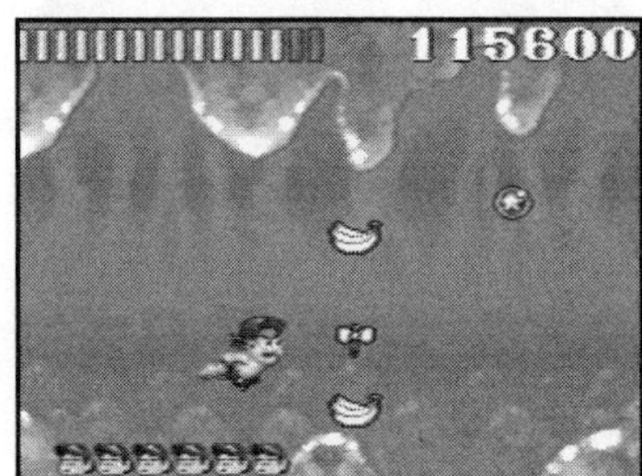

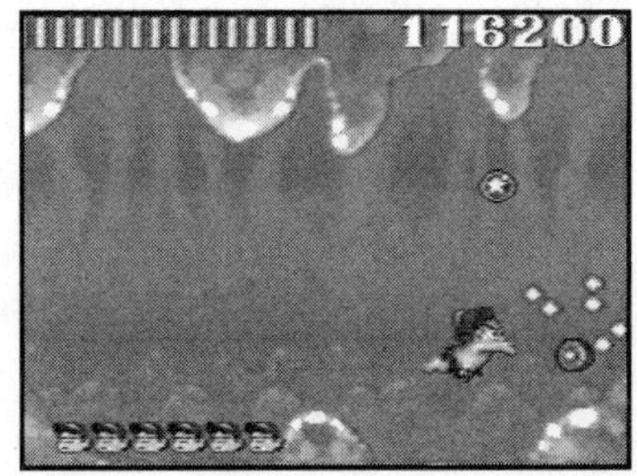

Round 2-4

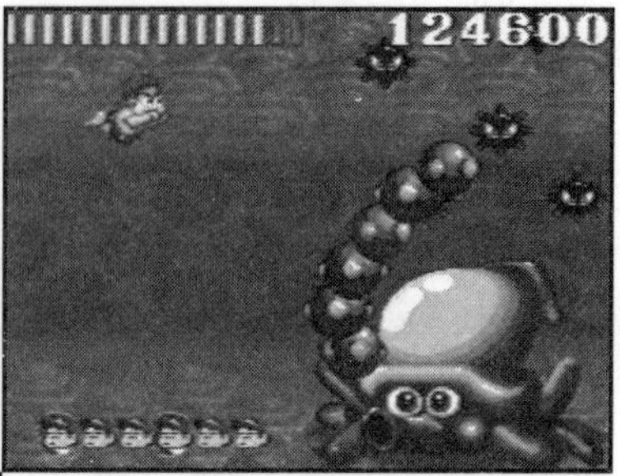

Swim through the black urchins until Kraken appears on the screen. Stay in the upper-left corner of the screen and swim in place. When Kraken lowers his tentacle,

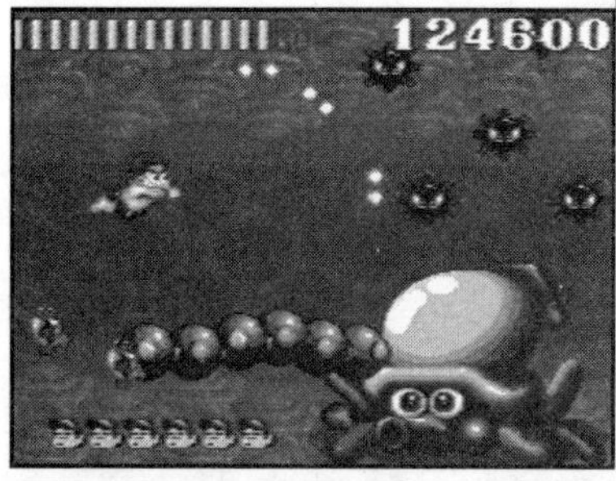

throw some Axes into his head. Kraken will shoot fish that swim upward at you, but you'll always have enough room to dodge them. Don't swim too far to the right, or your Axes will strike the black urchins above Kraken.

If you're stuck with the Boomerang, you'll have to swim directly in front of Kraken, and throw the Boomerangs when he lowers the tentacle. It's very tough to defeat Kraken with the Boomerang, so next time, bring the Axe!

Round 3-1

Enemies: Beezer, Shelly

The best advice for this Round is to move up the three slowly. If you jump upward too fast, you're guaranteed to run into an unexpected enemy, like a Shelly or Beezer. The Beezers are exceptionally tricky in this Round!

There are both types of weapons to be had in the tree, but most of the fruits, both visible and hidden, are on the left branches. Search these branches by throwing your weapon to reveal goodies. Even the Starball is on a left-hand branch (at the top of the tree, naturally).

Round 3-2

Enemies: Bamboon, Blue Reptilly, Skizzer

There's a Skateboard near the beginning of the Round, but it's not easy to get to the end of the Round with it. A large number of bogus Bamboons stands between you and the Starball. Get the Boomerang, since it's a more effective weapon against the Bamboons (especially on the Skateboard).

Round 3-3

Enemies: Bloob, Smokestack Sammy

This abandoned mine has several minecarts. Jump into a minecart and it will start rolling down the tracks. The tracks in this mine are rotted away, so be ready to leap out of the cart when it falls off the tracks and drops off the bottom of the screen.

When you're riding in the second minecart, leap out to grab the fruits in the air. You should be able to land in the minecart again and continue your ride. At the end of the second minecart ride, leap over the gap and you'll snag a Boomerang as you land on the rocky ledge.

The third minecart will take you to the Starball at the end of the Round. With good timing, you can leap out of the minecart and touch the Starball without landing on the ground.

Round 3-4

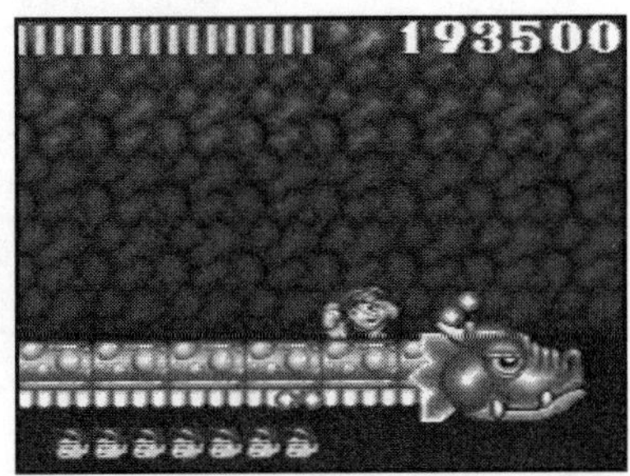

Lavaslither is a tough Boss Master! Shoot his head with your weapon and tears will well up in his eyes, showing that you're doing damage. The more damage you do, the faster Lavaslither will move.

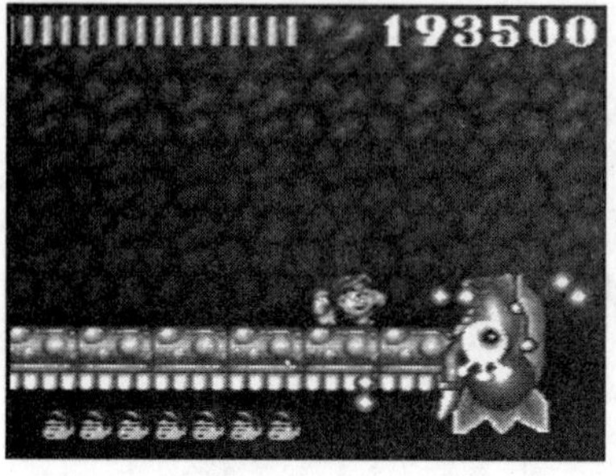

Don't fall off Lavaslither, or you'll tumble into the lava pool below!

The black caves in this Round spew out lava at regular intervals. If you see smoke coming from the mouth of a cave, get away before the lava stream pours out! Don't stay too close to Lavaslither's head or you won't see the smoking caves until it's too late.

Round 4-1

Enemies: Beezer, Blue Reptilly

There are several shielded enemies in this Round. Use the Boomerangs as you did before, throwing them behind the shielded enemy so they strike him from behind as they return to you. There's a Skateboard near the end of the Round; use it to Super Jump over the final shield enemy.

Round 4-2

Enemies: Blue Reptilly, Skullfoot

Collect the Boomerang and hang onto it! You'll need to fire above you, below you, and to the sides, something you can't do with the Axe.

Take your time jumping up the rocky ledges. As in the previous climbing Round (3-1), if you jump upward too quickly, you'll run into enemies without having a chance to attack. Stay on the ledges to the sides and you'll find fruits floating in the air.

When you're almost at the top of the mountain, Skullfoots will appear below you and start jumping upward. Scamper to the highest ledge, then High Jump or Super Jump to the right and touch the Starball. If you miss the Starball, steer yourself to the left as you're falling.

Round 4-3

Enemies: Flounder, Lectron, Wally

This swimming Round is about as easy as the last one. Hold onto the Boomerang, swim to the right, and shoot anything that gets in your way! Don't pick up any Axes along the way, because you'll want the Boomerang against the Boss Master.

Round 4-4

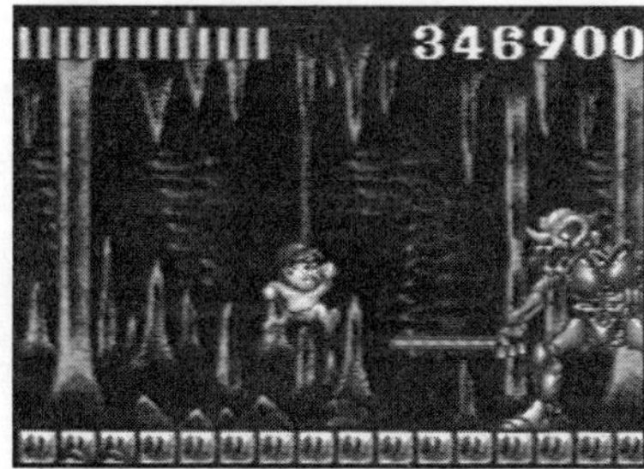

You'll immediately be thrown into the battle with King Reptilian. When he stops walking, move to the left. When the King swings his sword, leap over it and shoot him with the Boomerangs. He'll crumble into a pile of bones, but only for a moment. Run back to the left as he re-forms himself.

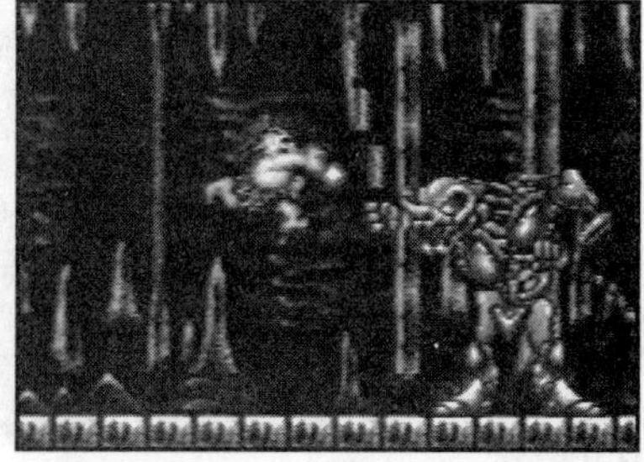

Sometimes, instead of swinging the sword when he stops, the King will leap to the left instead. Run underneath him while he's in the air. If you don't, he'll force you all the way to the left side of the screen.

If your Boomerang is powered up, you'll only need to hit the King three times to defeat him. Weaker weapons will obviously require more hits. Take your time and fight your way to the final Round!

Round 5-1

Enemies: Bamboon, Peppy

This snowy Round will have you slippin' and slidin'. Use quick, light presses of the Control Pad to keep Higgins under control. If you move too fast, you'll slide out of control (and into an attacking Peppy or Bamboon).

There's a Skateboard roughly a third of the way through the Round. The Axe is the better weapon to have while on the Skateboard, because it will strike your enemies as you skate down the snowy hills. If you've got the Boomerang, throw it downward as you skate along.

Round 5-2

Enemies: Skullfoot, Smokestack Sammy

The spotlight is on Master Higgins in this Round! A small circle of light surrounds Higgins at all times, but the rest of the screen is very dark. You can still make out enemies and items, but it's not easy! Look at the top of the screen, since that's where most of the fruits will be.

Starting halfway through the Round, spikes will appear in the floor. Use small jumps to get over the spikes. There's one group of spikes with only a single brick on the left side; use a Super Jump or High Jump to leap over this group.

Round 5-3

Enemies: Bloob, Skizzer, Smokestack Sammy

You're almost there! This final Round takes place inside Dark Cloak's castle. The first part of the Round is simple; just jump to collect the fruits and the weapons (you should use the Boomerang). You probably won't be challenged until you reach the floating platforms.

The normally harmless Skizzers become deadly in this Round because the floating platforms will carry you up into them! Throw the Boomerang straight up to strike the Skizzers before they attack you.

There's an Axe to be had to the left of a group of five fruits. Take the Axe, because you'll need it against Dark Cloak. After the Axe, you'll have to jump up a narrow shaft of floating platforms before you find the Starball. Don't fail now!

Round 5-4

Dark Cloak has several different attacks. The first, and deadliest attack, occurs if you stand too far away from him. Dark Cloak will transform and shoot three white fireballs at you. These fireballs are almost impossible to dodge!

Stay close to Dark Cloak, chucking Axes at him. The Cloakmeister will either run straight at you or jump over you. When he charges at you, leap over him. When he jumps over you, you can either run underneath him or leap even higher than he does (by using the Super Jump).

After you do some damage to Dark Cloak, he'll transform into a huge pink monster! Stand underneath him and trick him into smashing a hole through the floor and into the lava pit. He needs to smash the same part of the floor three times before he'll fall through. Defeat Dark Cloak and you've saved Adventure Island!

SHH . . . THE SECRETS

Star Bonus Rounds

There's a Star Bonus Round hidden in each Area of the game. Use the pictures and text descriptions below to find each of the Rounds. Remember, to reveal the hidden Star, jump into the air above the "tinging" area (see the manual for more details on "tinging").

Round 1-2

The hidden Star is about halfway through the Round. on the right side of a short wall. The wall is to the right of a Shelly.

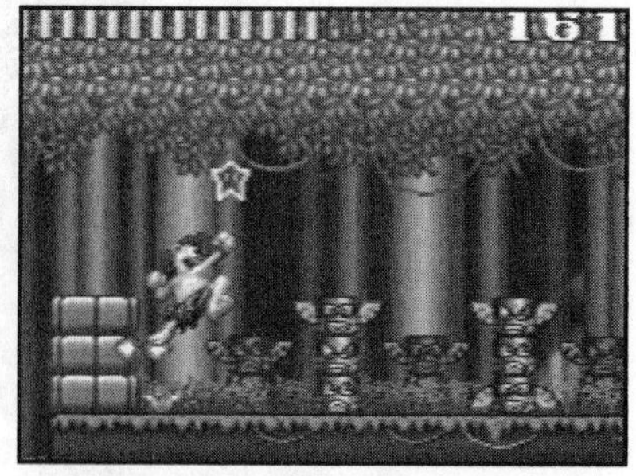

Round 2-2

The hidden Star is above the stationary island near the end of the Round.

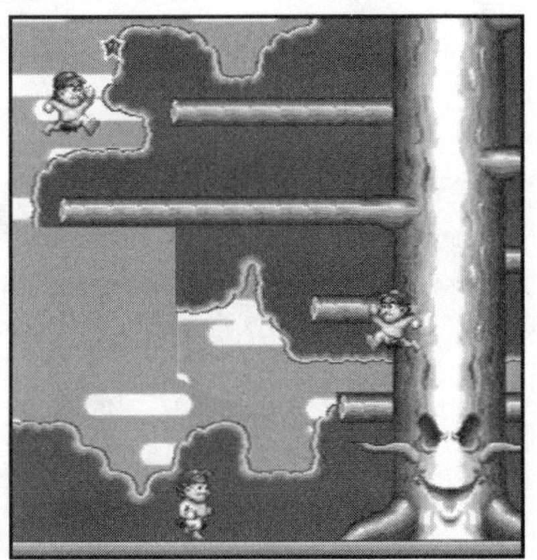

Round 3-1

The hidden Star is on the far left side of the first left-hand branch on the tree.

Round 4-2

The hidden Star is all the way to the right side, about three ledges from the bottom.

Round 5-3

The hidden Star is above the stationary ledge with two green fruits located to the right of it, and a Skizzer above it.

CHAPTER 14

Super Mario World Part 2

By Nintendo of America

In late 1991, we published *Super Mario World Secrets*. At the end of the book, we asked you, our readers, to send in your tips and secrets. The response has been overwhelming! We've received more great tips on Super Mario World than any other game we've ever covered. For this reason, we decided to feature an entire section of exclusive Super Mario World game tips from our awesome readers! If you sent us a tip on the Super Mario World game, look for your name at the end of the chapter. (We received many duplicate tips from different readers, so only the name of the first person to send in a particular tip is listed.)

Keep in mind that this chapter doesn't cover the entire game. It only shows some interesting secrets in some areas of the game. If you want a detailed guide to the Super Mario World game, you want *Super Mario World Secrets*. See the end of the chapter for more details.

GENERAL STRATEGIES

Mario Maneuvers

Here are a few of the more interesting moves Mario can accomplish in the game.

- **Swimming:** Press Up and A or B to swim up through the water at amazing speed. (Can Mario get the bends?) Press Down and A or B to "tread water."
- **Climbing Vines:** It's possible to carry an item up a vine. Pick up the item you want to carry, then walk to the vine. Press Up and release the X or Y button to throw the item straight up. Start climbing the vine and you'll catch the item while climbing!
- **Holding Two Items:** Mario can carry two items at once. Stack the items by taking one of the items to the same space as the other, then pressing Down and X or Y. When the items are in the same space, press X or Y again to pick up both items. This trick is most useful when you're crossing the Giant Gate (to make more bonuses appear).

Giant Gates

If you carry an object across the Giant Gate, you'll get a bonus item. The item you receive depends on several factors.

- If you're a Small Mario, you'll get a Super Mushroom.
- If you're a powered-up Mario, but the Reserve Box is empty, you'll get a power-up equal to your current power. Super Mario gets a Super Mushroom, Fire Mario gets a Fire Flower, and Caped Mario gets a Cape Feather.
- If you're a powered-up Mario, and there's an object in the Reserve Box, you'll receive an Extra Mario Mushroom!

Yoshi

There are four different Yoshis (Blue, Red, Yellow, and Green), and four different Koopa shells. Different combinations of Yoshi and Koopa shell produce different effects.

- Any Yoshi can fly with a Blue Koopa shell in his mouth.
- Any Yoshi can spit fireballs with a Red Koopa shell in his mouth.
- Any Yoshi can stomp dust clouds with a Yellow Koopa shell in his mouth.
- The Green Koopa shell doesn't give any special powers.
- Blue Yoshi can fly with any color of Koopa shell in his mouth.
- Red Yoshi can spit fireballs with any color of Koopa shell in his mouth.
- Yellow Yoshi can stomp dust clouds with any color of Koopa shell in his mouth.
- Green Yoshi doesn't have any special powers unless he has a non-Green Koopa shell in his mouth.

After a certain period of time, Yoshi will swallow any shell in his mouth. You can prevent this from happening by using a simple trick. Press Down and X or Y and Yoshi will spit out the shell. Press X or Y once more and Yoshi will swallow the shell again.

You can also use Yoshi's wondrous tummy to restore Switch Blocks (also known as Pows, Pow Blocks, and P-Switches). Jump onto the Switch Block and have Yoshi swallow the "smoke" of the Block. When Yoshi starts to swallow the Block, press Down and X or Y. Yoshi will spit out a new Switch Block!

WORLD 1: YOSHI'S ISLAND

Yoshi's Island 2

Five 1-Ups

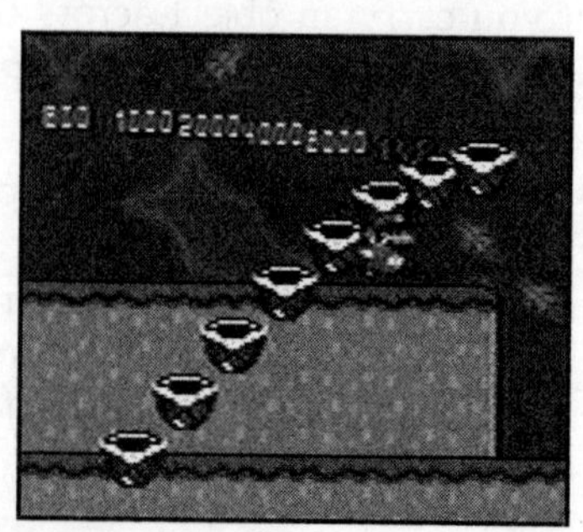

At the start of the level, pick up the Koopa shell and throw it along the ledge of Koopas. Run along behind the shell to the left, and keep running. If you're fast enough to keep the shell on the screen, you'll collect four more 1-Ups as the shell hits more Koopas!

WORLD 2: DONUT PLAINS

Donut Plains 4

Red Apple Trick

To make this awesome trick work, you have to enter this World as Fire Mario, while riding Yoshi, and with a Cape Feather in the Reserve Box at the top of the screen. (You can do all this at the nearby Top Secret Area.) Position yourself so that Yoshi is directly underneath a Red Apple, and that the Reserve Box is directly overhead.

Push Select to drop the Feather out of the Box. Now, here's the tricky part: jump up to grab the Feather and make Yoshi eat the Apple at the same time. If your timing is perfect, the screen will freeze up, but the music will continue to play. Sometimes, your Coins will start shooting upward until you earn 99 lives! Use Start and Select to exit the World.

Donut Secret 1

Inflation Action

Look for an upside-down blue pipe. Swim up into it to enter a dry underground area. Hit the Prize Block and a Power Balloon will come out of it. Jump up and touch the Balloon to become the strangest-looking Mario in the game, Inflated Mario.

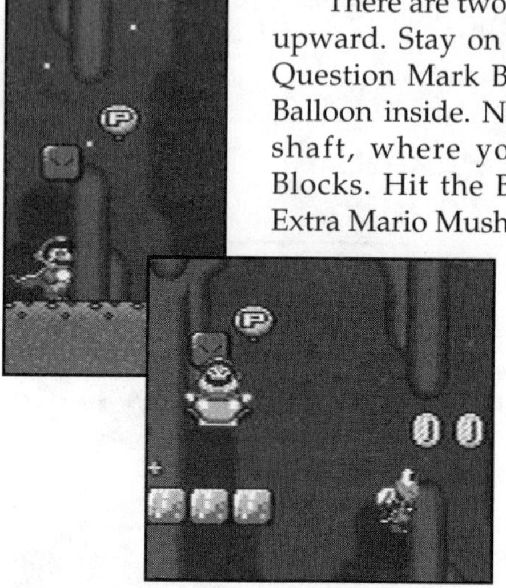

There are two ledges to find as you float upward. Stay on the left and you'll find a Question Mark Block with another Power Balloon inside. Now float to the top of the shaft, where you'll find two Rotating Blocks. Hit the Block on the right for an Extra Mario Mushroom.

Now float to the right side of the area until you're roughly four blocks away from the wall. Wait for the Balloon to wear off and fall straight down. You'll land on (or near) another Question Mark Block. This one contains a Fire Flower, which is very useful for shooting through the fish when you exit this area and return to the water.

Shell 1-Ups

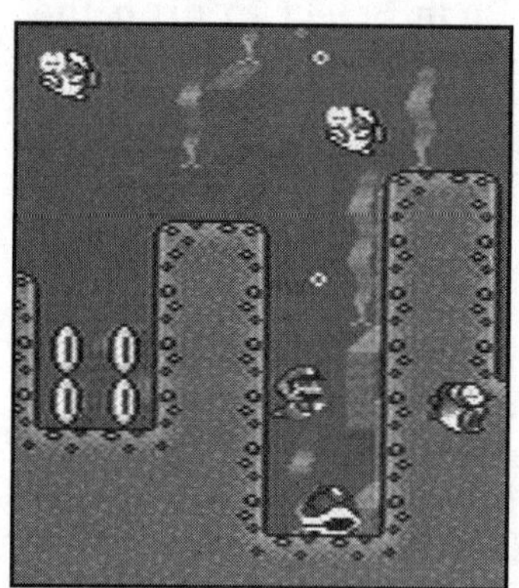

Go into the underground area described in Inflation Action above. Hit one of the Koopas and grab its shell. Take the shell with you as you exit the area. You'll still have the shell when you return to the water.

Drop the shell into the gap with the Dragon Coin, which is just below the exit pipe. Hit the shell from above as it bounces back and forth to earn 1-Ups.

Donut Secret 2

Coin Music Loop

Bring Yoshi to this World. Eat the first Koopa that appears, and walk all the way to the left. Turn around and spit the shell at the Prize Block on the ice. (Jump over the shell as it bounces back to

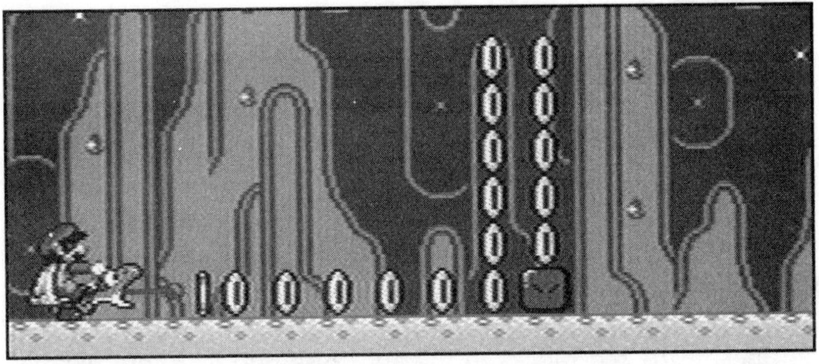

the left.) Steer the coin snake inside the Prize Block directly at Yoshi, and have Yoshi eat the coin at the "head" of the snake. The speedy coin music will continue to play throughout the World.

Morton's Castle

1-Up Pipe

There are two gaps in the roof at the start of the Castle. Bring a Cape here and get a running start to fly up into the leftmost gap. You'll enter a tunnel that takes you to a 1-Up Pipe!

WORLD 3: VANILLA DOME

Vanilla Dome 1

Alternate Path to Second Goal (To Vanilla Secret 1)

You normally get to the second goal by jumping up the red Exclamation Blocks that appear after you've been to the Red Switch Palace. There's a way to get to the second goal without the red Blocks, but you need Yoshi to do it.

Walk to the Prize Block on the ground. You'll see the outlines of the red Blocks in the air. Press B to leap into the air, then press A to jump off Yoshi and hit the Vine Block from below. Move to the right and press B and A again to leap onto the vine. From here, it's an easy climb to the second goal!

Vanilla Dome 2

Underground Mario

You need the Cape for this trick. Make it to the Midway Gate and let the Chargin' Chuck plow through the Rotating Blocks on the right. Defeat the Chuck, then walk up to the Rotating Blocks and use the Cape Spin. Move to the right while using the Spin, then stop and hold Down on the control pad. (You may not need to hold Down.)

Underground Mario — Part 2

You'll fall through the Blocks and into the ground! You can move left and right while underground. Jump up to get out of the ground. You may need to attempt this trick a LOT before it works, so keep trying!

Vanilla Dome 3

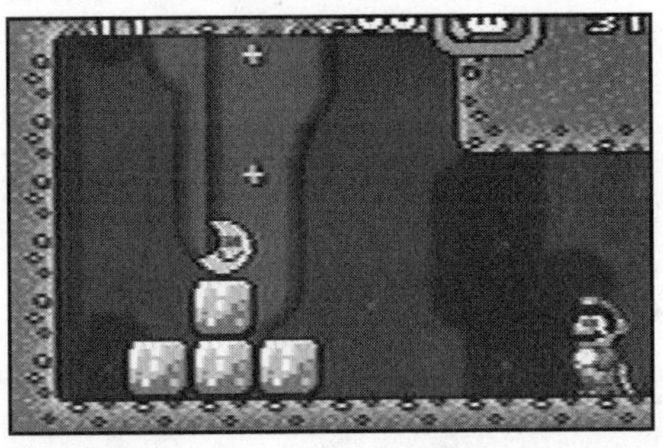

3-Up Moon

Come to this world as Cape Mario. When you reach the two orange pipes with the Invisible Block, take off into the sky and fly to the left. Zoom into the small corridor. At the end of the corridor, you'll find a 3-Up Moon on top of some stone blocks!

Vanilla Dome 4

Weird 1-Up

Walk to the right until you find a Prize Block with a brown Block beneath it. Jump counterclockwise around the brown block and a 1-Up Mushroom will spring forth! Grab the Mushroom quick!

Vanilla Fortress

Bony Beetle 1-Ups

Swim all the way through the Fortress until you reach the red door leading to Reznor. Instead of going through the door, start bouncing onto the two Bony Beetles. Since you're underwater, it's easy to keep from touching the ground, and you can keep hitting the Beetles until you start getting 1-Ups! The only problem with this 1-Up area is the Fishbone that keep swimming from the right side of the screen; he's a pain to avoid.

WORLD 4: COOKIE MOUNTAIN

Cheese Bridge Area

Second Goal (Leads to Soda Lake)

Come to the World with Yoshi and keep going until you reach the long ledge with the yellow pipe on the right side. Get a running start with Yoshi and take off to the right. You'll slowly start to fall. Bounce off a saw blade with Yoshi and keep floating to the right. When you reach the first Giant Gate, float underneath it, then use the Spin Jump to dismount Yoshi and jump onto the ledge behind the Gate. Move to the right for a 3-Up Moon and the second Goal!

Green Yoshi to Blue Yoshi

Bring a plain old Green Yoshi to this World. Hit the Prize Block just past the Midway Gate and grab Yoshi's Wings to enter a bonus Coin stage. When you finish the stage, your Green Yoshi will become a Blue Yoshi!

Ludwig's Castle

1-Up Pipe

The first section of the Castle is filled with Ball'N'Chains and Bony Beetles. You can get rid of the Bony Beetles entirely with the Cape. Otherwise, jump or spin jump onto them (when they're not in spike form) to disable them for a few moments.

Near the end of the section, you can jump upward and through one of the solid-looking blocks. Now move right and jump up the blocks, then go down the green pipe. You're in a 1-Up Pipe! When you exit this pipe, you'll begin at the second section of the Castle.

WORLD 5: THE FOREST OF ILLUSION

Forest of Illusion 4

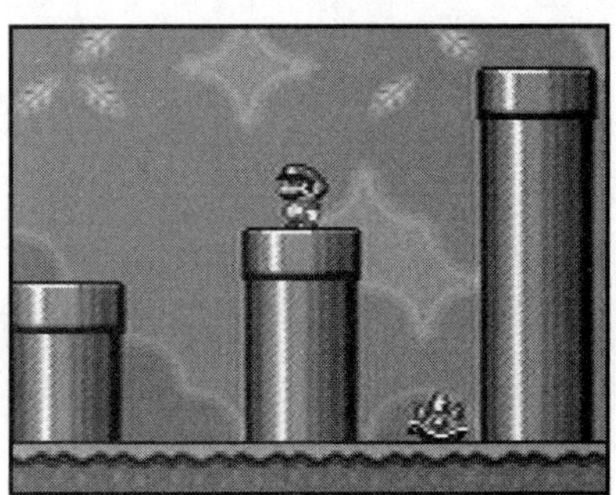

Coin Pipe

Look for a group of three green pipes between the Midway Gate and the Giant Gate. Go down the middle pipe to enter an underwater area with some Coins to collect.

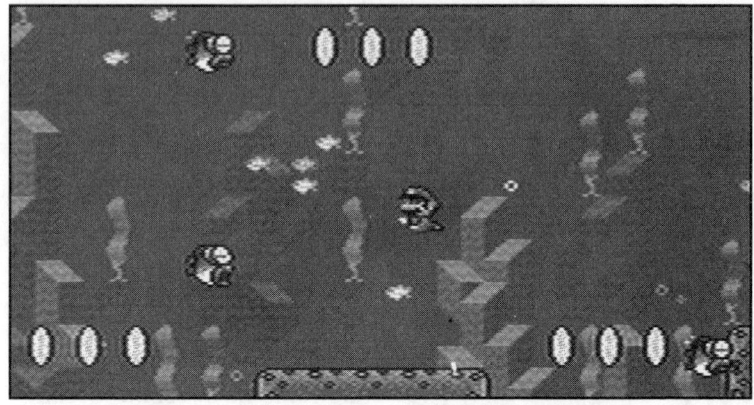

Water world in Forest of Illusion 4.

WORLD 6: CHOCOLATE ISLAND

Chocolate Island 2

Nine Areas

This World is made up of nine areas, but you'll only play through three of them each time you go through the Worlds. (You always start in Area 1.) The amount of Coins you collect, and the number on the Timer, affect which areas you'll visit.

Area 2-1 (Koopa Zone): Collect 0 to 8 Coins in Area 1.
Area 2-2 (Rex Zone): Collect 9 to 20 Coins in Area 1.
Area 2-3 (Flying Zone): Collect 21 or more Coins in Area 1.

Area 3-1 (Second Goal Zone): Complete Area 2 with 250 or more seconds left on the Timer.
Area 3-2 (Dino Zone): Complete Area 2 with 235 to 249 seconds left on the Timer.
Area 3-3 (Bubble Zone): Complete Area 2 with 1 to 234 seconds left on the Timer.

Area 4-1 (Finish Zone): Complete Area 3 with 0 to 3 Dragon Coins collected.
Area 4-2 (Another Finish Zone): Complete Area 3 with 4 Dragon Coins collected.

Sunken Ghost Ship

Bullet Bill 1-Ups

You have to be Super Mario to use this trick. In the first area of the Ship, swim against the bottom of the crate and face to the right. The cannon to the left will fire Bullet Bills into your feet! Keep swimming in place and you'll eventually start getting 1-Ups for each Bullet Bill that hits your feet.

1-Ups in the Water

When you plop into the water at the end of the Ship, don't jump onto the green sphere right away. Instead, swim down into the water. Swim against the wall on the right side of the screen for two 1-Up Mushrooms, and against the wall on the left side of the screen for a single Mushroom. These Mushrooms don't appear all the time, so don't be surprised if you don't find them.

WORLD 7: THE VALLEY OF BOWSER

Larry's Castle

A Wild Ride on the Brown Blocks

The first half of the Castle is a ride on a long brown block snake. Keep up with it as it wiggles and worms around the Ball'N'Chains. It will take quite a few plays before you start to memorize the snake's pattern, but keep at it. You may want to bring a Cape here for its floating ability.

There's an easy way to shorten your snake ride. Near the start of the area, wait until the snake goes past the first Ball'N'Chain and flattens out. Quickly jump up and left, then curve back to the right and land on the ledge above. Now you can wait here until the snake passes by! This will bypass about half of the snake ride.

It's also possible to avoid riding the snake altogether. To do this, try bringing along the Cape and flying the friendly screens. Take off at the beginning of the level and use The Pump (see the General Strategies) to stay airborne and gain altitude!

Midway Gate

To find the Midway Gate, ride the block snake until you reach the ledge with the door to the second half of the Castle. Don't jump onto the ledge. Instead, ride the snake straight down and it will take you to the Midway Gate (along with two Dragon Coins and a Super Mushroom).

Bowser's Castle

Battle Bowser the Hard Way

Do you find Bowser to be a real creampuff? Try this tough technique! You must make it to Bowser as Cape Mario. Now, instead of throwing the Mechakoopas up at Bowser, use the Cape to fly into the air and drop the Mechakoopas down at Bowser!

Mechakoopa Madness

Go into the Front Door of the Castle, then go into Door 3. Stomp onto a Mechakoopa with a regular jump (so you don't destroy it) and walk to one of the gray stone walls.

Put the Mechakoopa into the wall and wait for it to revive. The Mechakoopa will start vibrating rapidly inside the wall!

THE STAR ROAD

Star World 1

Pushy Blocks

Here's a strange way to lose a life. Get into an area with many Rotating Blocks. Hit some of the Blocks to make them spin, then get yourself trapped in the Blocks. If you do it correctly, the Blocks will push you to the left, into a wall, and kill you!

Star World 5

Second Goal (Leads to Special Zone)

To use this method of getting to the key, you must NOT have tripped the Blue Switch, and you MUST have the Cape. Take off at the start of the World and fly to the right until you hit the green pipe. Drop to the ledge below the pipe and knock away the Spinys with your Cape Spin.

Walk to the right side of the ledge and get a running start to the left. Fly straight into the air and through the small hole to the Key. It's tough, so if you miss, fall back down to the ledge and try again.

Yet another way to reach the key is to bring a Blue Yoshi to this World. Make it all the way to the green pipe and have Yoshi swallow the Koopa. Now you can fly up to the key.

THE SPECIAL WORLD

Metallic Music

When you walk onto the map of the Special Zone, let the music play for a few minutes and it will change into a steel drum version of the music from the original Super Mario Bros.!

Gnarly (Special World 1)

Extra Mario Mushroom

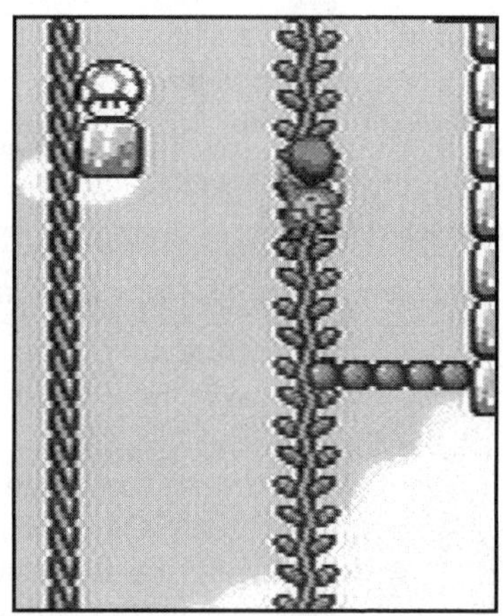

Here's an easy way to get the Mushroom in the upper-left corner of the first area in this World. Hit the second Vine Block from the left and start climbing up until you're at the top of the vine. When the vine is about to hit the Rotating Block, jump up and strike the block. The vine will keep growing, all the way up to the Extra Mario Mushroom.

Awesome (Special World 4)

Easy Clearance

Come to this World with the Green Yoshi from Way Cool (Special World 3). Play through the World until you reach the green flying Koopa. Have Yoshi eat the Koopa and you can fly through the rest of the World easily! (You can also have Yoshi eat the Rainbow Koopa shells at the beginning of the World for flying powers.)

Funky (Special World 8)

Speedy Music

You need to bring a Yoshi to this World for this trick (you can get Yoshi in Special World 5, Groovy). Walk to a Green Apple, but don't eat it immediately. Wait until the Timer falls under 100, then eat the Apple. Now run to the right and find another Apple. Wait for the Timer to go under 100 again. Keep repeating this trick until the music is playing at incredible speed!

SHH . . . THE SECRETS

1-Up Pipe

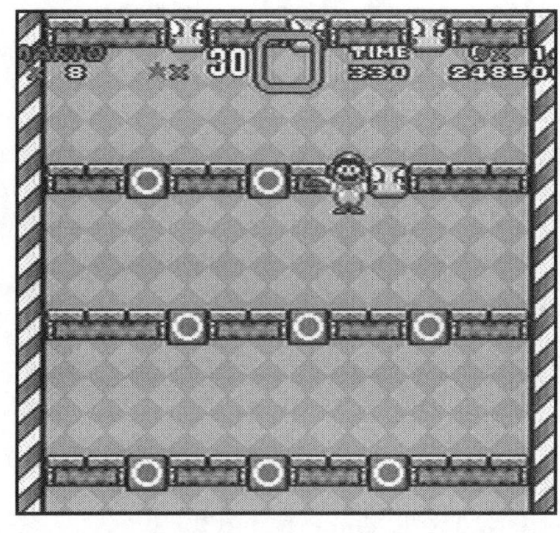

To get a 1-Up on every row of the Pipe, you need the Cape. Use the Spin Jump to hit the left side of each Question Mark Block with the Cape. Start with the left Block on each row, then hit the middle Block, then the right Block; if you don't hit them in this order, you won't get the 1-Up Mushroom. Do this trick correctly and you'll get five 1-Ups every time!

1-Up Timer

This trick isn't easy to do, but it's definitely interesting! You use the trick at the Giant Gate, when you break the moving tape to earn Stars. If the **first** digit of the number of Stars you receive equals the **last two** digits of the Timer, you'll earn a 1-Up Mushroom. For example, if you break the tape to earn **24** Stars, and the Timer says 1**22**, you'll earn a 1-Up Mushroom.

1,000 At A Time

Here's a trick you can perform in any area where you can perch underneath the Reserve Box at the top of the screen. Only two combinations will make this trick work. You must be a Caped Mario, with a Fire Flower in the Reserve Box; or you must be a Fire Mario, with a Cape Feather in the Reserve Box.

Maneuver yourself underneath the Reserve Box and start hitting the SELECT button rapidly. The power-ups will start falling from the Box, constantly changing Mario, and giving you 1,000 points every time! This trick will also slow down the game timer considerably, giving you plenty of time to rack up the points!

Blockless Challenge

One particularly daring reader sent in this challenge for Mario Masters: complete 92 goals without finishing any of the Switch Palaces (the Palaces are the other 4 goals). If you think the Super Mario World game is easy, you'll change your mind after taking on this challenge!

Dolphin-Safe Mario

In *Super Mario World Secrets*, we stated that Yoshi could eat dolphins. This is true for the Japanese version of the Super Mario World game, but in the U.S. version of the game, you can't munch the friendly cetaceans. Thumbs up to Nintendo for making Super Mario World a "dolphin safe" game!

Objects Into Objects

In some Worlds, you can kick objects into seemingly solid places! For example, in Vanilla Dome 2, you can boot the Switch Block into the hill. One reader reported kicking a Spring Board into an orange pipe in the Special World, Outrageous. Let us know where else you've been able to do strange stuff with objects!

Reader Roundup

Thanks to the following readers for their great Super Mario World game tips: **Tyler Baber** (Cartersville, Virginia); **Victor Ban** (Sugar Land, Texas); **Jonathan Brukirer** (Nepean, Ontario, Canada); **Jason Chan** (Westlake Village, California); **Angela Chapman** (Soquel, California); **Chris Crampton** (Washington, D.C.); **Jennifer, Amy,**

Anna, and John Dearinger (Santa Cruz, California); **Mario DeLecce** (Kihei, Hawaii); **Robert Scott Eckhart** (Virginia Beach, Virginia); **Stephen Esposito** (Hampton, Virginia); **Rebecca Lennen** (Burtonsville, Maryland); **Brad Loiland** (Grand Forks, North Dakota); **Timmy McIntosh** (Bellevue, Nebraska); **Stephen Mucchetti** (Lincoln, Massachusetts); **Sharon, Rachel, Sara, and Greg Prescott** (Macedonia, Ohio); **Grant Walker** (Highland, Illinois); **Chris and Jeremy Whitney** (Rutland, Vermont).

MORE SECRETS... MORE SECRETS...

Do you want to know everything about the Super Mario World game? There are a lot of other tricks, secrets, and hidden worlds. In fact, we had so much information about the Super Mario World game that there's no way we could have put it all into this chapter. So we wrote an entire book about it! It's called *Super Mario World Secrets*. It's by Rusel DeMaria and Zach Meston and it's available from Prima Publishing.

Super Mario World Secrets has all the information you'll ever need about the Super Mario World game—where to find every World, how to find every goal, and super-secret tricks you won't find anywhere else! Look for *Super Mario World Secrets* at your nearest bookstore, or see the order form at the end of this book!

The One-Page Goal Checklist

- ___ Yellow Switch Palace
- ___ Yoshi's Island 1
- ___ Yoshi's Island 2
- ___ Yoshi's Island 3
- ___ Yoshi's Island 4
- ___ Iggy's Castle
- ___ Yoshi's House

- ___ Donut Plains 1 ___
- ___ Donut Plains 2 ___
- ___ Green Switch Palace
- ___ Donut Ghost House ___
- ___ Top Secret Area
- ___ Donut Secret 1 ___
- ___ Donut Secret House ___
- ___ Star Road
- ___ Pipe to Donut Secret 2
- ___ Pipe from Donut Secret 2
- ___ Donut Plains 3
- ___ Donut Plains 4
- ___ Morton's Castle

- ___ Vanilla Dome 1 ___
- ___ Vanilla Dome 2 ___
- ___ Red Switch Palace
- ___ Vanilla Ghost House
- ___ Vanilla Dome 3
- ___ Vanilla Dome 4
- ___ Lemmy's Castle
- ___ Pipe to Cheese Bridge Area
- ___ Vanilla Secret 1 ___
- ___ Star Road
- ___ Pipe to Vanilla Secret 2

- ___ Vanilla Secret 2
- ___ Vanilla Secret 3
- ___ Vanilla Fortress
- ___ Butter Bridge 1
- ___ Butter Bridge 2
- ___ Cheese Bridge Area ___
- ___ Cookie Mountain
- ___ Soda Lake
- ___ Star Road
- ___ Ludwig's Castle

- ___ Forest of Illusion 1 ___
- ___ Forest Ghost House ___
- ___ Forest of Illusion 2 ___

- ___ Blue Switch Palace
- ___ Forest of Illusion 3 ___
- ___ Forest of Illusion 4 ___
- ___ Forest Secret Area
- ___ Forest Fortress
- ___ Star Road
- ___ Roy's Castle

- ___ Chocolate Island 1
- ___ Choco-Ghost House
- ___ Chocolate Island 2 ___
- ___ Chocolate Island 3 ___
- ___ Pipe to Chocolate Secret
- ___ Pipe from Chocolate Secret
- ___ Chocolate Fortress
- ___ Chocolate Island 4
- ___ Chocolate Island 5
- ___ Wendy's Castle
- ___ Sunken Ghost Ship

- ___ Donut Secret 2
- ___ Chocolate Secret
- ___ Valley of Bowser 1
- ___ Valley of Bowser 2 ___
- ___ Valley Fortress
- ___ Back Door
- ___ Valley Ghost House ___
- ___ Valley of Bowser 3
- ___ Valley of Bowser 4 ___
- ___ Star Road
- ___ Larry's Castle
- ___ Front Door

- ___ Star World 1 ___
- ___ Star World 2 ___
- ___ Star World 3 ___
- ___ Star World 4 ___
- ___ Star World 5 ___
- ___ Star Road to Special Worlds

- ___ Gnarly
- ___ Tubular
- ___ Way Cool
- ___ Awesome
- ___ Groovy
- ___ Mondo
- ___ Outrageous
- ___ Funky

CHAPTER 15

Wanderers from Ys III

by American Sammy

WHAT'S GOING ON?

The adventurous Adol and his best friend Dogi were exploring the world when they started to hear strange rumors about Felgana, Dogi's homeland. They traveled to Redmont, the town where Dogi had been born, to find out what was going on. What they discovered was the beginning of their greatest adventure ever!

PLAYERS

Wanderers From Ys III is for one player only.

SCORING

Like most RPGs, you don't score points in this game. Instead, you earn Experience Points and Gold for each monster you defeat. As you build your Experience Points, you'll reach higher levels of strength. You'll use the Gold to buy weapons and special items.

LIVES AND CONTINUES

Adol has one life, and his strength is measured with Hit Points. Every time Adol gets hit by a monster, he loses Hit Points. If he runs out of Hit Points, the game is over.

You can save the game at any point (except when you're in battle against a Boss creature). There are three save slots on the cartridge. Save often! If you die, you'll be allowed to load a game from one of the save slots.

CONTROLS

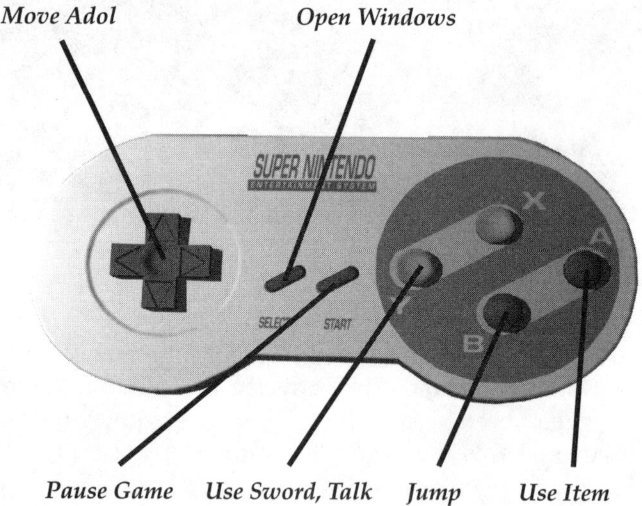

WEAPONS

There are five different swords in the game. You'll start the game completely unarmed, so buy yourself a weapon from Adniss' Tool Store right away!

The **Short Sword** is weak, but inexpensive.

The **Long Sword** is an improvement over the Short Sword, but it's still a puny weapon.

The **Broad Sword** is strong. This is the best sword you can purchase at Adniss' Tool Store.

The **Banded Slayer** will be given to you by Dogi's Master when you reach the Mountain Hut in the Eldam Mountains.

The **Flame Sword** is found deep within Ballacetine Castle. It's the strongest weapon you can have!

ARMOR

There are five types of armor, and five shields. Some of them can be purchased in Adniss' Tool Store, but the strongest items will have to be found on your adventures!

Armor

Leather Armor is weak, but it's all you can afford at first.

Chain Mail is stronger than the Leather Armor. You'll want to buy this Armor as soon as you can afford it.

Plate Mail is excellent armor. You'll find it inside the Warehouse at the Tigray Qurray.

Banded Armor is for sale at the Tool Store, but you'll need a whopping 8,000 Gold to buy it!

Battle Armor is the strongest armor of all. You'll find it in Ballacetine Castle.

Shields

The **Wooden Shield** isn't much protection, but it's better than nothing!

The **Small Shield** can be found in the Ilvern Ruins. By the time you find it, you may already own the Large Shield!

The **Large Shield** is excellent protection, but it's expensive.

The **Banded Shield** is the most expensive shield in Adniss' Tool Store.

The **Battle Shield** can be found in the Ballacetine Castle.

SPECIAL ITEMS

There are two types of Special Items: Magic Rings and items for sale in Cinthea's Supply Store.

Rings

Magic Rings are powered by your Ring Points. You earn a few Ring Points every time you defeat an enemy. You can have a maximum of 255 Ring Points. If you run low on Ring Points, you can buy Ring Point recharges at Cinthea's Supply Store for 100 Gold (and you'll probably want to do this, since it takes a long time to regain Ring Points by killing monsters). There are five different Rings in the game.

The **Power Ring** doubles the damage you cause with your attack. Handy against strong Bosses!

The **Shield Ring** halves the damage you take from enemy attacks.

The **Heal Ring** exchanges Ring Points for Hit Points. Obviously, it sucks away a lot of Ring Points if you're low on Hit Points.

The **Time Ring** slows down your enemies. Helpful against fast enemies.

The **Protect Ring** keeps you from suffering any damage whatsoever. A very handy Ring against one Boss in particular.

Other Items

The **Herb** fully restores your Hit Points.

Brocia's Secret Medicine fully restores your Ring Points.

The **Illusion Mirror** will freeze any monsters on the screen. Use it too much and it will shatter!

The **Amulet** destroys all the enemies on the screen. It only works three times. It won't destroy a Boss, but it will do some damage.

The **Fairy Necklace** is like an extra life. If you run out of Hit Points, the Fairy Necklace will restore all your Hit Points automatically. This is different from the Herb, which you have to access the Menu Screen to use.

FRIENDS

Redmont is full of friendly folk that will gladly talk your ear off. Talk to them whenever you're in town to see if they have anything new to say. One of these townsfolk, Ellena, is especially fond of Adol, and you'll meet up with her several times during the quest.

ENEMIES

You've got a ton of enemies to face. They're described in detail throughout the Strategy Session. Read on!

STRATEGY SESSION

General Strategies

• Save the game whenever you enter a dangerous new area, or just before you enter battle with a Boss. If you mess up, load the saved game and try it again.
• Return to Redmont often to see if you can buy better weapons at Adniss' Tool Store. The better your sword and armor, the better you'll do in the game. Don't be afraid to spend Gold—you'll always be able to earn more.
• Purchase the Amulet to use against enemy Bosses. It won't do much damage, but every little bit helps!
• We've provided detailed maps of each of the locations in the game. The Strategy Session will refer to certain Areas on reach Map that you have to visit. These Areas will be plainly labeled, so you'll be able to locate them on the map with no problems.

Redmont

Head for Adniss' Tool Store right away. Buy yourself the Wooden Sword, Leather Armor, and Wooden Shield. Remember to equip them all from the Menu Screen. You'll have 100 Gold left over to buy an Herb at Cinthea's Supply Store. Buy it and head out of town. Talk to the guard before you walk out of town and head for...

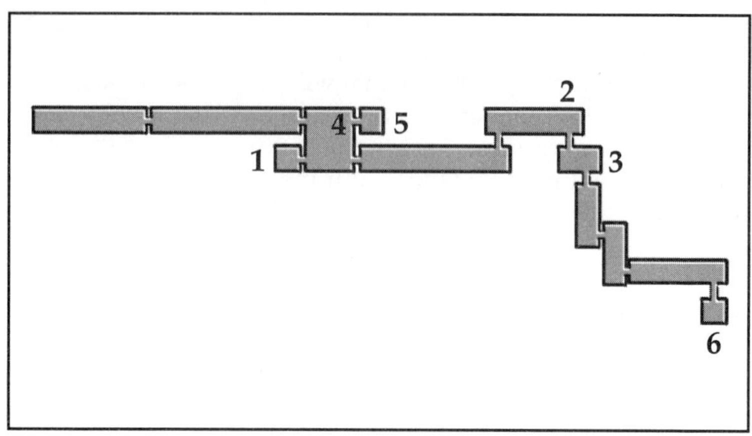

Tigray Qurray

You're very weak at the start of the game, so your first objective is to build your Experience Points. Stay at the beginning of the Quarry, using your sword to slash the Gulmurus and Keyrons. There's one spot next to the entrance where Keyrons will come onto the screen endlessly (see The Secrets for details). If you run low on Hit Points, run outside and you'll be healed. Save the game before you go back inside.

You should build yourself up to at least Level 5 before you start your real quest into the Quarry. Your first destination is Area 1, where you'll find a locked door and a treasure chest. Open the chest to find the Power Ring! You won't be able to unlock the door for a long time yet, so ignore it for now.

Run back outside the Quarry after obtaining the Ring. Save the game and go back to Redmont for an Herb (and better weapons and armor if you can afford it). Return to the Quarry. This time, go to Area 2. You'll find a chest with Robert's Pendant inside. Take the Pendant back to Redmont and go into Aida's house (she's in the building to the left of the Supply Store). She'll notice the Pendant and give you the Shield Ring.

Your next goal in the Quarry is Area 3, where you'll receive the Warehouse Key. After you collect it, you're ready for your first Boss encounter. Save the game, return to Redmont for any supplies, and then go to Area 4. To get there, jump into the upper-right corner of the large room in the Quarry (with the waterfall in the background). Leap up the rocks and go off the screen to the right.

Area 5 is the hideout of Dulan! Put on the Power Ring and use it against Dulan. Hold the controller Down and use the Crouch and Thrust move.

It may take you a few tries to beat Dulan, so make sure you've saved the game before you go into battle.

When Dulan goes down, you'll earn the Long Sword. Excellent! Equip the Sword and check your Gold. If you've got 1500 or more Gold, go back to Redmont and buy yourself the Chain Mail (if you don't already have it). You need the Chain Mail before you go to Area 6 and fight Elefeir.

Crawl on your belly until you're close (but not too close) to Elefeir. Duck under the three lighting bolts that Elefeir shoots at you. After the third bolt passes over you, stand up, run to the right, leap straight up, and slash Elefeir. Run back to the left before Elefeir fries you with lightning. This move takes some timing. Don't try to Jump and Slash as you're moving, or you'll jump into Elefeir and take damage.

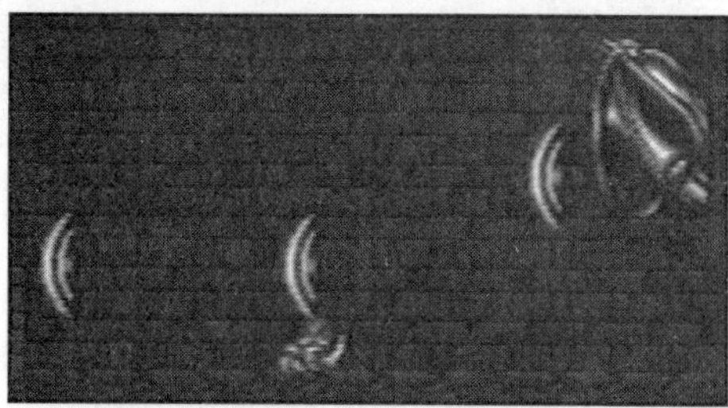

Crawl toward Elefeir . . .

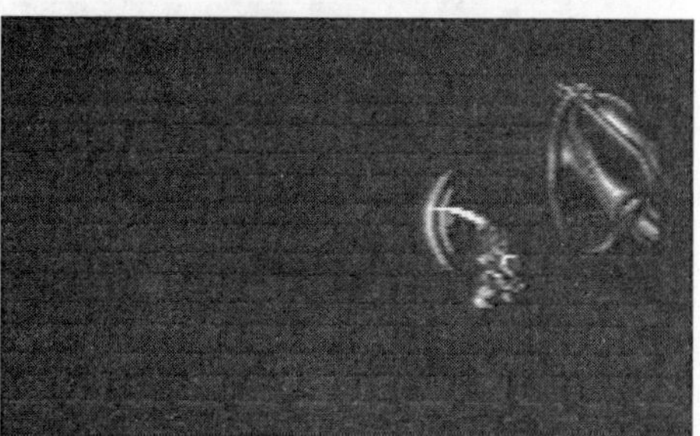

Jump and strike . . .

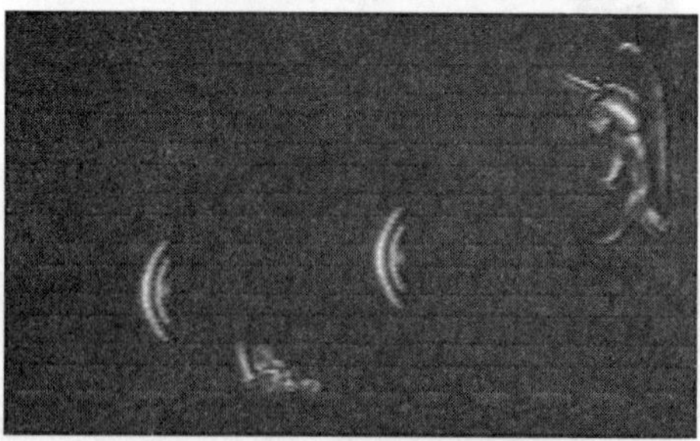

Then quickly retreat!

When you take out Elefeir, you'll get a Statue. Walk into the room to the right and you'll find two people: Chester and Mayor Edgar. Chester will leave. Walk up the stairs and talk to Mayor Edgar. You'll leave the Quarry.

Return to Redmont and go to the Inn. Talk to Ellena and Dogi, and you'll be ready for your next destination...

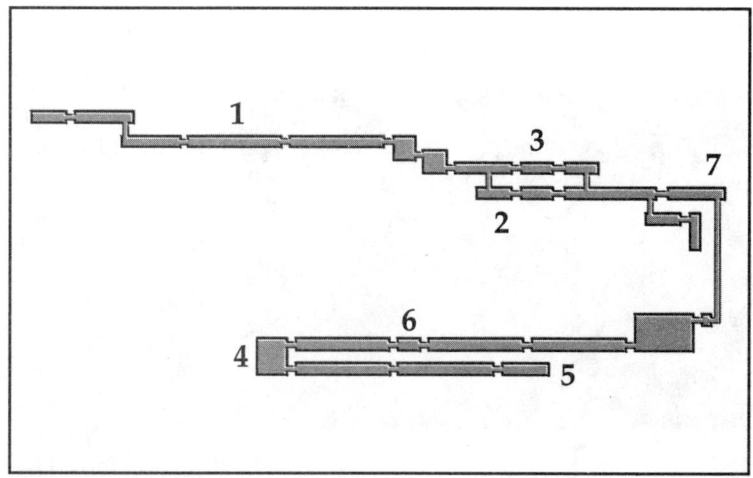

Ilvern Ruins

Your first task in the Ruins is to build up your Experience Points. You'll want to be at a minimum of Level 7 or 8 to face the dangers ahead. Travel to Area 1 on the map, where you'll be attacked constantly by Fuzzles. Stand in one place and use the Thrust Up maneuver continuously to strike the Fuzzles as they swoop at you. You'll earn 20 Experience Points for every Fuzzel that you strike. The Fuzzles will wear your Hit Points down quickly, so be ready to run back to Redmont to recharge yourself.

Once you're strong enough to adventure on, journey to Area 2 on the map. You'll find the Small Shield. Go to the Menu Screen and equip yourself with the new Shield.

Walk to Area 3 on the map. You'll overhear Cleric Pierre, the man from the Tigray Qurray, talking with Chester, Ellena's brother! Unfortunately, neither of them are particularly happy to see you. After being captured, you'll be cast down into the lava pit.

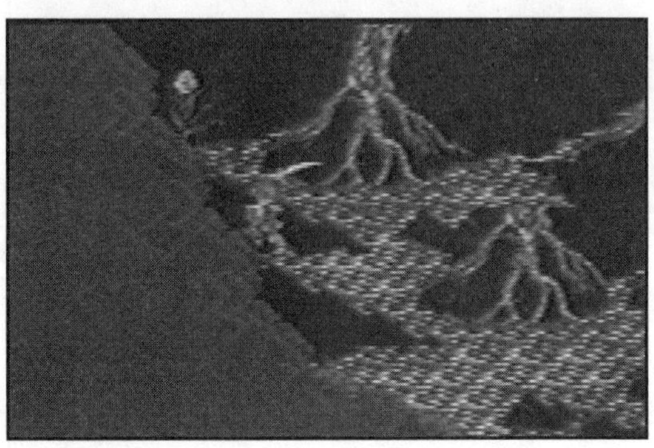

You'll land at the point indicated on the map. Travel to the left and fight through the lava monsters to reach Area 4. Jump up the rocks on the left side and you'll see a flower. Press the B button to collect the flower, which is an Herb! Use the Herb, walk off the screen, and then come back. You'll find another Herb to take!

With the Herb in your possession, walk to Area 5. At one point during your journey, you'll be chased by huge streams of lava! Jump over any rocks in your way and keep running to the right, or you'll be fried.

When you reach Area 5, get ready to fight Gilan, a mighty fire dragon! Gilan erupts from the ground and flies around in the air for a few seconds. He then drops to the ground before starting his aerial attack again. Use the Thrust Up and the Jump and Swing techniques to strike Gilan in the head. You should use the Power Ring (for double damage) or the Shield Ring (to protect yourself from Gilan's fiery body). When Gilan is defeated, you'll earn the Fire Dragon's Amulet.

You've got a long walk up to Area 6. When you reach it, walk next to the lava flow. You'll use the Amulet to dry up the flow! Now you can walk across safely.

Travel to Area 7. You'll meet Ellena along the way. After some interesting plot developments, you'll be in front of the door that leads to Gyalva! Save the game at this point. By now, you should have at least 8,000 Gold. (If you don't, go build up your Gold at Area 1.) Return to Redmont and buy the Broad Sword at Adniss' Tool Store. You need its strength to fight against Gyalva. You should also buy an Herb if you need one.

Before you fight Gyalva, make sure you're powered up to Level 9 or 10. You'll need to be strong for your next Boss battle!

Once you've achieved Level 9 or 10, return to Area 7. Save the game and go through the door. Walk to the right until the music changes. This tells you that Gyalva has arrived!

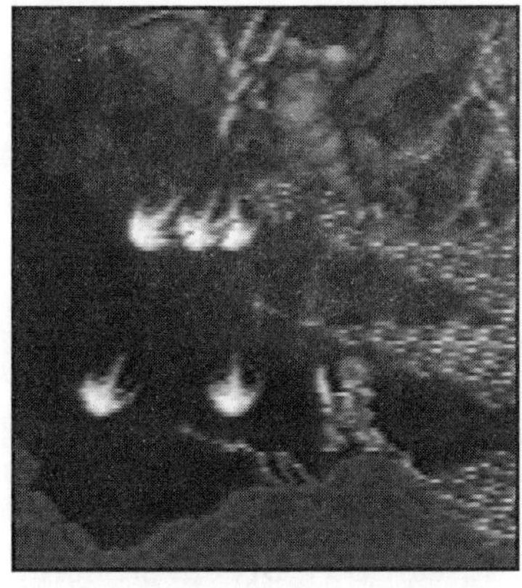

Gyalva starts to fly very fast before unleashing a barrage of fireballs. Stay below and to the right of Gyalva to dodge he fireballs. After Gyalva has attacked, climb onto the stone pillar and use the Jump and Slash to strike. Use the Power Ring to cause additional damage. If you get dangerously low on Hit Points, use the Herb. When you defeat Gyalva, you'll earn the Star Statue.

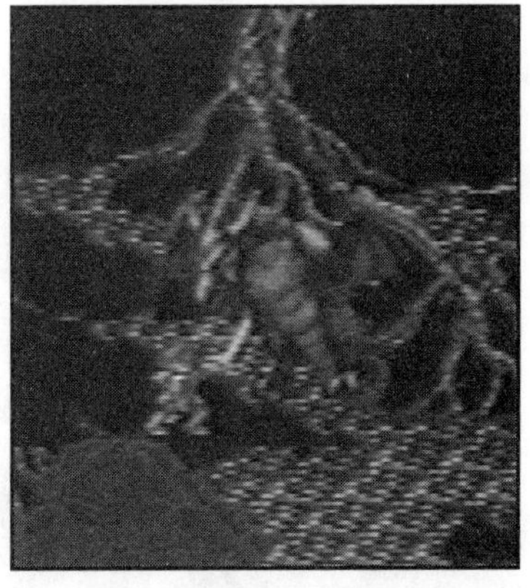

Return to Area 7 and you'll encounter Chester. He'll be about to attack you when Ellena intervenes. She'll travel back to Redmont with you. Walk into town and Dogi will tell you that he's leaving. He'll also mention that Mayor Edgar wants to talk with you.

Go into Mayor Edgar's house. Accept his offer to join and he'll give you the Time Ring! Now you must travel back to...

TIGRAY QURRAY

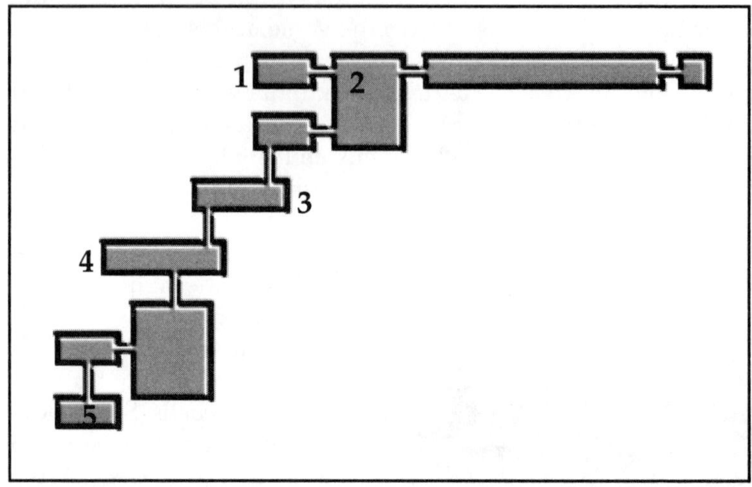

Remember the locked door next to the chest with the Power Ring? Walk down to it (it's located at Area 1 on the map). You'll meet someone there who will explain the situation. Go through the door. This section of the Quarry is Map 2 (the other area of the Quarry is Map 1).

Walk to the left to reach Area 1. The chest contains the Shining Crystal. Return to Redmont with the Crystal and enter Cinthea's Supply Store. Now you can buy Brocia's Secret Medicine, which recharges some of your Ring Points. The Medicine costs a steep 1000 Gold. Purchase an Herb if you need one and return to the Quarry.

Travel to Area 2 on Map 2. At this point, crawl underneath the wooden platform to fall down the shaft. Watch out for the Rowbals along the walls of the shaft. If you land on a Rowbal, jump away quick!

Move on to Area 3. The three men can't open the treasure chest, but you can, thanks to the powers of your statues. Inside the chest, you'll find a Tablet. Once you take the Tablet, the entire Quarry will begin to shake! When the earthquake is over, you'll be told of the legend on the Tablet.

Time to move on to Area 4, where you'll find a treasure chest with Plate Mail inside. Equip yourself with the Armor and make your way down to Area 5. Save the game before you enter into battle. You should have an Herb (and Brocia's Secret Medicine) with you. If you don't, go back to Redmont, buy them, and return here.

Istarjibar is a really tough creature! You should be at Level 11 or higher before you enter battle. There are two ways to attack. You can use the Shield Ring to protect yourself from damage, or use the Power Ring to do extra damage. (The Power Ring worked better for us.)

Leap up into the air to Jump and Slash. Land on the rocks below Istersiva so you can slash him repeatedly! With the Power Ring activated, you'll be able to damage Istarjibar faster than he damages you.

When Istarjibar is beaten, you'll gain the Flash Statue! Find your way back to the door and you'll automatically be taken back to the Quarry entrance. Walk back to Redmont and enter Mayor Edgar's house. Mayor Edgar will give you Edgar's Letter and direct you to the next area...

Eldam Mountains

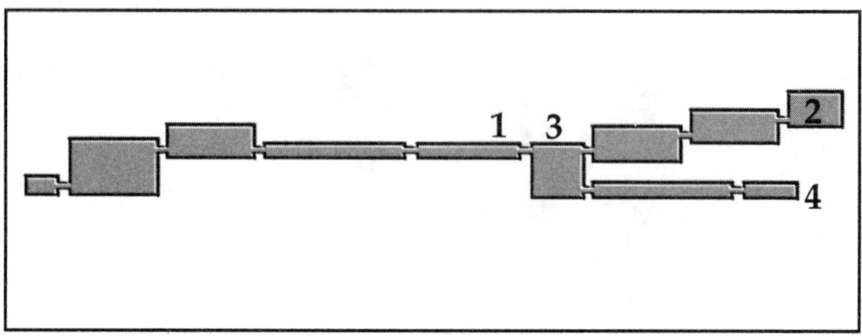

Before you start exploring, check your Experience Level. If you haven't reached Level 12 yet, go to the Tigray Qurray or Ilvern Ruins and build your experience. You'll need to be pumped up to survive the attacks of the monsters in these mountains!

You should also have the Banded Shield by now. If you don't, return to the Quarry or Ruins and earn 10,000 Gold, then go to the Tool Store and buy it. You'll need its defensive strength.

Travel to Area 1 on the map. Keep jumping into the air to avoid the attacking Halics and Iruvas. The Halics are especially vicious creatures. When you reach Area 1, Dogi will come out of the Mountain Cabin to greet you.

You'll be taken inside and given the Banded Sword. Equip it and prepare yourself for the next part of the journey. (Whenever you're in the Eldam Mountains and running low on Hit Points, return to the Cabin and talk to Dogi's Master. Your Hit Points will fully recharge!)

Travel to Area 2. Along the way, you'll pass Area 3, where a Silent Statue sits. You won't be able to do anything here yet, so keep going.

In Area 2, you'll encounter Ligaety, a flying harpy who shoots lightning balls at you! Use the Power Ring as you Jump and Slash Ligaety. You'll do double damage and make short

work of her. When she's beaten, you'll gain the Judgment Staff.

Return to Area 3. You'll use the Staff to melt away the snopw beneath the Silent Statue. Now you have access to Area 4, but you should be at Level 13 or higher before you go there. If you need to build your Experience Points, go back and forth between the start of Eldam Mountains and the Mountain Cabin. You'll be able to continually replenish your Hit Points as you power up.

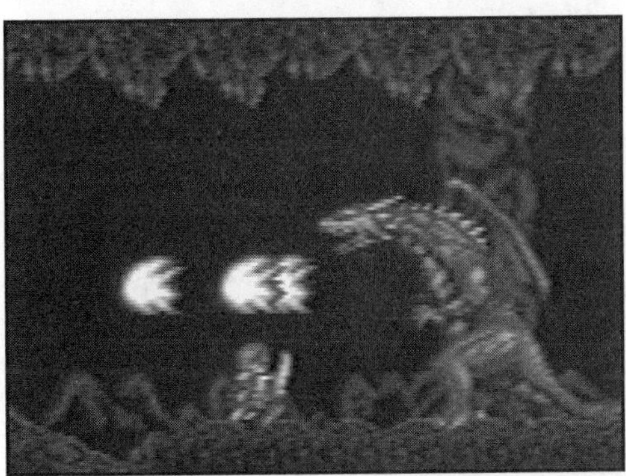

Once you're at Level 13, go to Area 4. Gildas is waiting here for you! Equip yourself with the Power Ring, then Jump and Slash Gildas' head. He'll try to toast you with fireballs, but as long as you keep jumping and attacking, you'll kill him before he kills you! When Gildas is defeated, you'll get the Dark Statue.

At this point, the evil Chester will walk onto the screen and demand the Dark Statue! He won't have a chance to take it, because a massive cave-in will trap you with Chester! Move to the left and talk to Chester. This will be the start of a long sequence. When the sequence is over, you'll be back in Redmont with Dogi and receive the valuable Healing Ring! The people of Redmont have been kidnaped and taken to...

Ballacetine Castle

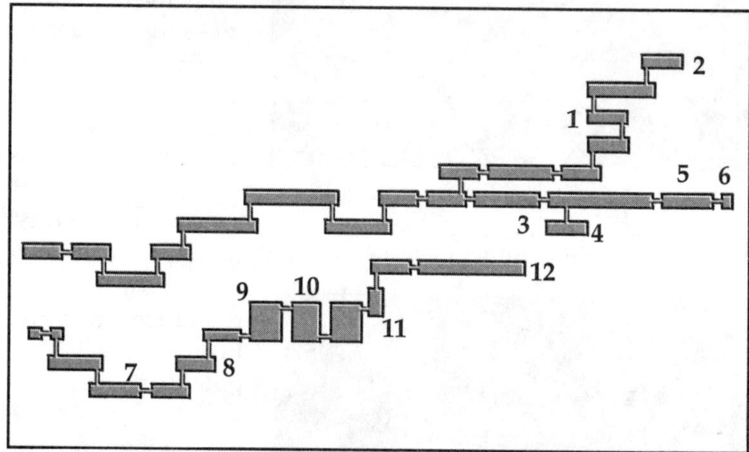

The Castle is extremely dangerous! Make sure you've got the Banded Armor and Banded Shield from the Tool Store before you travel here. You should also boost your Experience Points up to Level 14 or higher.

Once you're inside the Castle, make your way to Area 1. You'll find a treasure chest with the Battle Shield inside. Equip it. If you've got an Herb and lots of Hit Points, go to Area 2. Otherwise, leave the Castle and return after recharging your Hit Points.

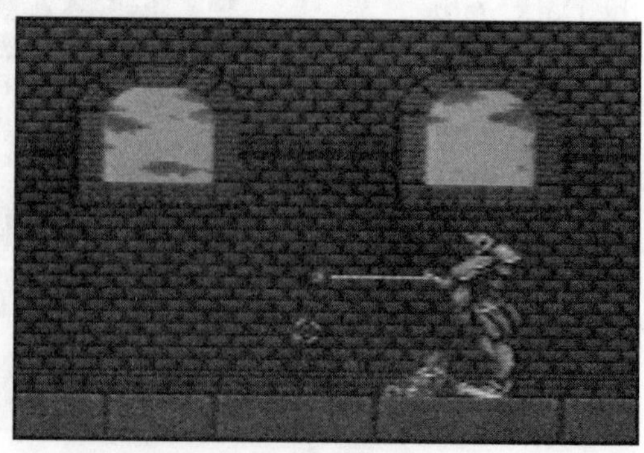

Area 2 is the home of Mace Man! Activate the Power Ring and crawl toward the Mace Man, underneath his twirling weapon. Strike with the Crouch and Thrust or

Crawl and Cut. Either of the attacks will quickly wear down the Mace Man. When he is defeated, you will receive the Garnet Bracelet.

Travel to Area 3 with the Bracelet in your possession. The statue of the Blue Knight, which is blocking the path, will disappear. Move on to Area 4, where you'll find the Battle Armor. Equip it and travel to Area 5 to fight the Fire Dog.

Use the Power Ring or the Time Ring (to slow down the Fire Dog's attacks). When the Dog leaps at you, jump into the air and use the Thrust Down attack. You shouldn't have any problems defeating the Dog.

After you've won the battle, walk to the right and enter the church. Ellena will appear with the knight of King McGaya. The knight will open a secret passage. Go through the passage and into the second section of the Castle.

Head directly to Area 8. You'll pass by Area 7, a dungeon cell, but you won't be able to open it yet. When you reach Area 8, you'll find the Jilduros statue again. This time, Jilduros will spring to life! He moves slowly, so hack him and move to the left before he can strike. If he reaches the far left side of the area, he'll teleport back to the right and start coming at you again. You can use the Power Ring or Shield Ring if you want to, but you can beat the Knight without using any Rings at all.

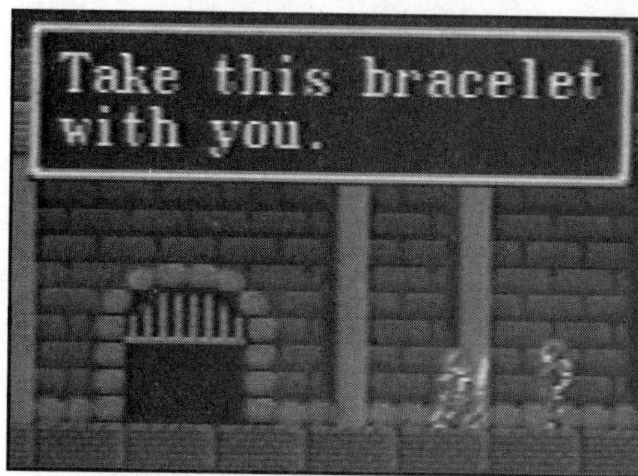

When Jilduros is beaten, you'll earn the Prison Key. Return to Area 7 and unlock the prison. Go into the prison and talk to everyone. The prisoner on the right side of the cell will give you the Blue Bracelet.

Once you have the Bracelet, go to Area 9. Climb up the gears to the top of the room. Look for a treasure chest on the left side of the room. This chest contains the Protection Ring. Take the Ring, then go to the right side of the room to find the exit to Area 10.

There's another chest in Area 10. This time, travel to the upper-right corner of the room. Open the chest to find the powerful Flame Sword! Equip the sword, then make your way down the right side of the room to find the exit.

You've got to pass through a third clock room before you reach Area 11. The guardian here is a real wimp. Thrash him and a chain will appear. Jump onto the chain and ride it up to the next room. Now walk to the right until you reach Area 12.

At Area 12, you'll meet up with Garland! When he transforms, activate the Protect Ring and start attacking him. If

The evil Garland zaps you with lightning, but the Protect Ring keeps you safe .

Garland disappears off the screen, take off the Ring to conserve Ring Points. Put the Ring on again when Garland reappears.

When you defeat Garland, King McGaya will invite you into his throne room. He'll give you the Dark Night with which to reach Galbalan's Island. You'll then meet up with Ellena, but the evil Galbalan will capture her.

Return to Redmont. Talk to Dogi, then go to Mayor Edgar's house. He'll give you the Ogre's Ball of Fire. You're almost ready for the final battle. Go to Cinthea's Supply Store. Buy an Herb, Brocia's Secret Medicine, and the Fairy Necklace. Leave the town and go to...

Galbalan's Island

Adol sets sail for Galbalan's Island.

When your boat lands on the island, walk to the right. The Dark Night will open the way for you. Continue to the right until you enter a dark screen. Call up the Menu Screen and select the Orge's Ball of Fire. A beam of light will illuminate the screen to let you see where you're going.

The dark Island passages are tough to navigate, so instead of providing a map, we've given you precise instructions on how to get through them. Don't get lost or you'll have to find your way back out!

From the start of the maze, walk to the right until you find a platform. Stand on the platform and let it drop all the way down the shaft. Do **not** jump off into the passage to the left. It leads to a dead end.

At the bottom of the shaft, walk to the right and into the next area. You'll find some stairs. Kill the skeleton at the top of the stairs, then jump into the shaft on the right side of the stairs. Move Adol against the left side of the shaft.

Keep holding the controller to the left as you fall and Adol will eventually land in another tunnel. All you need to do from this point is follow the tunnel. There won't be any other paths, so you won't get lost.

You'll eventually find yourself in a lit room. Walk to the right until you find Garland. You defeated him before, and you'll have to fight him again! Use the same technique as before (put on the Protect Ring and slash away). When you beat Garland for the second time, walk to the right.

Climb up the tower and continue toward Galbalan. Before you reach him, Chester will stop you. Walk to the right again. Galbalan will use his powers to capture Chester! When the platform appears, walk onto it. Galbalan will transport you to his chamber for the final confrontation.

Galbalan has two attack patterns. In the first pattern, he fires three lightning balls from each arm, descends to the ground, takes off again, and repeats. Jump over the lightning balls and slash one of Galbalan's arms while he's on the ground.

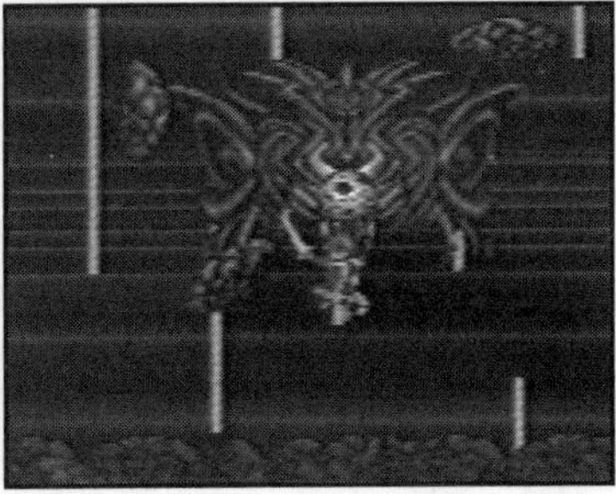

Once you've destroyed both arms, Galbalan will use his second attack pattern. After firing three fireballs from his mouth, Galbalan will use one of two attacks: a lightning beam that zips along the ground, or a crushing attack using his own body. After either of these attacks, Galbalan's chest will be exposed for a few moments. Jump and Slash Galbalan's chest, then get ready to dodge his next round of attacks. Put on the Power Ring when you attack Galbalan to do extra damage, then take it off to conserve Ring Points.

After you've beaten Galbalan, you'll return to Redmont. Talk to everyone to say your goodbyes, then leave town to see the ending sequence!

SHH... THE SECRETS

Power-Up Areas

There are several areas in the game where you can power-up by standing in one place and using the Thrust Up move constantly. Powering up is excruciatingly boring, but it's the best way to prepare for the dangers ahead. Here are three great power-up areas we've discoverered (the second one is the best).

Tigray Qurray

There are two great power-up spots in the Quarry. At the first spot, you'll be attacked by an endless stream of Keyrons, worth 4 Experience Points each. At the second spot, you are attacked by monsters worth 10 Experience Points each. You must position yourself at the precise spot indicated in the pictures. Don't try the second area until you're pumped up enough to kill the monsters there with one swing of your sword.

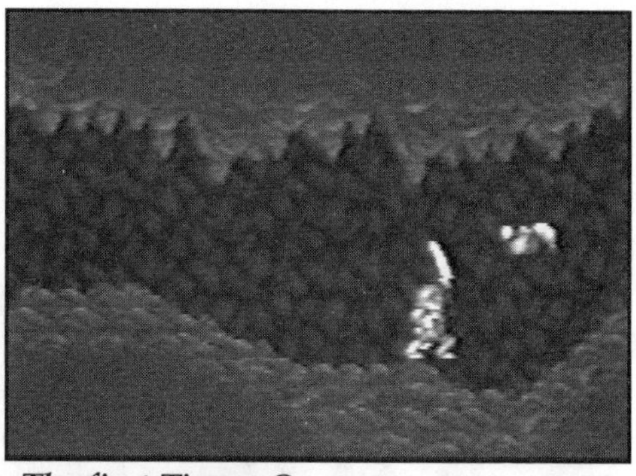

The first Tigray Quarry power-up spot.

The second Tigray Quarry power-up spot.

Ilvern Ruins

Go to Area 1 and slice and dice the Fuzzles for 20 Experience Points each. The Fuzzles will wear your Hit Points down, so you'll have to recharge every once in a while.

Last-Minute Secrets!

See the Short Tips section at the end of this book for some hot secrets on Wanderers from Ys III; a Sound Test and an Invincibility Mode (which is tough to activate, but worth the effort).

CHAPTER 16

Wings 2: Aces High

by Namco

WHAT'S GOING ON?

Wings 2: Aces High is loosely based on the Amiga computer game Wings, released by the now-defunct Cinemaware (although several Cinemaware employees went on to found Acme Interactive, the company that programmed this game).

Wings 2 is set in the skies of Europe during World War I. You're the commanding officer of a British fighter squadron of five pilots. Your goal is simple: help all the pilots survive to see the end of the war!

PLAYERS

Wings 2: Aces High is for one player only.

SCORING

The only scoring in Wings 2 is the number of enemy "kills" you achieve. Each enemy plane you shoot down counts as one kill. If you rack up enough kills, you'll earn war medals and promotions.

LIVES AND CONTINUES

There are five pilots in the squadron. You have to choose one of the pilots to fly each mission. If a pilot gets shot down, he's dead and you continue the game with your remaining pilots. If you lose all five of your pilots, the game is over.

Every time you complete a mission, whether your pilot lives or dies, you receive a password. If you crash and burn, you can reset the Super NES and use the last password you got to start the mission over again, with the same pilot or another one.

CONTROLS

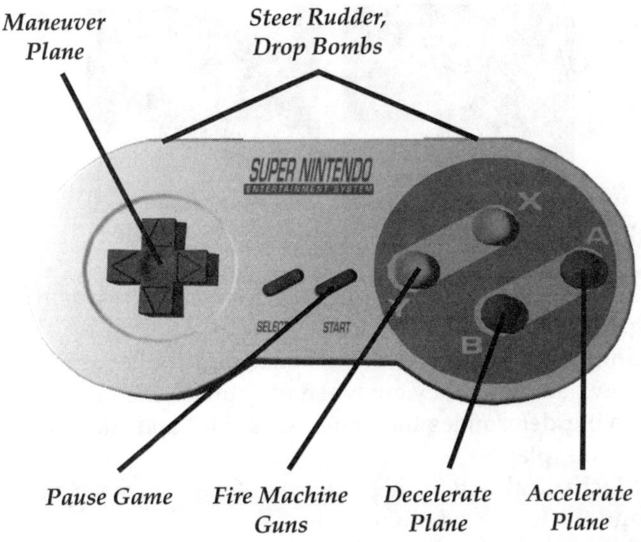

WEAPONS

During the Dogfighting and Strafing sequences, you're armed with machine guns. During the Bombing sequence, you're armed with bombs. You have infinite ammunition during all of the sequences.

SPECIAL ITEMS

None.

FRIENDS

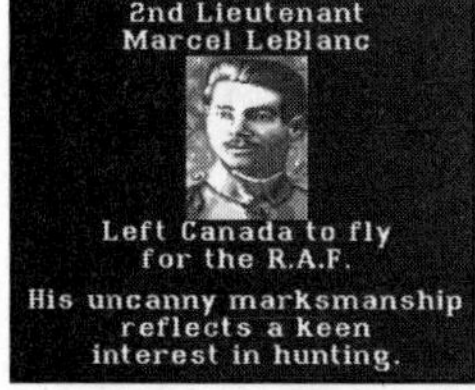

Marcel LeBlanc

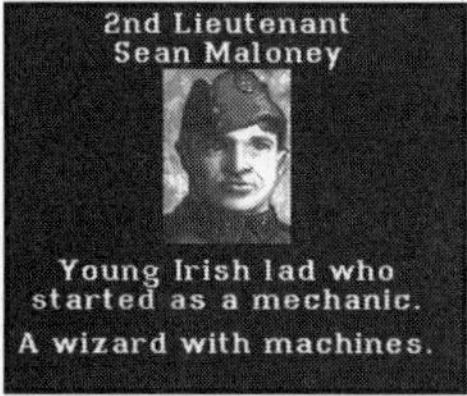

Sean Maloney

John Hargreaves

Charlie Dexter

Lawrence Wolfe

Each of the pilots in the game has four statistics: Shooting, Flying, Mechanical, and Stamina.

Shooting determines the distance your bullets travel, and how damaging they are when they hit an enemy plane.

Flying determines the maneuverability and turning speed of your plane.

Mechanical determines the rate of fire for machine guns, and the top speed of the plane.

Stamina determines how many hits your plane can take

before you crash.

ENEMIES

In **Dogfighting** missions, your enemies are the enemy planes! Shoot 'em down!
In **Bombing** missions, your enemies are the "ak-ak" anti-aircraft guns.
In **Strafing** missions, there are no enemies.

STRATEGY SESSION

General Strategies

The Wings 2 manual recommends spreading out your missions among the pilots, but we suggest just the opposite. Concentrate on powering up one or two pilots, and use them throughout the game.

If you fail a mission by crashing or being demoted, reset the Super NES and enter your last password to try the mission again. There's no point in continuing to play if you've lost an ace pilot.

Dogfighting

• The maneuver referred to in the Wings 2 manual as a "Split S" is actually an Immemann Roll, but we digress. It's not a particularly useful maneuver to use in combat. Tight turns, using the L and R buttons, are much more effective at getting you lined up behind enemy planes.

• Once you've got an enemy in your sights, cut back on the

throttle. The biggest danger in a dogfight is lining up for the kill and then slamming into your target!

• The color of an enemy plane indicates the skill of the pilot. There are seven colors: Light Blue (easiest), Dark Blue, Green, Dark Red, Gray, Black, and Bright Red (hardest). There's only one Bright Red plane in the game, and it appears in the final dogfight of the 20th mission, escorted by two black planes.

Bombing

• Stay at maximum altitude throughout the mission. It's harder to bomb targets from higher altitudes, but you'll be much safer from anti-aircraft fire.

• You have an unlimited number of bombs, but only two bombs can be in the air at a time. Don't drop more than one bomb at a target.

• It's possible to bomb and destroy the AA guns. No big deal, but it sure feels good to fire back at the suckers!

Strafing

• Some strafing missions are won simply by flying straight and shooting, but other missions require you to do a little steering back and forth. Try to memorize where the targets are, so you can start steering ahead of time.

• Watch the shadow of your plane to judge your altitude. Don't get too low!

SHH... THE SECRETS

Passwords

Use these passwords to start at any of the first 20 missions in the game. Two pilots in your squadron will be powered up: Marcel LeBlanc and Sean Maloney (Sean is stronger in the earlier passwords). The type of mission is listed before each password. Remember that some missions start out as one type, but become another; for example, getting into a Dogfight after a Bombing mission.

Mission 2: FGYHMBQ!nG!xD!

Mission 3: r5zKNJC2pf!V

Mission 4: HCcMJ6H!brG!s!

Mission 5 (Dogfight): VrDPMPBHvw!G

Mission 6 (Bombing): F!RLBMDLw!!!KRV

Mission 7 (Dogfight): Bt!jhD!dGLZLT

Mission 8 (Strafing): BQ!WC5YsCGwL

Mission 9 (Dogfight): MG!YPDY4lV!Zc!

Mission 10 (Bombing): hB003GjWBH!B

Mission 11 (Dogfight): R6!2xG!7WcL!Bz

Mission 12 (Strafing): !!4Tb!JGPMWvs!m

Mission 13 (Dogfight): G!!dNNG1B7FD6

Mission 14 (Bombing): ChD8ZCDcrW!Z

Mission 15 (Dogfight): NH7CJwblHXQ

Mission 16 (Strafing): z!!BFlBBPhK7d

Mission 17 (Dogfight): zFMg2NG8jd!r

Mission 18 (Dogfight): !c!FKvGdKhGSj

CHAPTER 17

Xardion

by Asmik

WHAT'S GOING ON?

In the distant future, the Alpha 1 solar system is in the middle of interplanetary war when a bizarre "living planet," NGC-1611, invades. The three worlds of Alpha 1 end their conflict and unite their three greatest warrior robots: Triton, Alcedes, and Panthera. The robots have to stop NGC-1611 by finding and resurrecting a legendary cyborg with extraordinary powers. The cyborg's name: Xardion!

PLAYERS

Xardion is for one player only.

SCORING

No points in this game. Instead, you earn Experience Points (XP for short) when you zap a bad guy. There are two numbers in the upper-right corner of the screen. The left number shows your current XP; the right number shows the amount of XP you need to advance to the next Experience Level. There are 12

Levels altogether. A robot's stamina and weaponry improve with higher Levels.

LIVES AND CONTINUES

The Xardion cartridge is equipped with an automatic battery backup system. The game saves the XP and weaponry of each robot, and keeps track of all the Stages you've reached in the game. This kinder, gentler save system makes losing a life almost painless, since you always keep your XP, and you can start from any Stage you've reached.

Each robot's strength is indicated by the Life Meter in the upper-left corner of the screen. As the robot is hit by enemies and enemy bullets, the Meter decreases. When the Meter runs out, the robot explodes, and you'll have to start the Stage over again. It's not that bad, though. When a robot "dies," it is instantly "resurrected" with full Life and Ammo Meters, along with all XP it earned up to the moment it exploded. Neat!

CONTROLS

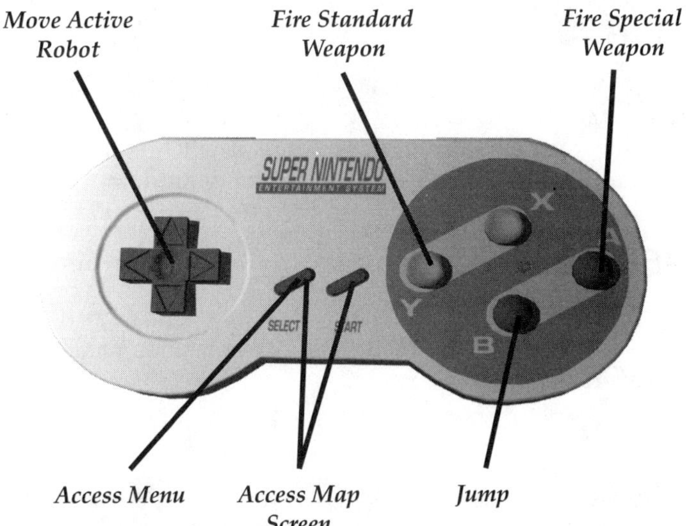

WEAPONS

Each of the three robots is equipped with an unnamed "standard weapon." Triton and Panthera's standard weapons are machine guns; Alcedes' weapon is a wave whip. As the robots increase in Levels, they earn the use of special weapons. Triton and Panthera have four special weapons by the end of the game; Alcedes only has one. Special weapons have limited ammunition, indicated by the Ammo Meter in the upper-left corner.

In addition to special weapons, the robots have two "shared" weapons: **T (Time) Bombs** and **Missiles**. Time Bombs blow up walls, while Missiles home in on enemy targets. You can have up to five of each.

SPECIAL ITEMS

The **Ammo** item fully recharges the Ammo Meter.

The **Save** item saves your progress, and your exact position, within a level. If your robot is destroyed, it will begin from the place where you used the Save item. This is not the same as the battery backup save.

The **Subtank** recharges the Life Meter.

FRIENDS

Your friends in Xardion are the three robots: Alcedes, Panthera, and Triton. Near the end of the game, Panthera gets destroyed by a tidal wave of acid (don't you hate it when that happens?) and is replaced by a fourth robot, the mighty Xardion.

ENEMIES

Some games have names for the bad guys, and some don't—Xardion is one of the don'ts. We'll make up names as we go along in the Strategy Session.

STRATEGY SESSION

General Strategies

• There are two ways to play Xardion. The first method is totally obvious: blast through each planet and build your robots' Levels as you go. The second way is to play through the first Stage repeatedly, powering up all of your robots to Level 12 (the highest level) before continuing. Either method works well, but beginners will find the second method to be the better one, since powered-up robots can survive longer in the higher Stages of the game. Choose the method that you like best!

• Triton is the best of the robots, Panthera is a close second, and Alcedes is a lame-a-zoid. You'll use Triton against the Bosses of the first six Stages, while Panthera will fight the Bosses of Stages 7 and 8. During these Stages, Panthera is equipped with the Invisible Shield, which makes him completely invulnerable to attack (and therefore the best choice to fight against Bosses).

• Don't forget your shared weapons! We haven't mentioned them in the Strategy Session because we assume you'll use them against the Bosses. You can visit earlier Stages to build up your weapon stocks.

Stage 1 (Oceansphere)

After you pass through the "yellow" part of the Stage (with the blue sky at the top of the screen), drop down the shaft on the right. When you land on the lower of the two ledges, walk to the left and drop straight down. After you land, jump to the left, then fall to the left to obtain the item.

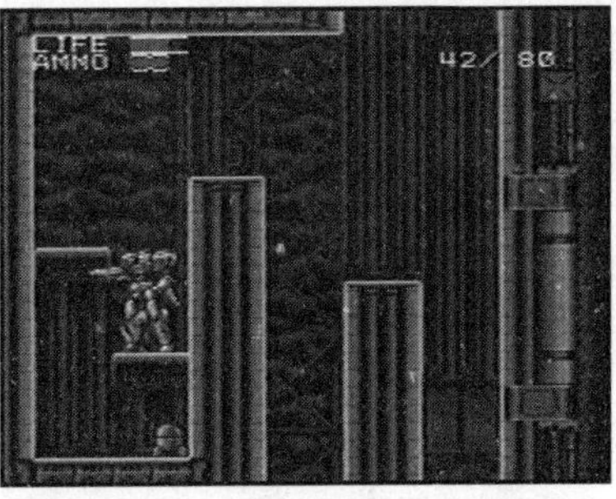

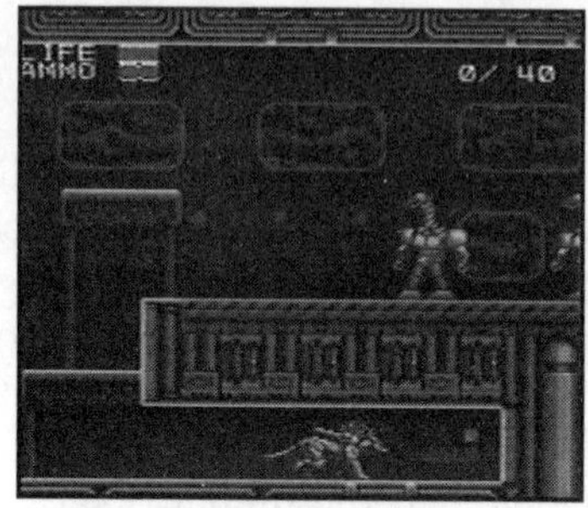

When you reach the transport switch, change to Panthera and walk to the end of the tunnel. Touch the switch and return to the left. Jump into the beam and you'll shoot upward into an area with a few enemies and a few items to grab.

The Boss is named Arms, but he should've been called Ugly! Arms attacks in three different ways. The first attack is a simple spread of three bullets; stand on the left ledge and the bullets will miss you. Jump into the air to shoot Arms's eyeball between attacks.

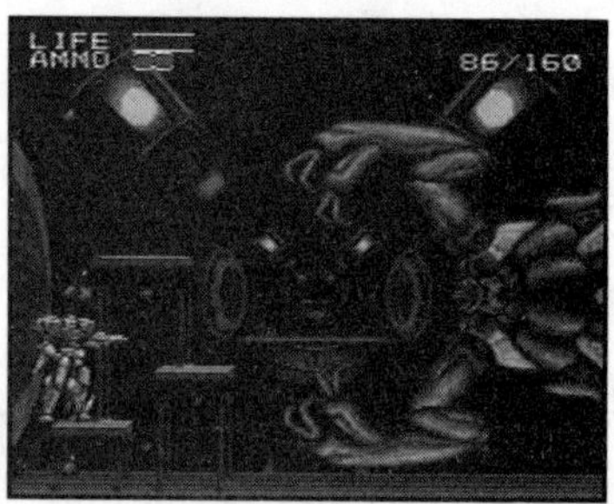

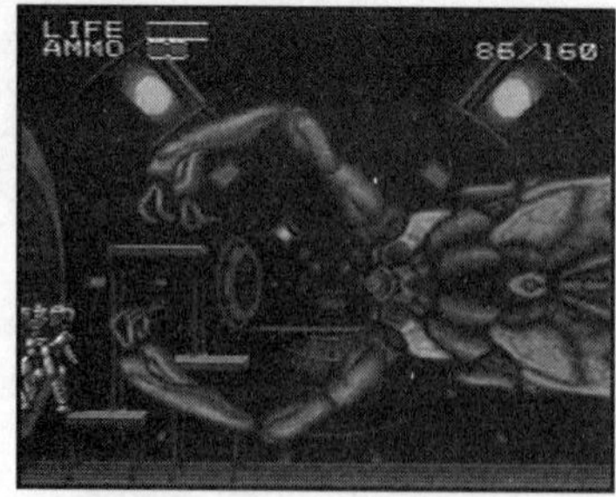

In the second attack, Arms shakes violently, then slides to the left in a frenzy. When Arms uses this attack, move to the far left side of the screen and he won't be able to reach you.

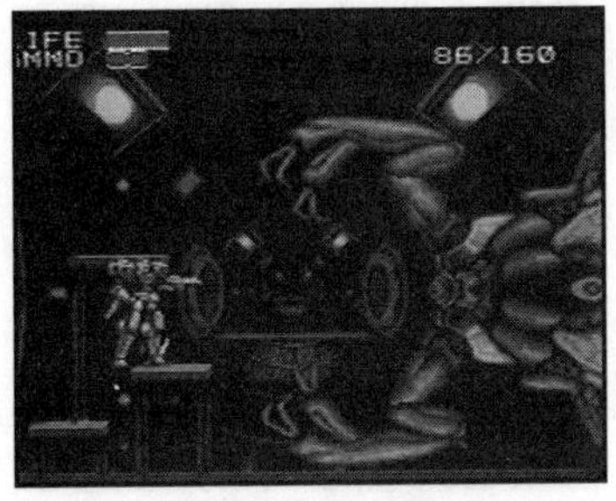

In the third attack, Arms shoots two circling gray bullets. Jump onto the right ledge and fire to the right; the bullets won't hit you, and you'll have a wide-open shot at Arms's eyeball. Move back to the left ledge when the gray bullets disappear.

Stage 2 (Oceansphere)

There's a Life recharge placed behind some solid bricks. Plant two T Bombs to destroy the blocks. (The blocks will stay destroyed permanently.)

You'll find a hole at the bottom of the water beneath the ship, but don't go into the hole yet. You'll return here when you've got the mighty Xardion in your group of robots.

Before you can face off against the Boss, you have to destroy the underwater control unit. Your weapons can't destroy the unit, but don't worry. All you have to do is move in front of the unit and jump. When you land, you'll destroy the unit under your heavy metal feet!

The watery Boss is a real wuss. Stay on the left side of the screen and shoot to the right. Jump over the bullets that the Boss shoots from his mouth. The hopping water sprites take a few hits, so you've gotta be quick on the fire button.

Stage 3 (Hollowsphere)

When you fall out of the trees, you won't lose a life, but you'll appear back at the start of the Stage. Take your time and make your jumps!

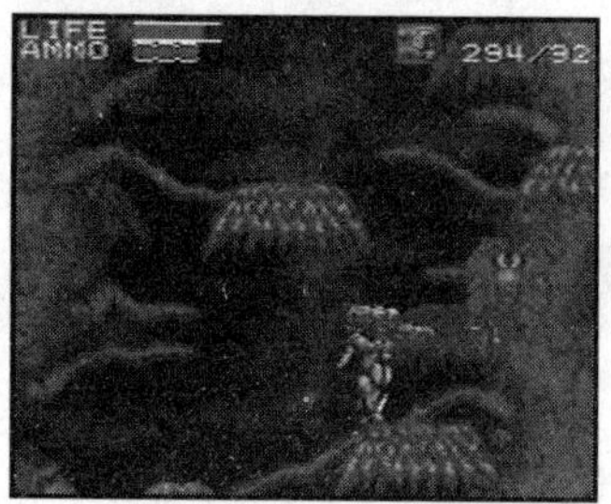

Watch the right edge of the screen for the psycho butterflies. Shoot them while they're still partially offscreen, since they won't attack you until their entire bodies appear on the screen.

Triton is usually the best robot to take through this area, because he can fire straight up, unlike the other robots. It helps to be able to blast enemies running on the ledges above you. Otherwise, they'll throw deadly boomerangs at you.

When you reach the giant roses, you've reached the end of the Stage. Walk off the right side of the screen, but remember this spot; you'll be coming back here later!

Stage 4 (Hollowsphere)

Before you fight the Boss, you have to scale the pillar. Jump from ledge to ledge and blast anything that gets in your way. Watch out for the flying fish in the waterfall. You can't shoot them, but they can damage you on contact.

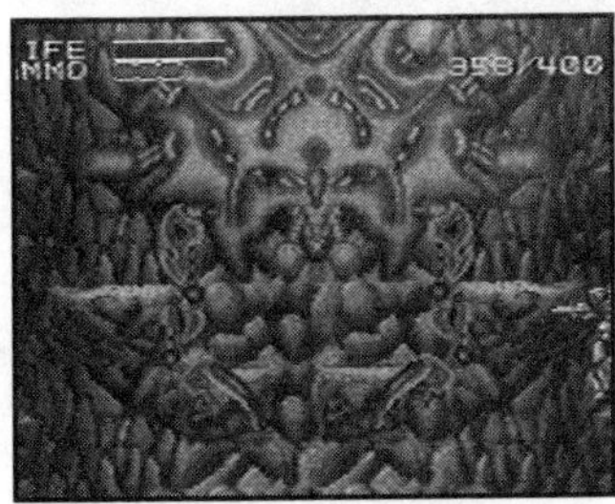

Use Triton against the Boss. You'll need his upward-shooting ability. The Boss' attack pattern is simple. He starts the pattern by swatting at the ground with his arms. Stand on the far left or far right side of the screen and shoot at the arms.

After the swatting attack, the Boss shoots aliens out of its head! Stand directly underneath the claw of either arm and shoot straight up. You'll hit the claw, and hit the aliens as they fly past you. Your positioning is crucial. If you aren't in the right spot, the aliens will hit you as they dive.

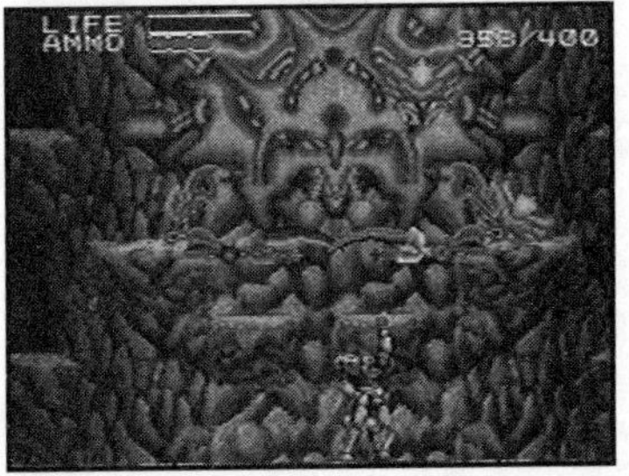

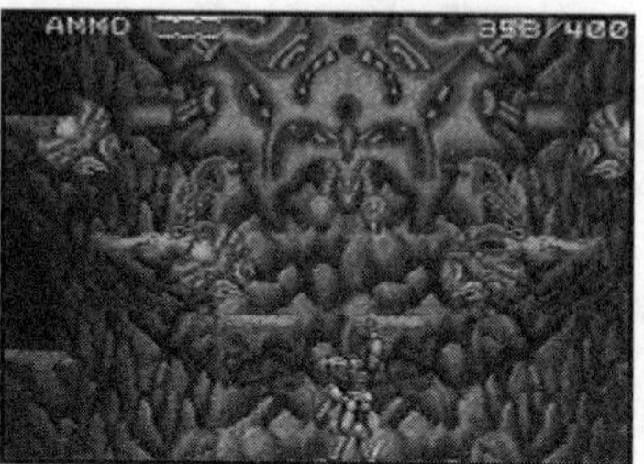

Once you've destroyed both claws, the Boss starts playing rough! Stand underneath it and shoot the small pods underneath its eyes. He'll shoot groups of four aliens down at you. You can avoid the aliens by running to one side of the screen and shooting upward. Run back to the pods between attack waves.

When you defeat the Boss, you'll appear in a completely mental upside-down bonus area! Grab what you can, then move to the left and you'll fall to the next Stage.

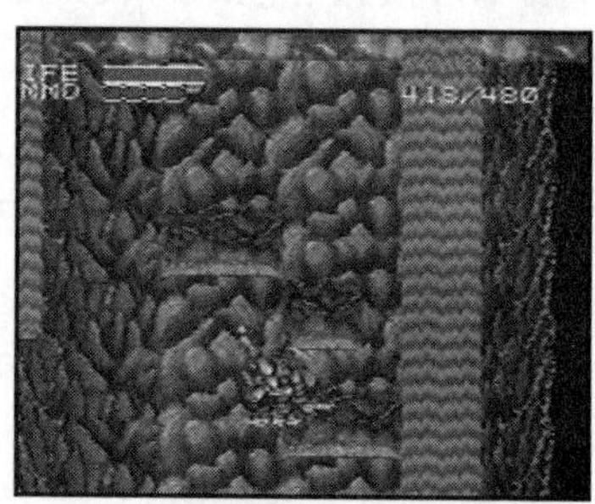

Stage 5 (Fiera)

When you get the "Careful" message on the screen, jump down the hole. This is the only way to get through the Stage (and to the Boss).

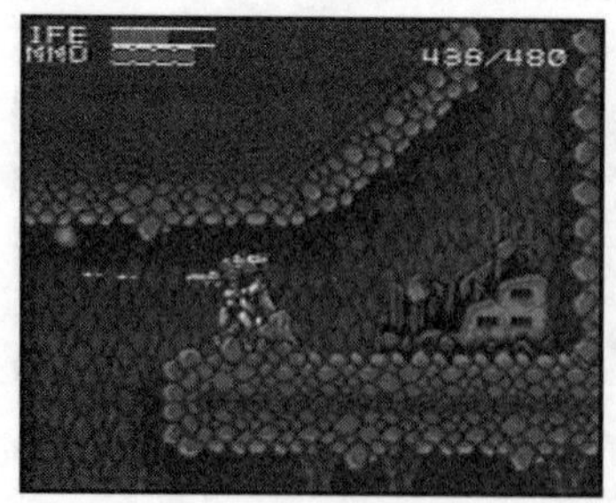

The most dangerous enemy in the underground tunnel is the green slime. Look closely at the roof of the tunnel for these nasty ooze-beings. When you see one, jump into the air and shoot it. If you walk underneath a slime, it'll drop two nasty enemies onto you.

When you reach the tank turrets at the end of the tunnel, don't stand on the cannons themselves. The cannons will tilt downward and cause you to fall.

The Boss has a complex pattern, and takes a lot of damage. Select Triton as your robot and activate the Shield as your special weapon. Keep using the Shield, putting up a new one as soon as the old one dissipates.

The Boss starts it's attack by dropping bombs. Shoot upward at the Boss, then duck whenever a bomb is dropped. A few of the bombs won't hit the ground, but instead will fly at your head. If you duck, the bombs will miss.

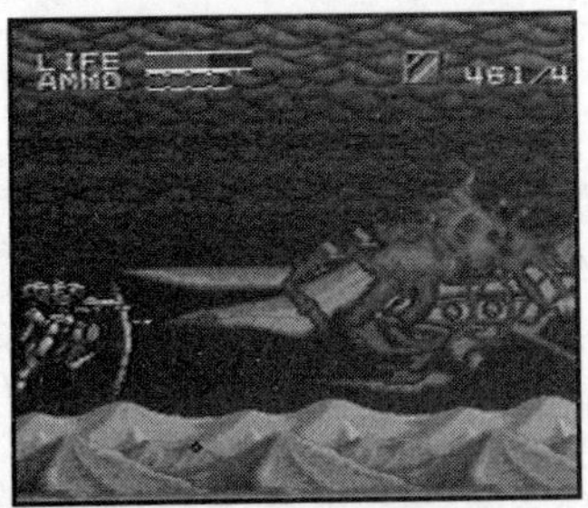

After the bombing run, the Boss floats down into the lower-left corner, then moves away to the right. Keep your shield up, because the Boss takes shots at you with a machine gun while moving to the right.

When the Boss reaches the right side of the screen, it fires a laser and a homing missile. Block the laser with your Shield and jump over the missile to dodge it. The Boss will start to repeat its attack pattern, so keep repeating your dodging maneuvers and shooting like crazy.

Stage 6 (Fiera)

This Stage takes place in an orbital elevator. There are several floating ledges that you have to use to move upward. To make a ledge start moving, stand on it and press Down on the controller for a few seconds.

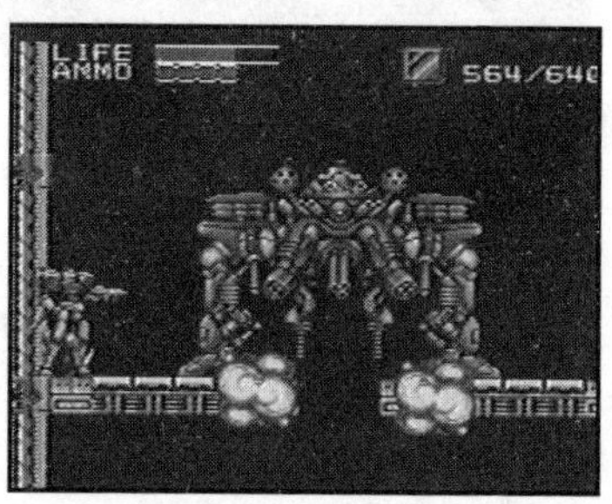

The Boss may seem like too much to handle, but you don't have to fight him at all! The moment you enter the Boss area, jump up and left until you've standing on the same ledge as the Boss, on the far left side of the screen. Stay still and the Boss will destroy its own ledge. What an intelligent opponent—not!

Stage 7 (Space Ship)

When you pick up the goofy-looking item at the beginning of the Stage, Panthera will gain the Invisible Shield special weapon (presuming his Level is high enough). This rad-ilicious weapon protects Panthera from all damage. Don't use Panthera to play through the Stage;

save him for the Boss, using Triton or Alcedes instead.

The Boss is a giant parasite in the antimatter generator. Activate Panthera, use the Invisible Shield, and jump into the air to blast the parasite. Turn on a new Shield as soon as the old one wears out.

Stage 8 (NGC-1611)

Watch the ground for strange green patches. There are creatures underneath the patches who'll pounce at you when you get close. Watch out for the killer trees, too. The rule for this Stage: if it's green, shoot it!

The Boss of the Stage is a big blob o' faces hacking white "loogies" at you! Gross! Activate the Panthera robot and stand on the top ledge. Shoot to the right and destroy the first two faces (they'll explode into skulls when you've done enough damage).

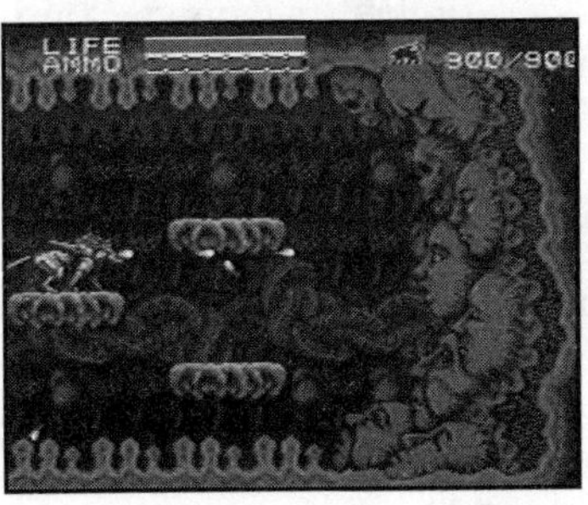

With the first two faces gone, move to the ledge on the far left and shoot the middle face. Destroy it and drop to the ground to destroy the final two faces. Use the Invisible Shield to prevent any stray loogies from damaging you.

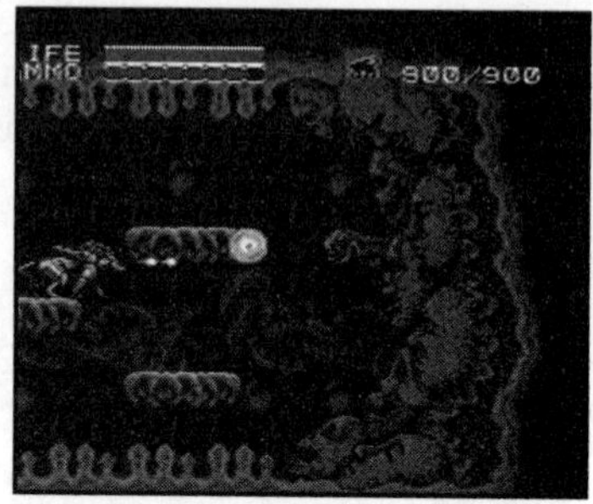

After all the faces have been destroyed, a snake will appear on the right side of the screen. Stand on the far left ledge and wait for the snake to appear. It will always appear horizontally aligned with one of the ledges. Move onto the proper ledge to shoot the snake. Keep using the Invisible Shield and keep shooting. When you fry the snake, jump to the right and walk through the hole.

Intermission Stage (Panthera Bites the Dust)

You'll get to watch a short intermission after finishing Stage 8. A huge wave of hydrochloric acid will take out poor Panthera. Don't worry, be happy, because the remaining two robots will make an awesome discovery. They'll find and reactivate the mighty Xardion!

You'll appear in Stage 9, but you're not ready for it yet. Press SELECT and START to exit to the Stage map. You've got three tasks. Number one: power Xardion up to Level 12. Number two: find the three treasures. Number three: defeat the final Stage. Let's start from the top, shall we?

Stage 1 (Oceansphere)

This Stage is perfect for power-up purposes. You'll earn about 80 XP every time you play through the Stage. Keep playing through the Stage until Xardion has 600 XP. (You'll earn 200 more XP, and hit Level 12, by defeating the Boss in Stage 2.) Time to get the treasures!

Stage 2 (Oceansphere)

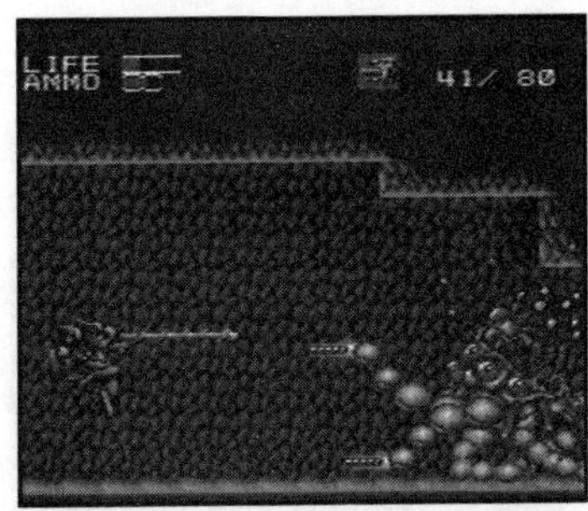

Remember that hole we told you not to go into? Drop into the hole and walk to the right to face off against a big ugly bad guy. This brainy Boss shoots fireballs your way. Activate Xardion's Hyper Beam, then jump into the air and fire the Beam at the Boss's brain. A few solid hits will destroy the Boss with ease. Pick up the white container that appears to collect the first treasure.

Stage 3 (Hollowsphere)

Play through to the end of the Stage and you'll find the second treasure on the branch above the giant roses.

Stage 5 (Fiera)

Drop into the hole in the sand. You'll spot the third treasure in a small tunnel. If you're at Level 12, with all of the treasures, it's time to rock and roll!

Stage 9 (NGC-1611)

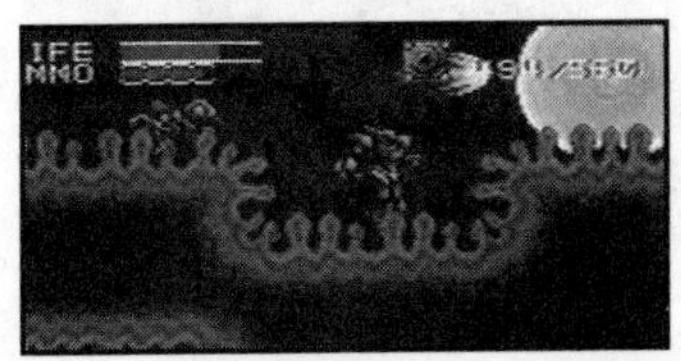

When you appear at the start of the Stage, jump up and to the right. You'll find what looks like an artificial sun. Activate Xardion's L-Arrow and blast the sun to smithereens. Follow the tunnel until you reach the three entrances. Use the middle entrance to reach the Boss.

The final Boss has a severe identity crisis; it will transform into more powerful forms four times! We'll start our strategies with the third form (the creature with the l-o-n-g neck).

Third Form: *Stand about an inch away from the left side of the screen, jump, and shoot the Boss in the head. When the Boss shoots its homing bullets, wait until the bullet is about to hit you, then jump high into the air, The bullets should pass harmlessly by. The timing is crucial!*

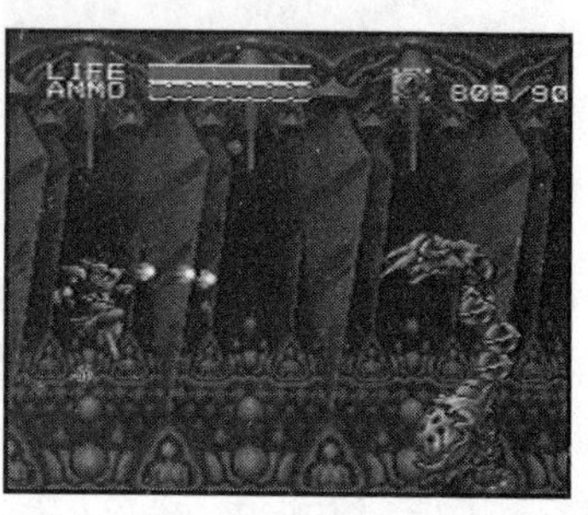

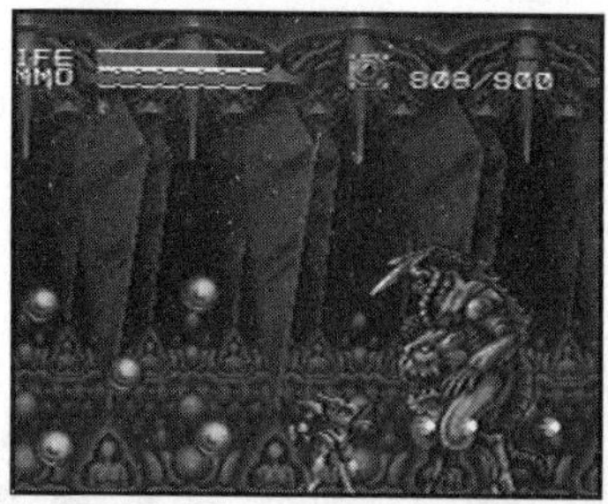

Fourth Form: *The colored spheres are a real pain in the robotic rear end! Don't try to dodge them. Instead, run up to the Boss and shoot from ultra-close range until he transforms.*

Fifth Form: *Easy. Stand on the far left side of the screen. Jump over the laser waves that the Boss shoots at you. When the colored spheres appear above you, aim upward and shoot the spheres as they fall. (Watch out for the laser waves, even when the spheres are overhead.) Use all of your Ammo, because this is the final form! When the Boss walks off the right side of the screen, sit back and get ready for a nice, long reward sequence!*

CHAPTER 18

Superstar Sports Games

The Super NES is building up a strong library of sports titles. Golf is by far the most popular Super NES sport (yes, golf), with baseball just slightly behind. There's a lack of football, basketball, and hockey games, but that will change rapidly over the coming months. (We're anxiously awaiting the Super NES version of NHL Hockey!) Read on for some great tips on the "first wave" of Superstar Sports Games!

HOLE-IN-ONE GOLF

by HAL America

Metal Clubs

Enter your name as METAL PLAY (with a space). You'll now be equipped with metal clubs that hit the ball for longer distances.

Passwords

Use either of these passwords to witness a hole-in-one:

CQJB83CFDFJ#H?LBBT7BJCF

and

B!5B9GB5SFGB3J5BB?GMBYQ

JOHN MADDEN FOOTBALL

by Electronic Arts

See the Crowd

At the title screen, hold down any button, and then press START several times to begin a game. The screen will blank for a few seconds, and then you'll get a close-up of the fans! Release the button you're holding down to continue the game.

SUPER BASEBALL SIMULATOR 1.000

by Culture Brain

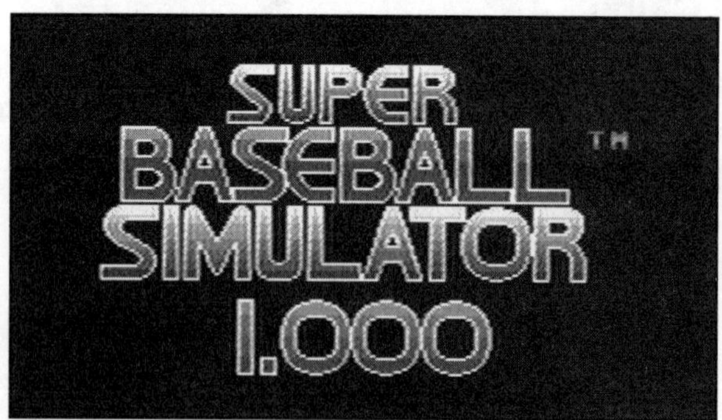

Batting

It's very easy to hit the ball in this game. You should almost never strike out, and you will VERY rarely draw a walk. Just move to the top of the batter's box and you'll be able to hit practically every pitch (except the Ultra Pitches, naturally).

When you get runners on base, don't try to steal. It's almost impossible to do. You can, however, play "hit and run" (telling the runner to steal and then swinging at the pitch), and you should play hit and run when you've got slower runners on base. This gives them a "head start" when the ball is hit into play.

There are six stadiums in the game. Some of them are "hitter's parks," where the walls are close in. Others are "pitcher's parks," meaning that it's harder to hit homers. Here's a list of the six stadiums and their measurements. The smaller the numbers, the smaller the stadium.

Stadium	LF Line	Deep CF	RF Line
Brown	85	120	85
CB	90	110	90
Dome	100	120	100
Grass	100	122	100
Harbor	90	112	90
Town	85	122	85

Pitching

The computer batter will go fishing for outside curves, but generally hits the ball almost as often as you do. This is a hitter's game, so the trick is making the batter ground out or fly out. Don't ever throw the ball down the middle of the plate—keep it inside or outside.

In a normal game, pitchers grow fatigued quickly. The longest a strong starter can go without becoming totally exhausted is five or six innings. After that, you'll have to put in a reliever. You've got six pitchers on your squad; the first four are starting pitchers, while the final two are the relievers.

Fielding

When you move a fielder into the right position to catch a fly ball, he'll raise his hands. Stand still and the ball will drop right into your glove. Easy!

The throws in this game are weak. Most throws from the outfield will hit the ground and roll into the infield. Learn to use the "relay man" between the outfield and the infield.

If a pop fly drops in for a hit, let the computer runner keep going. He'll often try to stretch a single into a double. You can gun the ball to second, then whip it to first for the easy out.

Ultra Play

In Ultra Play mode, the competing teams can use Ultra Powers when batting, pitching or fielding. You can set the number of Ultra Points given to the teams before the game. Give both teams unlimited Ultra Points for a truly insane matchup!

When you're playing an Ultra game against the computer, don't waste your Ultra Points (if you have a limited number). Wait until the computer uses an Ultra Power, then use one of your own. Ultra Powers don't cancel each other out, but it will even the odds.

The only time to break this rule is in critical situations; if you have the bases loaded and want to use your hitter's Ultra Power, or if you're pitching and need a strikeout desperately. Use your best judgment, and save some Ultra Points for the final innings!

Some of the Ultra Powers are useless against the computer, but work well against another player. Here's a list of the Ultra Powers, and whether they work against the computer.

Ultra Batting Power	Works?
Hyper Hit	Yes
Missile Hit	Yes
Tremor Hit	Yes
Bomb Hit	Yes
Shadowless	No
Invisiball	No
Meteor Hit	Yes
Squirrel Hit	Yes

Ultra Batting Power	Works?
Spinner Hit	No
Leaf Hit	Yes
Shadow Hit	No
Hyper Run	Yes
Freak Hit	Yes
Dizzy Ball	No
Orbit Hit	Yes

Ultra Pitching Power	Works?
Fire Ball	Yes
Stopper Ball	Yes
Phantom Ball	No
Snake Ball	Yes
Ninja Ball	Yes
Spark Ball	Yes
Iron Ball	Yes
Speeder Ball	Yes
Photon Ball	Yes
Zig Zag Ball	Yes
Spiral Ball	Yes
Jumper Ball	Yes
Tremor Ball	Yes
Change-Up Ball	Yes
Floater Ball	Yes
Multi Ball	No
Fadeout	No
Warp Ball	Yes
Lotta Ball	No
? Ball	Yes

SUPER TENNIS

by Nintendo of America

Serving

The key to serving is learning how to use the L and R buttons to put spin onto the ball. If you position yourself correctly behind the service line, you can hit spinning serves that are nearly impossible for the other player to return.

The other key to service is timing your button presses. While the manual says to press the button when the ball is at the top of its arc, you don't have to. In fact, a better way to serve is to hit the X button twice rapidly. No muss, no fuss!

Against a human opponent, use some "fakes." Press the X button once, but don't serve the ball. Just let it fall back into your hand. After a few fakes, your opponent won't know when you're going to serve, and you can (hopefully) blow the ball past him.

Returning

There's one strategy that works like magic against the computer, and it's rather easy to do. All you have to remember is not to move off the baseline. If you do, you'll mess the strategy up.

When the ball is hit to you, lob it to one side of the court (press the Y button and Left or Right on the Control Pad). Position yourself near the middle of the court.

When the computer smashes the ball back at you, hit the ball to the opposite side of the court from the one the computer player is on. If you do this properly, the computer won't have a chance of returning the ball—and if it does, by some miracle, rush the net and use the A button to knock the ball to the opposite side again and win the point.

Don J

If you're playing on the Men's Circuit, and manage to win the Grand Slam—that is, win the Melbourne, Paris, London, and New York Opens—you'll take on an outrageously good player named Don J. Don lives on an island that you can't see on the world map. The colors of the court on Don's island are very strange. Even the ballboys here look bizarre!

Don is an incredibly fast player who loves to rush the net. The only way you can beat him is to use the Returning strategy listed above. If you don't use it, you'll lose. It's as simple as that.

Your match against Don is only an exhibition, so you won't win any extra prize money. What you will win is a secret code that allows you to change the music (see below).

New Music

On the Select Player screen, press these buttons on Controller One: L five times, X, R seven times, and X. The music will change to a different tune!

Passwords

Use these passwords to take controls of John (Men's Circuit) in various stages of the game. The Grand Slam password will take you to the exhibition match with the incredible Don J!

Won Melbourne Open:
NJ5QCHT JWM5JVD5GNYCR2 5376D6QFLVTK8X D3HRFTLWJPY2PP 1JK
Won Paris Open:
GXM9QL4 1ND6DFSWGWLYKQ F6HQZFS47365C6 PDJSTK8XD39RSX TBJ
Won London Open:
2B5RZO? 2L7WRBNV48699F 8TJLVYMC?H3HRF TLWJPC2GNY4SD9 6M4
Won Grand Slam:
K8XD3HR FTLWJPC2GNYBQ1 4065C6PDJSTK8X D3HRFTLWJPPDLW 1RK

Player Editor

This fantastic trick lets you fool around with the stats of your player! Press SELECT during the match to bring up the score. Press R, R, Left, Down, B, A, L, and L on Controller Two. You'll hear a smattering of applause. Press A or B on Controller One and four rows of eight characters will appear on the screen. Each row indicates the stats of a player. In a singles match, only the two rows on the top have stats; in a doubles match, all of the rows have stats.

You can change each number to increase or decrease a player's skills. From left to right, the eight characters represent the following skills: Forehand, Lob, Left/Right Speed (how fast the player runs left and right), Back/Forth Speed (how fast the player runs up and down), Volley, Serve, Jump, and Backhand.

Set each character by pressing the X button. The lowest setting is 0, while the highest setting is F. Give your character a row of Fs for maximum results. (In a one-player game, your stats are on the top, while the computer player's stats are on the bottom.)

TRUE GOLF CLASSICS: PEBBLE BEACH GOLF LINKS

by T&E Soft

Teeing Off

For the longest drives, wait until the red mark goes across the third row (moving from right to left). Depending on the wind, you should hit closer to the range of the club's maximum yardage.

Trying to whack the ball at maximum power can be risky. If you go even a single "click" beyond maximum strength, the power meter will drop back to minimum strength. Not too fair, but that's how the game works, and the chance you've gotta take to hit long drives.

On the Fairway

When you're on the fairway, you can use the Wood clubs for long yardage. For this reason, you should always try to keep your tee shot on the fairway. If you knock the ball into the rough, your longest club choice is the 2-Iron, with a distance of 200 yards (compared to a 3-Wood's 236 yards).

A good rule of thumb is to move your stance, the spot on the ball (to put "English" on the spot), or the direction you're aiming, about one notch for every 6 MPH that the wind is blowing. Adjust this figure based on your own personal experience.

Putting

Some approach shots may appear to have hit the green, but actually curl off onto the fairway just outside the green. If you're gutsy, and 20 yards or less from the hole, you can try an extra-long putt. Set the club to the Putter, and hit the ball at roughly three times the normal power for the distance of the putt. You can't call up the contour grid, so you won't be able to read the green's break before the shot.

CHAPTER 19

Short Tips

When one of the Short Tips listed below says to press the L or R button, this means the L and R buttons on top of the controller. When a tip says to press Left or Right, this means to press Left or Right on the control pad. Don't get them mixed up!

BATTLE BLAZE

What's Going On?

There's a perfect way to describe Battle Blaze: a medieval version of Street Fighter. Take control of one of the six different contenders in the game and use your fighting skills to defeat any and all challengers!

The Hero

You control Kerrel on his quest to defeat Adrick, Gustoff, Shnouzer, Tesya, and Autarch, the Dark Lord. Autarch doesn't appear until you've beaten the first four opponents.

The best strategy against the first four opponents is to use the Tornado Kick as much as possible. Even if you miss with the Tornado Kick, you will be in perfect position to use the Inferno Slash. The Kick and Slash combination can be truly devastating.

When you're fighting Autarch, the Dark Lord, don't attack directly. Move to the left side of the screen and use the Tornado Kick repeatedly, jumping straight into the air. Autarch will be struck by your Kick as he attacks. Wait in between Kicks to lure Autarch into attacking.

Use the Tornado Kick to make short work of the evil Autarch.

The Battle

If you play through The Battle in one-player mode and defeat all the challengers, you'll get a reward sequence where you speak with the King. This isn't the true ending of the game, though. You've got to beat The Hero mode for that.

DARIUS TWIN

49 Extra Ships

At the One Player/Two Player screen, hold down L and R on Controller Two, then press SELECT and START on Controller One.

Level 1 Safety

In the first level of the game, position your ship above the last three digits of the high-score. You won't be hit by any enemies. This trick works until you reach the Boss.

No Enemy Demo

Play the game and beat the high score of 100,000 points, then lose all your lives intentionally. On the high-score screen, enter your initials as ZZT. Wait for the game to demo itself and there won't be any enemies on the screen!

EARTH DEFENSE FORCE

Invincibility

During the game, press START to pause. Now press A, B, X, Y, L, R, Up, Down, Left, and Right. Unpause the game and you'll be untouchable.

Strange Title Scroll

Turn off the Super NES. Hold down the START button on Controller 2, and hold the control pad on Controller 2 Up. Now turn on the Super NES while holding down both buttons. The title screen will scroll differently.

FINAL FANTASY II

Defeat Zemus/Zeromus

Use FuSoYa's and Golbez's combined Meteo spell to destroy Zemus in the first round of combat. He'll come back from the dead! Use the Crystal to transform Zemus into Zeromus, then start attacking. Have Rosa cast the White spell and Rydia use Bahamut summoning. If you need to heal, use Rosa's Cure 4 and Rydia's Asura. Support your magic-users with physical attacks: Cecil's Crystal Sword, Kain's Jump Attack, and Edge's Spoon Dagger (foolowed by Ninja Stars). If you're at Level 60 or higher, you'll outlast Zeromus (and his 110,000 hit points!) and win the game.

GRADIUS III

Controller Reset

Hold down L, R and START, then press SELECT and the game will reset just as if you pressed the RESET button on the Super NES!

Mega Demo

Hold down the A button on the title screen and wait for the game to start its self-running demo. You'll see an incredible display of how to play this game!

HYPER ZONE

Sound Test

At the title screen, hold down L and R and press START. The Sound Test menu will appear on the screen.

JOE AND MAC

Extra Lives

Play through any level with a 1-Up (this doesn't include the bonus stages). Return to the level, collect the 1-Up, then press START and SELECT to exit the level. Repeat until you've maxed out your lives.

LEMMINGS

Passwords

On the next two pages, you'll find an awesome list of 125 passwords for every level in this game, including the super-tough Sunsoft levels. Have fun!

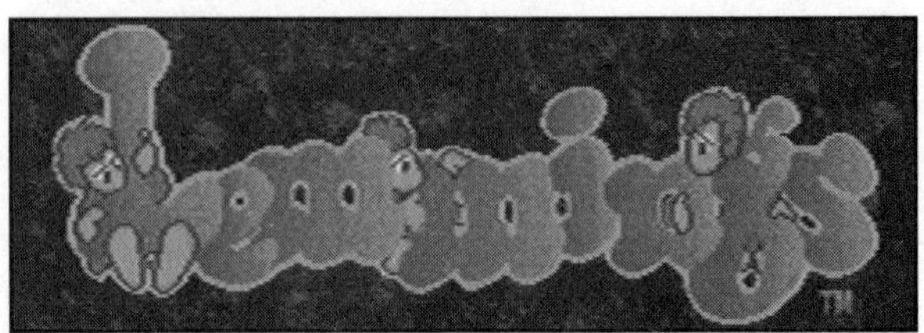

Fun

Level 1: No Password	Level 16: HMHRSDR
Level 2: MJDVLXT	Level 17: MFLFHSH
Level 3: ZBHPRLQ	Level 18: QXPKCHB
Level 4: GWSXMHK	Level 19: MWRTLNR
Level 5: NCDKKWG	Level 20: GMXCWPS
Level 6: CKWDRKV	Level 21: KGXNLPB
Level 7: HCBSMGV	Level 22: DVJJBGM
Level 8: JBKZQGS	Level 23: LGSSCZL
Level 9: MMDMKKX	Level 24: MVGDKVX
Level 10: SKFKNNB	Level 25: LSQHCQS
Level 11: LXNLJCP	Level 26: SXRQMVR
Level 12: MTPCTNP	Level 27: PMQJPMX
Level 13: PCLSRCP	Level 28: DHBPTWQ
Level 14: KPMDGXZ	Level 29: BCXLWVV
Level 15: TLVKLSW	Level 30: FXWBBSL

Tricky

Level 1: MGQZMGG	Level 16: JQXRNGJ
Level 2: LXSFDXB	Level 17: WFVHQQT
Level 3: ZRVXBWQ	Level 18: KWVBVJP
Level 4: NKVKRTB	Level 19: TTKLKZT
Level 5: GJWDHMG	Level 20: NNFFQPV
Level 6: DJCQQZT	Level 21: ZNXBKMP
Level 7: JHSVCQL	Level 22: QSLQWTJ
Level 8: RCHFGNN	Level 23: BGFVMFR
Level 9: BJWVRCQ	Level 24: PQZWDKM
Level 10: RFPZFBJ	Level 25: SBCMSJS
Level 11: JKJBRMQ	Level 26: BDGQRNX
Level 12: MZDCDTC	Level 27: XPPBQWL
Level 13: ZVMQKXB	Level 28: JHQSPRH
Level 14: ZZRHJPL	Level 29: GCLKJMQ
Level 15: JFLKJPX	Level 30: SRWGXZM

Taxing

Level 1: PQFPTBP	Level 16: PFVFXCR
Level 2: BPLHRXL	Level 17: NKVCKDN
Level 3: CPZRSRV	Level 18: QPDDJFB
Level 4: SMSWSPW	Level 19: QBGBPSW
Level 5: DXCQKRX	Level 20: JLXJWNW
Level 6: MDGMJLV	Level 21: JLHFSRF
Level 7: WZWSDMK	Level 22: WCLJNNK
Level 8: HZBCFQM	Level 23: LVFHHMM
Level 9: SPRPVHR	Level 24: MHNNCPC
Level 10: BWCBKXJ	Level 25: RNMKXLP
Level 11: WRFVJDL	Level 26: XZZSDDN
Level 12: GGBCXXS	Level 27: BBTSGZC
Level 13: TTXQXQL	Level 28: LXFLJPX
Level 14: DCBBWNH	Level 29: QKZVKFT
Level 15: WCBLDQX	Level 30: WFCSHNT

Mayhem

Level 1: XNMTWVD	Level 16: LGJCRKM
Level 2: KDTJQQR	Level 17: SQXKBZN
Level 3: VNTGWRB	Level 18: WXTBWCB
Level 4: SQDLCRR	Level 19: NPKNRKV
Level 5: JHQTCPD	Level 20: PZQWRGP
Level 6: RQXNVNP	Level 21: DZTHVNL
Level 7: CBWMMLG	Level 22: RMDTBFQ
Level 8: LCVDQWL	Level 23: FCSLSPK
Level 9: KDHWTJL	Level 24: RNHQXVM
Level 10: GVNKKJL	Level 25: LTGNDXH
Level 11: DXCDGNH	Level 26: LHLTDDW
Level 12: GWJTPLW	Level 27: HCBBKHV
Level 13: LNZNHWM	Level 28: MWLGVQJ
Level 14: MZXZKZC	Level 29: GSPQCRQ
Level 15: RWLTTCQ	Level 30: ZTTGRFH

Sunsoft

Level 1: TPCWFMP	Level 4: HZSQQNV
Level 2: WSJCLDX	Level 5: KCGHCNC
Level 3: PVNRCMV	

PAPERBOY 2

Password

To start the game on Hard Way, use this password: **6479**

ROMANCE OF THE THREE KINGDOMS II

What's Going On?

This historical wargame is based in 2nd century China. The Han Dynasty has fallen (and can't get up), and a variety of groups are fighting for control of the land. Assume the identity of a powerful general and battle for power!

Quick Victory

Use this walkthrough to finish the game in roughly an hour. Remember that this walkthrough is a quick, dirty way to win. You'll get the most of this great game by playing fair and square against the computer (or human opponents).

Setting It Up

Choose Scenario 5. Select a four-player game. Set the difficulty level to 1. Choose not to view other wars. Begin the game. (If a plague occurs at the start of the game, reset and try again.)

First Commands

Meng Huo: Move all generals except for Meng Huo into province 41. Take all food and gold supplies. Appoint Meng You as Governor of 41.

Sun Quan: Rest all provinces except 40. Send one general from province 40 to attack province 41. Don't request reinforcements for Meng You, and don't sens any generals into war to help Meng You. When the battle begins, Flee Meng You and the entire army to province 36.

Liu Bei: Rest all provinces except 34. Send one general from province 34 to attack province 36. Meng Huo's army has no food or gold, and will lose the war in the second round of combat.

Cao Cao: Use the command Person/Delegate and delegate authority to provinces 3, 4, 5, 7 and 9. Delegate any type of rule. Rest all of Cao Cao's provinces.

On The Attack

Now you have to expand Cao Cao's territory by attacking border provinces, one at a time. You're guaranteed to win since you're controlling both the attacking and the defending army!
Attacking Army: You only need to send one general into battle. You don't need to bring gold, but always bring one month's supply of rice. Don't initiate or accept personal combat. Send generals of high War Ability when possible, to have extra Mobility. After you win a war, recruit all of the prisoner generals.
Defending Army: Don't call for reinforcements. Send only the province ruler to war by selecting END at the General Selection Screen. Don't initiate or accept personal combat. Flee the battle on the first turn. If you can't flee, move out of the castle and let the attacking army occupy it.

Wrapping It Up

Once you've destroyed Sun Quan and Liu Bei, you need to occupy provinces 1 and 15. Move the following generals in order. Move Zhang Lu from 13 to 14. Move Yu Lin from 8 to 6. Move Xiahou Hui from 29 to 13. Move Jia Xue from 6 to 2. Move Li Tong from 2 to 1. Move Hou Xuan from 14 to 15. Now keep resting until you receive the ending sequence!

SIMCITY

Extra Maps

Choose "Start New City" on the menu screen. Choose any map from 1 to 999, then click on OK. Now choose the "Go To Menu" icon. Don't save the game. Choose "Start New City" again. After a few moments, you'll see a different map with the same number as the one you chose before. You can use this trick with any of maps, giving you a total of 1,998 maps to choose from.

One Million Dollars

The first step to this trick is to spend all the money you begin with. Do this by building ONLY Fire and Police Departments. If you still have a bit of money left, construct some train tracks. You've got to get your funds down to $0.

When the Tax Info screen appears at the end of December, hold down the L button, then exit the Info screen and go back to the game screen. Continue to hold down the L button and re-enter the Tax Info screen. Set the budgets for Transportation, Police and Fire to 100%. Exit the Info screen a second time and release the L button. After a few moments, you'll go from $0 to $999,999! Now you can build the ultimate Megalopolis!

SUPER CASTLEVANIA IV

Invisible Stairs

On the screen just before the final confrontation with Count Dracula, you'll see some stairs. Instead of climbing them, walk to the end of the ledge and take a large jump to the left. You'll land on an invisible ledge! Walk to the left and climb down the invisible stairs. Move as far left as possible and power-ups will start to fall from the top of the screen! Wait until you've collected 99 hearts, a Triple Boomerang and the best Whip. Now climb back up the stairs, jump back to the visible ledge and climb up the stairs to fight Dracula!

SUPER GHOULS'N GHOSTS

Change The Music

Use the Sound Test/Stage Select trick below. Choose one of the sounds from D5 to EA; these are the musical tracks. CHoose a music track, then select sound B5. When you press the button to hear the music, you'll hear drum beats instead of the normal instruments.

Sound Test and Stage Select

Go to the Option Screen and move the cursor to the EXIT option. Hold down L (not Left) and START on Controller 2, then press START on Controller 1. You'll enter a special screen where you can choose your stage, area, and listen to the sound and music.

SUPER OFF-ROAD

Always Finish Third

If you're playing by yourself, but don't want to risk finishing in last place, play by yourself in the two-player mode, and let the blue truck stand still. This guarantees you at least a third-place spot in every race.

SUPER R-TYPE

Fade Out the Music

Use the sound test to play a musical score from the game, then hit the R button. The music will start to fade out. Each press of the R button makes the music fade faster.

Level Select

When the title screen appears, press R nine times, then Up nine times. You'll hear a sound. Start a new game, then press START to pause the game. Press R, A and SELECT simultaneously. A number will appear in the lower-left corner of the screen. Use the controller to select a level.

Weapon Select

This is a complicated trick, so follow along carefully. On the title screen, press Down, R, Right, Down, Right, Right, Down, Right, Down, Down. You'll hear a chime. Press START to begin a new game. When the game has begun, press START again to pause. Now press R, Right, Down, Y, Down, Right, Down, Left, Right, Down, Right, Right, and then the buttons for the laser and missile you want. Make sure you select the laser first, then the missile. See the lists below to figure out which buttons to press for the weapons you want. Once you've selected your weapons, unpause the game and start shooting! You can use this trick with each new life, and you can also use it with the Level Select trick.

Lasers
Ring Laser: Button A
Air-to-Surface Laser: Button B
Reflective Laser: Button X
Spread Laser: Button Y

Missiles
Mega Bomb: Button R
Homing Missiles: Button A
Air-to-Surface Missiles: Button X

U.N. SQUADRON

Hidden Difficulty Level

Go to the Option Mode and highlight the difficulty setting. Hold down A and X on Controller Two, then change the difficulty using Controller One. A new skill level, GAMER, will appear. Select this level for some awesome action!

WANDERERS FROM YS III

We got these super-secret hints just before this book went to press, so we weren't able to place them into the Ys chapter, but we were able to list them here. The invincibility trick may take you a lot of attempts before it works, so keep trying.

Invincibility

Start the game, then press RESET on the Super NES to reset the game. When the American Sammy logo appears, press Up, Down, Up, Down,, SELECT, and START on Controller Two. You have to wait until the logo fades in completely before you start to enter the code, and you have to punch the entire code in before the logo starts to fade out. It's not easy to do!

When the Start/Continue Screen appears, use Controller One to select the Continue option. Use any saved game on the cartridge. When you enter the saved game, press Select on Controller One to call up the Menu. Go to the Status subscreen. When the Status screen appears, press START on Controller Two. The word DEBUG will appear next to STATUS, and you'll be invincible!

Sound Test

Press SELECT on Controller One to bring up the regular Menu, then press SELECT on Controller Two to call up the Sound Test Menu. Press Up and Down to select a sound, and press B to hear the sound.

Got any other great tips? Let us know! Write to:

Game Tips
P.O. Box 1260
Rocklin, CA 95677-1260

CHAPTER 20

Peripherals

Every great video game system has its fair share of add-on devices, known as peripherals. 8-bit NES owners are familiar with peripherals such as the Zapper (an infrared light gun), the Advantage (a multi-featured joystick), the Power Pad (a huge floor mat with buttons you press with your feet!), and the now-extinct R.O.B., or Robotic Operating Buddy, a bizarre "robot" packaged with some of the earliest NES decks.

A wide assortment of peripherals has begun to appear on the Super NES, and this chapter features three of our favorites. Look for more great peripherals in future editions of Super NES Games Secrets!

asciiPad Controller

Yep, you're reading that name correctly. This controller is called the asciiPad, with a lowercase "a." Don't let the English-teacher's-nightmare of a name give you the wrong idea, though; this outstanding controller has sent our original Super NES controllers into the closet.

The first feature about the asciiPad that we liked was the colorful buttons. The purple-and-gray Super NES controllers look totally drab next to the lively asciiPad color scheme. (The Super Famicom, the Japanese version of the Super NES, comes with colorful controllers much like the asciiPad; Nintendo decided to change the Super NES controller colors to purple and gray for reasons unknown.) Of course, the asciiPad doesn't just have looks, it's got great features too.

In the middle of the controller are six rapid-fire switches, one for each of the six action buttons: L, R, X, Y, A and B. Each switch has three settings: Off, Turbo (20 shots per second when you hold down the button), and Auto (20 shots per second whether you're holding the button or not). The rapid-fire switches come in extremely handy for some games. (We'll be listing recommended rapid-fire settings for the games we cover in future editions of Super NES Games Secrets.)

If the rapid-fire isn't enough, you also have a slow-motion switch. For games that use the START button to pause, the slow-motion feature works like a charm. (We'll be mentioning which games slow-motion works with in future editions of Super NES Games Secrets.)

If you're looking for the great features of the 8-bit NES Advantage joystick, combined with the comfort and ease of play that a joypad provides, the asciiPad is the controller you're looking for.

THE MIRACLE PIANO TEACHING SYSTEM

The goal of The Miracle Piano Teaching System is to make learning to play the piano an exciting, enjoyable experience. The tutorial system was written by professional music educators to be fun for students of all ages.

The Miracle package comes with a full-sized, 49-key, velocity-sensitive keyboard and a Super NES cartridge. You plug both The Miracle and the cartridge into the Super NES, turn 'em both on, and start learning!

The cartridge is equipped with 36 tutorials, each of which has several lessons. You start by learning basic stuff, such as hand position on the keyboard and the names of the notes and keys. As you advance through the tutorials, the lessons become more advanced to match your improving musical skills.

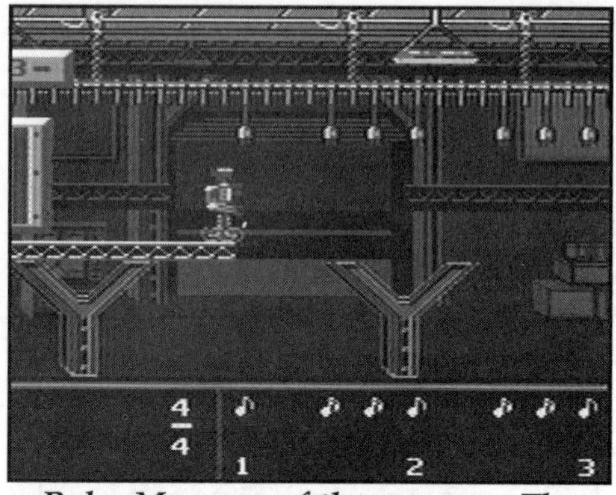

Robo-Man, one of the games on The Miracle cartridge.

The Miracle tutorials aren't just screen after screen of musical notes, either. The "serious" lessons are mixed with neat games like Robo Man (which teaches rhythm and timing) and Shooting Gallery (which teaches note reading).

The Miracle keyboard is teeming with features. It's equipped with 4" stereo speakers, 128 instruments and sound effects, headphones, a sustain pedal (actually a rubber pressure pad), and MIDI-compatible jacks. MIDI stands for Musical Instrument Digital Interface, which is the world-wide standard for computerized music. MIDI keyboards can "talk" to each other and create sounds you couldn't achieve with a single synth.

The Miracle has a premium price, but you're getting a near-professional-quality keyboard and a great tutorial system for the money. If you want to learn the piano, you want The Miracle.

SUPER SCOPE

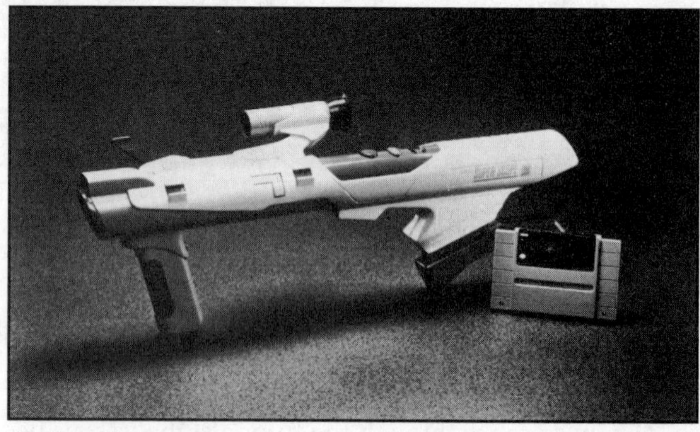

The Super Scope gets our award for the scariest-looking peripheral ever built! This mega-whopping light gun measures

23 inches in length, and it looks like a missile launcher straight out of a Rambo film. It's also the most original and exciting peripheral we've seen yet for the Super NES.

The Scope itself is wireless, and takes six AA batteries. An included Receiver Module plugs into the second controller port of the Super NES. You place the Module on top of your TV to allow the Scope to operate properly.

The Scope is contoured to rest comfortably on big and small shoulders alike, and the gunsight can be adjusted so both left

Mario and Bowser make cameo appearances in the Lazerblazer game for theSuper Scope.

and right-handed players can use the Scope equally well. There are three buttons on the Scope: Cursor, Fire, and Pause. (There's also an on/off switch that doubles as a Turbo switch for rapid-fire shooting.)

The Cursor button, in certain games, will display a red point on screen, similar to the aiming laser seen in movies like Predator or The Terminator. The Fire button does what it sounds like. The Pause button also does what it sounds like.

The Super Scope is miles ahead of the 8-bit NES light gun, the Zapper, in several categories. While the Zapper is only accurate to about an inch, the Super Scope is accurate to almost a single television pixel! And do you remember that annoying screen flash when you shot the Zapper? There's no flash whatsoever with the Super Scope.

The Super Scope comes packaged with an 8-meg cartridge simply named Super Scope 6. The cartridge includes six games separated into two groups: Blastris and Lazerblazer.

The Blastris games are a variation on the Tetris theme. You use the Super Scope to zap the falling Tetrads so that they'll fit together. Don't let the blocks pile up to the top of the screen!

Also included in the Blastris group of games is a completely silly game called Mole Patrol. If you've ever played Whack-A-Mole in an arcade, you already know what to do in this game. Shoot the blue Moles, but don't hit the pink ones!

In the Lazerblazer games, your home base is being attacked by enemy ships and missiles. You have to shoot down the attackers in three different games: Intercept, Engage, and Confront. Each of these games has 30 levels.

Nintendo is already working on two new games for the Super Scope, and Nintendo's third-party licensees are also creating hot new titles for this amazing peripheral. These future games will take advantage of the Cursor and Turbo features, neither of which is used by Super Scope 6.

Overall, we're thrilled with the Super Scope. Our only wish is that the Super Scope had an auto shut-off feature. Even without auto shut-off, we highly recommend the Super Scope. It's an outrageous way to play!

NOW AVAILABLE

Super Mario World Secrets $12.99
Nintendo Games Secrets, Volumes 1, 2, and 3 .... $9.99 (each)
Super NES Games Secrets $9.99
Nintendo Game Boy Secrets, Volumes 1 and 2......... $9.99 (each)
Sega Genesis Secrets, Volumes 1, 2, and 3 .... $9.99 (each)
TurboGrafx-16 and TurboExpress Secrets,
Volumes 1 and 2.................................... $9.99 (each)
GamePro Presents:
Nintendo Games Secrets Greatest Tips.............................. $9.99

UPCOMING VIDEO GAME BOOKS
Coming Soon

Super NES Games Secrets, Volume 2 ....$9.99 (Jul)
GamePro Presents:
Sega Genesis Games Secrets Greatest Tips .... $9.99 (Aug)
The Legend of Zelda:
A Link to the Past Game Secrets...............................$9.99 (Aug)

And there's a lot more where these came from....

COMPUTER GAME BOOKS

SimEarth: The Official Strategy Guide....................................$18.95

Harpoon Battlebook..$18.95

Wing Commanander I and II..$18.95

The Official Lucasfilm Games
Air combat Strategies Book...$18.95

Chuck Yeager's Air Combat Handbook.................................$18.95

Sid Meier's Civilization, or Rome on 640K a Day $18.95

Ultima: The Avatar Adventures..$18.95

MORE COMPUTER GAME BOOKS TO COME

JetFighter II: The Official Strategy Guide....................$18.95 (Aug)

The Official Lemmings Companion (w/disk)............$24.95 (Sep)

Global Conquest:
The Official Strategy Guide (w/disk) ....$24.95 (Sep)

V for Victory: The Utah Beach Battle Book ....$18.95 (Sep)

A-Train: The Official Strategy Guide ....$18.95 (Sep)

Falcon 3: The Official Combat Strategy Book
(w/disk)..$27.95 (Oct)

TO ORDER BOOKS ONLY

Please send me the following items:

Quantity	Title	Unit Price	Total
______	______________________________	$______	$______
______	______________________________	$______	$______
______	______________________________	$______	$______
______	______________________________	$______	$______
______	______________________________	$______	$______
______	______________________________	$______	$______
______	______________________________	$______	$______
		Subtotal	$______
		7.25% SALES TAX (California only)	$______
		SHIPPING $3.00	$______
		TOTAL ORDER	$______

HOW TO ORDER

By telephone:
With Visa or MC, call (916) 786-0449. Mon.–Fri. 9–4 PST.
By Mail: Just fill out the information below and send with your remittance.

My name is____

I live at ____

City ____________________ State________ Zip____________

Visa/MC# ___________________________ Exp.____________

Signature____

PRIMA PUBLISHING
P.O. Box 1260 SNESB
Rocklin, CA 95677
(Satisfaction unconditionally guaranteed)